GW00362220

STRATEGIC SURVEY 1988-1989

Published by **Brassey's** for

THE INTERNATIONAL
INSTITUTE FOR
STRATEGIC STUDIES
23 Tavistock Street London WC2E 7NQ

STRATEGIC SURVEY 1988–1989

Published by Brassey's for
The International Institute for Strategic Studies
23 Tavistock Street, London WC2E 7NQ

Director   Editor
François Heisbourg   Sidney Bearman

This publication has been prepared by the Director of the Institute and his Staff, who accept full responsibility for its contents. These do not, and indeed cannot, represent a consensus of views among the world-wide membership of the Institute as a whole.

First published Spring 1989

ISBN 0 08 037556 1
ISSN 0459-7230

Printed and bound in Great Britain by Nuffield Press, Hollow Way, Cowley, Oxford OX4 2PH

CONTENTS

Perspectives

When historians review 1988, they may well see it as the year in which the Cold War ended. Much depends on how the two super-powers adjust to the new world that is being created – a very different world from the one which emerged from the ashes of World War II. The threatening but stable post-war strategic order has entered a state of flux, characterized by new uncertainties and corresponding challenges and opportunities. After more than forty years of confrontation and conflict, it is little wonder that each power is approaching the other gingerly. The habits of thought and action developed over that time are difficult to shed. Yet the leaders of both super-powers are increasingly forced to recognize that economic and social imperatives at home, and a declining ability to influence the world abroad, call into serious question the shibboleths that have guided their countries' past behaviour.

This is clearest in regard to the Soviet Union. Mikhail Gorbachev's much-vaunted 'new thinking' in international affairs turns out to be pragmatic common sense, something that the United States has always prided itself on exercising, even if this was not always readily apparent to the detached observer. But it is truly new thinking in the USSR. Soviet leaders at last seem prepared to accept what many foreign observers have always known: that to begin to deal with the appalling failures of the Soviet economic system and the consequent societal tensions, the aggressive forward thrust of Soviet foreign policy, and the concomitant costly and politically unrewarding expansion of the military machine that supported it, would need to be curtailed. What has perhaps been most surprising to foreigners has been the boldness with which Gorbachev has moved and, within the limits of Leninism and undiminished Party control, how far he seems willing to go to assure that his restructuring of the Soviet economy will succeed.

The West has so far done little to compete with Gorbachev for the limelight. This is partly because 1988 was an election year in the United States, and the government's attention was seriously divided. But it is also because much of what Gorbachev has been doing is to adopt parts of long-standing Western positions, programmes and policies. If it was heartening to find that the USSR has agreed that it should withdraw its forces from Afghanistan, it requires nothing from the West but to accept graciously what it had been demanding for nine years. If Gorbachev now recognizes an asymmetry in favour of the Soviet Union in the force balance in Europe, and is prepared to do something about it, this too is an acceptance of Western positions. Yet, both to encourage further Soviet moves and to prevent the Kremlin from scoring heavily with world public opinion, the West now needs to advance its own vision and practical ideas for further progress towards a more stable and secure order in a post-Cold-War world. In its own interest, the West should be establishing the standards which it considers the Soviet Union should meet in order to be treated as a positive contributor to the international system.

The Promise of Peace

The sense that 1988 was a year in which the nations of the world may have set a new course was fed by the extraordinary change during the year from a world dominated by long-running conflicts to one in which settlement through negotiations became the more expected norm. While in most cases events have not yet reached the stage that guarantees complete peace, the change from the beginning of the year to the end has been momentous. All around the globe belligerence gave way to compromise.

For well over a year the Soviet Union had been talking about bringing its troops out of Afghanistan. In April 1988, although unable to gain assurances from the *Mujaheddin* or their supporters that the Communists in Kabul would be allowed to play a significant (if not leading) role after Soviet troops left the country, Gorbachev agreed with UN negotiators on a firm schedule for withdrawal. The troops began to leave in May, and on 15 February 1989, precisely on schedule, the last Soviet soldier, the commanding General, walked across the border out of Afghanistan. A nine-year effort to force the Afghan people to accept an alien governmental philosophy had ended without success; it left in its wake a devastated country, with over five million people driven from their homes to foreign lands, and the minority Communist government still in the same precarious state as it had been when Moscow began its rescue mission.

The fighting in Afghanistan is far from over, and the future of that troubled country far from clear. The departure of the Soviet forces has robbed the *Mujaheddin* of their most hated enemy and the focus of their unified efforts. Their continued cohesion now looks less certain, and it may not be quite so easy for the *Mujaheddin* to topple the Najibullah regime as many had thought. Nevertheless, the significance of the Soviet withdrawal is hard to exaggerate. It provides confirmation that much of the new foreign policy that Gorbachev has been erratically evolving over the last four years is not just a jockeying for international advantage, but derives from genuine changes in policy objectives on which the USSR is prepared to act. It is a firm 'deed', such as sceptics have been demanding, and one that underpins the 'words' that they distrust. Coupled with other Soviet actions throughout the year, it represents a profound shift in the USSR's attitudes and behaviour on the world scene.

In two other regional conflicts Soviet influence was exerted to reduce the level of violence. Partly because of Soviet pressure, an agreement was reached in southern Africa for Cuban troops to be withdrawn from Angola in return for parallel South African withdrawal from that country and Namibia, so as to allow UN resolutions on Namibian independence to be implemented. And in South-east Asia, Vietnam has pledged the withdrawal of its troops from Kampuchea before 1990, opening the way for a possible settlement of the war there. In neither case, though, have these developments meant an immediate end to fighting. UNITA, under Jonas Savimbi, still insists that it will overthrow the present Angolan government, and in Kampuchea the tripartite opposition coalition, headed by Prince Sihanouk, insists that the Communist Heng Samrin regime must be replaced. But in each case the spiral of violence has wound down, and the future looks brighter than it has for almost ten years.

In the Gulf, the longest conventional war of this century, after raging for just short of eight years, ended with a cease-fire in July. Although the peace talks which began at the same time have moved in fits and starts, more off than on, neither war-weary nation seems ready to go back to the fighting that has cost hundreds of thousands of lives and devastated both economies. In Central America, the *Sandinista* regime and the rebel *Contra* forces have ceased fighting and have held a series of inconclusive talks. A settlement has not yet been signed and sealed, but the political and economic weakness of the Nicaraguan government and the denial of further military aid to the *Contras* by the US Congress guarantee that, here too, the shooting, if not the shouting, war is over. In north-west Africa, the Maghreb nations have begun a serious dialogue aiming at greater unity, and the struggle between Morocco and the Polisario for control of Western Sahara is moving away from armed conflict to negotiations.

Even Yasser Arafat, claiming to speak for the majority in the PLO, has joined in championing peace in place of war. His public acceptance in December of UN Resolutions 242 and 338, acknowledging Israel's right to exist, and his renunciation of terrorism, brought the United States to open a dialogue with him. Although Israel continues to insist that it will never deal with the PLO, its increasing isolation, its inability to bring the *Intifada* under control and its lack of coherent alternatives to an international conference or a direct negotiation all suggest that it will be making every effort to find a way to break the impasse.

Other tensions that have long marred the international order were also reduced during the year. The thirty-year dispute between the USSR and China has slowly dissolved; reciprocal visits by the two nations' foreign ministers in 1988 will be capped in May 1989 with a visit to China by Mr Gorbachev. With Sino-Soviet tension dissipating, and with Vietnam displaying readiness to withdraw from Kampuchea and promising to play a positive role in seeking a settlement there, the Chinese animosity towards Vietnam is also weakening. North Korea and South Korea are edging towards talks on improving their relations. India and Pakistan, under new and younger leaders, have expressed a desire to smooth their jagged relationship. In other areas of the world, too, old antagonisms are being rethought, and there is renewed hope that peaceful competition can replace active conflict.

Co-operative Super-powers?

The bare record of the outbreak of peace is impressive enough. But behind it are more fundamental and profound changes that explain why many very sober observers feel there is reason for cautious optimism. What has overwhelmingly polarized international relations in the past forty years has been the global confrontation between the super-powers, the clash between Soviet expansionism and US containment. Under Soviet direction, the Eastern bloc has pushed aggressively against all boundaries in search of advantage, while the West, under US leadership, has reacted vigorously to prevent the advance. The Soviet belief in the constancy of class warfare on the international stage, the inevitable victory of socialism, and the merits of revolutionary struggle as a means to that end, informed its bellicose, non-cooperative approach to the rest of the world, which created and sustained the Cold War. As Soviet beliefs and actions have changed under Gorbachev's tutelage, East–West tensions have eased, and a less harsh international environment has emerged.

Since his election as General Secretary of the Soviet Communist Party in 1985, Mikhail Gorbachev has been slowly, bit by bit, redefining Soviet approaches to the outside world. On 7 December 1988, in a magisterial speech to the United Nations, he assembled all the various pieces into a coherent expression of the whole of the Soviet 'new thinking' on international relations. Fundamental to this rethinking of the basis of Soviet policy is the jettisoning of the concept of class war and the division of the world into 'us and them'. In its place Gorbachev has elevated a belief in interdependence. According to this view, if one side gains, the other need not lose – both can, and will, gain through mutual efforts.

Gorbachev's thinking on security has also undergone a sea change. He recognizes that the devastating power of present nuclear arsenals ensures that nobody can win a war. Security is not a matter of military might (partly because in today's world much of that might cannot be used) but is dependent on social and economic strength at home. No one country can count on developing security through overwhelming military strength. This makes other countries feel insecure and forces them to build up their strength in reply, risking an uncontrollable arms race and creating mutual insecurity. In place of the goal of security through strength, he would put the notion of 'reasonable sufficiency'; in place of offensive doctrines, the idea of 'defensive defence'. Both concepts hold promise and convey reassurance; neither has yet taken on any clear and precise definition.

These ideas lie behind the admission that in many respects there is an imbalance between Warsaw Pact and NATO forces. In a first move towards rectifying these asymmetries, Gorbachev, in his UN speech, announced unilateral reductions in the armed forces of the Soviet Union: 500,000 men (50,000 to come from troops stationed in East Germany, Czechoslovakia and Hungary); 50% of tanks (including six tank divisions) stationed in the Central Front area; a large cut in artillery pieces; and the removal of assault landing (helicopter-borne) troops and assault bridging materiel, the prime function of which relates to offensive action. In January 1989 all the other Warsaw Pact countries except Romania announced unilateral reductions in their own forces. The Soviet Union has not requested any reciprocal moves by NATO (though it would surely welcome them) but has pointed out that in its opinion NATO holds an advantage in the size of its air and naval forces. Moscow can be expected to push for changes in the first of these two areas in the CDE talks on conventional arms reductions that began in March, while making the case for naval arms reductions in other fora.

Both in the unilateral conventional arms reductions it has already made and in the agreement on INF forces ratified in time for the Moscow summit in May, the Soviet Union has shown itself willing to back up its new thinking by reducing the disparities in forces that now exist. It has agreed, and is in the process of implementing, the destruction of a far larger number of intermediate-range nuclear weapons than the US. There are in fact numerous and welcome indications that it is prepared to act on the 'new thinking' it espouses.

Gorbachev does not hide his hope that the effort to play a more constructive role in international affairs will redound to Soviet advantage. If co-operation can achieve as much security as military might, the USSR can devote its resources of both money and manpower to rejuvenating its sagging economy. If outside fears can be quieted, trade and other barriers may be lowered, and vital Western low-cost loans, subsidized credits, technical aid and managerial know-how may be made available. The challenge for the Soviet Union, therefore, is to create an atmosphere of long-lasting confidence among the Western nations. However, this may not be possible if it continues to succumb to the temptation of advancing traditional proposals such as that on the denuclearization of Europe, whose sole purpose appears to be to attempt to split the Atlantic Alliance.

Unless Gorbachev's *perestroika* is a success, the Soviet Union will remain a second-rate economic power and can never be expected to keep up with developments in the technologically advanced world. Indeed, its economic performance will need to improve dramatically to ensure that the gap with the US, Japan and Western Europe does not widen further – and this may be the maximum realistic objective for *perestroika* for the foreseeable future. Today Soviet hard-currency exports are less than those of South Korea or Taiwan. Ultimately, the USSR's claim to super-power parity is threatened by its economic underperformance. The question is: how far can, and will, Gorbachev go in his reforms if they conflict with basic tenets of Soviet power, such as the leading role of the Communist Party?

In the face of the innovative flurry of Soviet words and actions, Western nations have appeared hesitant and unimaginative. The attention of US leaders was focused on the presidential election for the last six months of 1988, and the new President spent the first three months of 1989 trying to get his foreign-policy team into place. Those who had surmounted the hurdle of Senatorial confirmation were engaged in a series of sensible, indeed vital, but time-consuming reviews of foreign and military policy. And West European governments found it difficult to agree on what response to make to Gorbachev's moves, with reactions ranging from the more forthcoming attitude of West Germany to the tougher one of the United Kingdom.

While scepticism about Gorbachev's sincerity was subsiding among Western leaders, questions about his ability to succeed, and even to stay in power, abound. This remains a major impediment to rapid acceptance of the brave new world he is championing. Despite all the talk about a changing Soviet political and social reality, the USSR remains a country governed by men and not laws. Although Gorbachev has not criticized the tentative development of a multi-party approach to political life in Hungary, he has categorically ruled out such a development for the Soviet Union, characterizing such an idea as 'rubbish'. There can be little doubt that throughout Soviet society there is considerable opposition both to *perestroika* and to some of Gorbachev's projected social changes, and there is no assurance that a massive backlash against the hardship required by the efforts at economic reform might not result in his replacement as leader.

Other domestic threats also clearly exist. *Glasnost* may be building a desire for democratization that the limited measures so far announced will signally fail to satisfy. It has rekindled the fires of nationalism, most notably in the Baltic states and, together with some of the economic decentralization envisaged under the banner of *perestroika*, has raised the spectre of geographically differentiated prosperity, compounding problems of haves and have-nots. Nor have the problems of reconciling economic modernization with continued Party control yet been convincingly addressed. Continued progress along the road of reform is thus not assured. If the West adjusted itself to the new Soviet Union, would it then find itself at a great disadvantage if it should be faced once again by a more traditional Soviet leader, intent at least on slowing the pace of reform, if not halting it, and possibly bent on turning the clock back completely?

In the past four years the Soviet Union has become a very much more open society, but it is still difficult to see the workings of the highest levels of the government clearly. Once the USSR was an enigma wrapped in a riddle; now *glasnost* may have removed the riddle, but the enigma remains. All the same, it is reasonable to assume that most Kremlin leaders agree with Gorbachev's basic analysis of

Soviet life: the economy must be rejuvenated; some movement to a less centralized economy is required; to gain the help of the Soviet people, the relaxation of social controls, already started, must be continued; the world has changed radically, and the Soviet Union must change with it. While there is undoubtedly disagreement about the pace and scope of the present reforms – with some wishing to go further and faster than Gorbachev and others fearful of the unknown consequences of the present actions – the basic reforms probably command a consensus. It is too much to believe of any individual, even one as dedicated, energetic and imaginative as Gorbachev, that he can institute and implement the programme that is now evolving without the help and support of a majority of the leaders of the country.

The danger of failure, however, remains very high. It stems from the difficulty inherent in attempting to energize an encrusted economic machine in the face of the innate resistance to change of the workers and managers. They would like an immediate pay-off, not more sacrifice. But it is in the nature of what the leaders are trying to do that the pay-off will come only slowly, if it comes at all. Worker recalcitrance, plus the foot-dragging of those who really believe that reform of the kind now being attempted is apostasy, create a formidable barrier that may not be surmounted.

Another risk, equally serious, comes from the other end of the spectrum: those who are seizing on the new opportunities to advance ethnic and nationalist demands which may go so far that they frighten the Russian centre into a reaction that brings all advance to a halt. The Armenian riots of 1988 have subsided, and the ethnic feelings they excited are now simmering below the surface; but those feelings have not been assuaged, and at any time they may break out again with renewed fury and spread to as yet quiescent areas, such as the Ukraine. And the attempts by Latvia, Lithuania and Estonia to reassert part of the independence lost when Stalinist Russia gobbled them up at the end of World War II may overstep the present ambiguous bounds of permissible differentiation.

This lack of definition has also created considerable risks with regard to East Europe. The tight Soviet control maintained for so long seems to have been lifted far enough to allow a latitude for independent action that has not existed for forty years. In response, Hungary and Poland have begun to move well beyond the USSR in the political, as well as the economic, realm, while the other four satellite nations have thrown up barriers to change and now lag well behind it. The Soviet Union has indicated throughout the past year that the Brezhnev Doctrine, which set distinct and tight limits on the changes that would be allowed in Eastern Europe, is no longer valid, but there is no reason to believe that this means it would welcome, or allow, reformist Hungary (for example) to replace its Communist-Party-led government or to vote itself out of the Warsaw Pact. Yet there is a growing perception that in Eastern Europe some states, and some inter-state relations, are increasingly unstable, and there is a distinct danger that the strength of nationalist feeling, kindled by what the Soviet Union is both saying and doing (particularly in reducing its armed forces in East European countries), will burst forth in flames that Moscow will feel it essential to quench. The consequences, for both the Soviet Union and the West, would be disastrous.

Given so many uncertainties, there is good reason for Western statesmen to be cautious. But caution need not mean inaction. Co-operation with the Soviet Union in a number of areas (in his UN speech Gorbachev mentioned the environment, anti-drug trafficking efforts, support for UN peace-keeping) would not only test Soviet sincerity but, if successful, would help all the world's nations, while not prejudging the success or failure of the Soviet experiment at home. Of particular immediacy is the need to find a way to manage and control the spread of sophisticated weaponry to countries in the Third World, riven by national and territorial disputes and trembling on the brink of further conflict.

The Threat of Proliferation
One of the loud and clear messages of the Gulf War is that weapons of mass destruction are no longer a monopoly of the major industrialized countries. Another is that some countries in the Third World have little compunction about using them. Iraq used chemical weapons repeatedly to thwart massive manpower attacks by Iran; it did not hesitate to use them against its own citizens, the Kurds in Halabja. In 1988, in the so-called 'War of the Cities', the two countries launched up to several hundred missiles at each other, the largest number of ballistic missile attacks on civilians since the German V-2 attacks on England and Belgium during World War II.

Both missiles and chemical arms are rapidly proliferating in areas where animosities are high and relations are tense. This is particularly true of the Middle East. Israel has had a missile capacity for some time; with the development of the *Jericho* II missile, targets up to perhaps 1,450 kms away can be reached. Israel is also suspected of having a chemical-weapons capacity and is widely believed already to possess a nuclear-weapons capability.

While none of the Arab states is thought to be nuclear-capable, they have been acquiring ballistic missiles and chemical weapons at an increasing rate. Iraq and Iran have demonstrated their inventories. Syria has over 30 Soviet-supplied SS-21 launchers and is believed to be producing some form of nerve gas. China has sold a number of CSS-2 (DF-3) missiles (their range is approximately 2,200 km) to Saudi Arabia. Egypt is co-operating with Argentina to develop an intermediate-range missile to supplement the *FROG* and *Scud* it got from the USSR. Libya has been temporarily thwarted in its ambitions to finish building one of the world's largest chemical-weapon plants, but there is every reason to believe that it will go on trying to develop a capacity to manufacture chemical-warfare agents. There are also reports that Libya has been attempting to acquire missiles, with ranges of about 950 km, from Brazil. On the subcontinent, India has tested its own ballistic missile with a range of about 240 kms and is working on a much longer-range one. Similarly, Pakistan has flight tested a 300-km-range missile. Both countries could conceivably use such missiles to deliver nuclear weapons.

Both the US and the USSR have an interest in preventing the further spread of such sophisticated weapons to nations in areas of high tension. While they are not themselves directly threatened, the possible outbreak of hostilities brings with it the risk that what begins as a local war can expand rapidly and in unexpected ways. It will not be easy to find a way to stem the swelling tide of sophisticated, dangerous arms in the Third World. Many third-world nations feel that they are entitled to acquire such weapons, particularly chemical weapons (often dubbed 'the poor man's nuclear bomb'), so long as the major powers are unwilling to give up their own nuclear and chemical weapons. But it remains an area in which super-power co-operation can move from rhetoric to some co-ordinated action.

A Rosier Future?
The remarkable developments of 1988 have left a sense that the world has become a safer, saner place than it has been for many decades; it also seems likely that further improvement is on the way. One of the deepest reasons for optimism is the fact that both super-powers are approaching the 1990s with a greater focus on the need to improve their domestic assets than on thrusting outwards. The basis of the Soviet 'new thinking' is the need to repair the USSR's unworkable social and economic systems, a process that, under the best of circumstances, Gorbachev and his colleagues believe will take a number of five-year plans. The US is not in such dire straits, but it, too, has had its gaze turned inwards, with massive budget and trade deficits to overcome, and years of social neglect to put right.

As the tensions built up by antagonistic relations begin to subside, the structure of the post-war world is coming under different strains. It is now possible to begin asking questions about the need for opposing blocs and alliances, if the threat they were set up to meet is receding, and many on both sides of the divide are asking these questions. NATO has played a crucial role in guaranteeing security and stability over the past forty years. It may have an important part to play in the future, provided that this role can be redefined to fit a changing world and is seen as contributing positively to the change. To a large extent, it has been the Soviet Union that has been setting the pace. To ensure that the pace does not slacken, and that the direction of change remains beneficial, Western statesmen must begin to develop some new, and imaginative, political thinking of their own.

Strategic Policy Issues

MISSILE PROLIFERATION IN THE THIRD WORLD

Ballistic missile proliferation has emerged as a major problem for the international community. Thirty years ago, in the wake of *Sputnik* and the space race, several developing countries initiated rocket research programmes of their own; for years these were inconspicuous side-shows, curiosities seemingly without promise or danger. In the last two years, however, new ballistic missile programmes have been revealed throughout the Third World, ranging from small and inexpensive short-range systems to intermediate-range ballistic missiles larger than some of the missiles destroyed under the INF Treaty. (And Iran and Iraq fired hundreds of ballistic missiles at each other during the spring 1988 War of the Cities). Policy-makers in Washington, Moscow, Beijing and European capitals are already having to cope with the consequences of these events, but their approaches remain rudimentary and inconsistent, leaving much to be resolved.

It is ironic that recent East–West accomplishments have coincided with a dramatic intensification of the military competition elsewhere. Like the growing regional interest in chemical weapons and the steady pace of nuclear proliferation, missile proliferation poses global risks. While no developing country except China appears capable of producing an intercontinental weapon before the end of the century, space launch vehicles under development in Brazil, India, Israel and Argentina could form the basis for long-range missiles in the future.

The acquisition of advanced military equipment by countries in areas of conflict has long been recognized as contributing to instability in regional affairs. And some weapon systems are clearly more destabilizing than others – ever since the early 1970s, analysts have been stressing the dangers posed by precision-guided munitions. The trend towards greater sophistication in regional arsenals has led to re-evaluations of the risks to great powers trying to project power outside Europe. In the widely noted report, *Discriminate Deterrence*, a group of experts in the US acknowledged that the dangers of military conflict in the Third World may soon necessitate a reorientation of US armed forces from their traditional alliance obligations to cope with less predictable regional contingencies. The emergence of new ballistic missile forces can only hasten such pressures.

Despite continuous disclosures and intensive publicity, outside observers know about as much about regional ballistic missile forces today as they did about Soviet ballistic missiles in 1957, the year of *Sputnik*. Typically, this is only what might be seen at a military parade or deduced from a government press release. Data on range, payload, accuracy, armament and the number of missiles deployed can remain elusive until the systems are finally used in combat. This was the case with Iran and Iraq; the capabilities of their missile forces were revealed only when the weapons were fired.

Third-world Missiles Today

In all, more than twenty developing countries have ballistic missile programmes, more than a dozen possess operational ballistic missile forces, and others have on-going research and development programmes. Some countries – Argentina, Brazil, India, Iran, Iraq and Israel – have several continuing programmes, although some may be 'paper missiles', unlikely to progress beyond the drawing board. Other countries, such as North and South Korea, Libya and Taiwan, keep their programmes concealed behind a thick security screen.

There is usually adequate information to classify these programmes by missile range. Accuracy, armament and basing modes are also important, but more elusive, characteristics. The range categories used to define NATO and Warsaw Pact arsenals do not have much meaning in regional contexts, where strategic distances are so different. A missile considered short-range by NATO (that is, less than 500 km) may be able to reach strategic targets in several regional situations. In comparing third-world ballistic missiles three categories appear to be useful: 40–150 kilometres, 150–600 kilometres, and above 600 kilometres. These categories are based on technological similarities; those in each group share important advantages and disadvantages, strengths and weaknesses (see Table on p. 18).

40–150-km Range

At the lowest end of the scale are missiles which are inexpensive and relatively easy to manufacture. Weapons of such short range, which do not need complex engines, hard-to-handle fuels or elaborate guidance systems, are by far the oldest and most numerous ballistic missiles in third-world hands. The US sold *Honest John* missiles (range 40 km) to its NATO allies as well as to Korea and Taiwan in 1958–61. The Soviet Union has supplied *FROG*-4/-7 missiles (40–70 km) to over a dozen regional friends and allies since the early 1960s.

Despite their availability, many countries are developing similar systems of their own. China is marketing a family of missiles with various ranges under 150 km. Its first foreign customer was Iran, which used Chinese plans and assistance to manufacture the 40-km *Oghab* and the *Nazeat* and *Shahin*-2 with ranges of some 100–130 km. Egypt is building the 80-km *Saqr*-80 with foreign help. Other Arab countries have purchased the 68-km *ASTROS* II SS-60 from Brazil, and Pakistan is developing its own 80-km missile, the *Haft*-2.

Missiles of under 150-km range are easily acquired in large quantities, but their payload usually is not over 200 kg, and this is too small for a fission warhead of reasonable yield. Individually, they lack the accuracy to be militarily effective with conventional warheads. But there are several ways to make them more militarily effective. The most obvious is to procure large quantities, which appears to be the goal of countries which are producing the missiles themselves. Another approach is to rearm the warhead, replacing unitary explosive warheads with cluster weapons containing scores of small sub-munitions for use against soft targets like parked aircraft. Fuel/air explosives (concussion bombs) could have the same effect. The most widely discussed use for short-range missiles is to carry chemical weapons. Loaded with persistent chemical agents, even relatively small missiles could be effective against civilian targets.

150–600-km Range
Missiles in this class are more complex and expensive, but their greater capabilities better satisfy military and political requirements. With more powerful engines and high-energy fuels, they can carry most warheads, including nuclear weapons. And weapons in this range category can reach strategic targets in most regional areas. They can be relied upon to hit city-sized targets and, with inertial guidance systems, can be accurate enough to hit large military installations. They are also readily adapted to mobile launchers (usually hardened trucks), which reduces their vulnerability. A final advantage is their availability on the international arms market. For countries unable to buy them abroad, or preferring to manufacture types designed to their own national requirements, the large number of component suppliers facilitates development programmes at home.

The most common missile in this class is the Soviet *Scud* B (range 280 km). Hundreds have been supplied to at least five Arab countries since 1973, as well as to Afghanistan in 1988. A ubiquitous symbol in Middle East military parades, the *Scud* has become so plentiful that a lively second-hand market emerged in the mid-1980s, with purchases made by Iran, Iraq and Western intelligence agencies. Based on early 1950s technology derived directly from the German V-2, it uses storable liquid propellants and a rudimentary strap-down inertial guidance system. The design is hardly efficient by contemporary standards, but it is robust and reliable and can be modified or manufactured by nations without an extensive aerospace industry. North Korea appears to have reverse-engineered Soviet-supplied *Scud* for domestic production. Iraq, aided by an unidentified foreign assistant, had great success with its *al-Hussayn*, a modification of the *Scud* with its range extended to 600 km. Unveiled in August 1987, it was Iraq's most important weapon in the War of the Cities. (A 900-km *Scud* version, the *al-Abbas*, was announced in April 1988. This seems to have over-extended either the limits of the basic *Scud* design or Iraqi capabilities; only a few were used against Iran.)

There is no Western counterpart to the *Scud*. Third-world nations unwilling to buy from the Soviet Union, or with specific national requirements in mind, are developing their own weapons instead. Only one other regional missile in this class is operational at present: Israel's *Jericho* I, a 450-km system developed by France's Avions Marcel Dassault under contract in the 1960s. In 1985 Argentina unveiled the *Condor* I, a 150-km system test-fired in late 1988 with a cluster-munition warhead. Brazil is developing several missiles in this class, of which the most advanced are the *Sonda*-4, a large sounding rocket which could be used for long-range ground attack, and the Avibras SS-300, a 300-km missile similar to the *Scud* B. India tested its own *Scud* equivalent, the 240-km *Prithvi*, in February 1988. China is trying to become a supplier of similar missiles in the near future with its 300–600-km M series; these are designed to be launched from a Soviet *Scud* launcher, which leaves little doubt about whom the manufacturer, China Precision Industries, hopes to compete with. The M series is still in development and has aroused considerable interest among prospective clients like Libya and Syria.

600 km and Beyond
As their ranges increase, ballistic missiles require more elaborate and expensive development in order to perform adequately. Controllable-thrust engines, inertial guidance systems and heat shielding are necessary. Development and production costs mount, procurement numbers decline and, since few can be afforded, measures must be taken to protect them against surprise attack, which raises the costs further. Until very recently, speculation about such missiles in the Third World might have seemed over-imaginative. No developing country was thought to be able to undertake domestic development, and none of the traditional arms suppliers was willing to sell them. In 1974 Israel asked the US for *Pershing* Ia missiles (range 750 km) but was refused. In 1984 there were rumours that Moscow had supplied SS-12 *Scaleboard* missiles (range 900 km) to Iraq and Libya, but these appear to have been false.

In the mid-1980s the situation began to change. In 1985 it was revealed that Israel had been developing its *Jericho* II missile since the mid-1970s; test-fired in 1987, it flew 820 km and was said to be designed for a maximum range of 1,450 km, which would allow it to reach Soviet Black Sea bases and Baku. Soviet spokesmen have criticized the project and obliquely promised retaliation against any threats to Soviet territory. A version called the *Shavit* was used to launch a 75-kg Israeli satellite into low-earth orbit on 19 September 1988, provoking criticism from Arab governments and demonstrating a potential for longer ballistic ranges than those achieved by *Jericho* II.

On 18 March 1988 Washington announced that China had supplied DF-3 missiles (NATO designation CSS-2) to Saudi Arabia. About 50 or 60 of these second-hand missiles were retired from China's forces, refitted with conventional warheads and installed on fixed launchers south-west of Riyadh. With a range of at least 2,200 km, these are the most powerful missiles outside the arsenals of the five nuclear powers.

Proliferation of Ballistic Missiles in the Third World

	40–150 km[1]	150–600 km	600 km and greater
Afghanistan		Scud B	
Algeria	FROG-7		
Argentina		Condor I	Condor II*
Brazil	ASTROS II SS-60 EE-150*	SS-300* Sonda-4*	
Cuba	FROG-4/-7		
Egypt	FROG-7 Saqr-80	Scud B	Badr-2000*[2]
India		Prithvi*	Agni*
Indonesia	RX-250*		
Iran	Oghab Shahin-2* Nazeat (Iran-130)*	Scud B	
Iraq	FROG-7 ASTROS SS-60	Scud B al-Hussayn	al-Abbas*
Israel	MAR-350 Lance	Jericho I	Jericho II*
N. Korea	FROG-4/-7	Scud B	
S. Korea	Honest John Nike-Hercules[3]		
Kuwait	FROG-7		
Libya	FROG-7	Scud B ex-OTRAG*	
Pakistan	Haft-2*	Haft-1*	
Saudi Arabia	ASTROS SS-60		DF-3 (CSS-2)
S. Africa	*[4]		
Syria	FROG-7 SS-21 Scarab	Scud B	
Taiwan	Honest John Hsiung Feng		
N. Yemen	SS-21 Scarab[4]		
S. Yemen	FROG-7 SS-21 Scarab	Scud B	

* Currently under development.
[1] Missiles with a maximum range under 40 km are usually classified as artillery rockets. They equip most of the world's armies.
[2] Egyptian designation for the Condor II.
[3] A US-supplied surface-to-air missile modified without US consent for ground attack.
[4] Unconfirmed.

They could reach targets in Israel and the Soviet Union, although Saudi officials insist they are intended only to deter Iran. To appease critics of the deal, Saudi Arabia signed the Nuclear Non-Proliferation Treaty and promised not to retransfer the missiles to other countries.

Other countries are interested in acquiring, or developing, similar missiles, although their programmes have several years of development work left. In the late 1970s Taiwan's Institute of Science and Technology was believed to be developing a 1,000-km missile, but this apparently stopped in the early 1980s. Argentina's Condor II is a sophisticated 800-km missile under development since the early 1980s (see below). Brazil has talked of a comparable missile, the Avibras SS-800, but there is no evidence that it has progressed beyond the drawing board. India is planning to test a new ballistic missile called the *Agni*. Little is known about this, except that it relies on technology borrowed from India's large civilian space launch programme. Press reports say that it has a range of 2,500 km, but early versions will almost certainly be significantly less capable.

Missiles of such range are difficult to justify unless they carry nuclear weapons. Their cost is considerable (Saudi Arabia paid about $US 3.25 bn for its DF-3 force, approximately $54 m per missile), and, when conventionally armed, they lack the accuracy to be effective against military targets. The established nuclear powers have never deployed similar missiles with conventional warheads.

Recent Military Experience
Ballistic missiles have been used four times in regional conflict. In the 1973 Middle East War, Syria fired a few *FROG* against military bases in northern Israel, while Egypt fired a small number of its *FROG* and *Scud* from the south. In April 1986 two Libyan *Scud* B were fired at the US Coast Guard station on Lampedusa, off the Italian coast, in retaliation for the US air raid on Gaddafi's headquarters (they failed to hit the island). In November 1988 the Afghan Army displayed newly received *Scud* B systems in Kabul, and in subsequent weeks at least 50 of them were fired at suspected *Mujaheddin* positions – one fell on a refugee village in Pakistan, reportedly killing ten people.

By far the greatest use of ballistic missiles in regional conflict was during the Iran–Iraq War. Iraq began using its *FROG*-7 in 1980, in small-scale attacks against Iranian border towns. These were followed between 1983 and 1986 by over 100 *Scud* B attacks on more distant targets. Iran had no ballistic missiles until 1985, when it received its first *Scud* B (about 50 in all) from Libya. These were quickly used against Baghdad. The missile war abated soon afterwards, as both sides replenished their inventories.

Iraq acquired 300 or more additional *Scud* B from the USSR in 1986–7 and modified them into 600-km *al-Hussayn*, which could reach Tehran. Iran bought over 100 *Scud* from North Korea, and it turned to China for technical assistance in manufacturing the shorter-range *Oghab*, *Nazeat* and *Shahin*-2 systems. Both sides were well armed for the War of the Cities that started on 29 February 1988. The intensity of the missile attacks was limited mostly by the lack of launchers, which prevented Iraq and Iran from firing more than 10 and 3 *Scud* per day respectively – although Iran fired many more smaller missiles. When the attacks ended after six weeks, Iraq had fired about 190 modified *Scud*, and Iran over 80 *Scud*, about 250 *Oghab*, and other missiles: a total for the two countries of about 570 in all.

Perhaps the most striking aspect of regional missile warfare is how little impact it has had. To be sure, missile strikes on Tehran sapped

Iran's morale, but it was already weakened by other factors. Baghdad endured less physical damage with no visible effect upon Iraqi willingness to fight on at a time of ascendancy on the battlefield. To put these examples into perspective, they can be compared to the German V-2 missile attacks in 1944–5. Some 4,300 missiles were fired in the closing months of World War II in Europe, mostly against London and Antwerp – an effort far larger than any regional war has yet seen. The V-2 was not as accurate as the *Scud* B, but its warhead was comparable: one ton of high explosive. Several thousand people died in V-2 attacks but the effects on allied morale were minimal.

While experience shows that a few missiles with unitary conventional explosive warheads is not a reliably effective force, states that are acquiring missiles are now looking for different warheads, more accurate weapons, or larger quantities. The most serious danger is from nuclear-armed missiles, for nuclear armament alone can guarantee a massive destructive capability. It is no surprise that many leading missile proliferators are also high on the list of likely nuclear proliferators. Israel is widely believed to have nuclear weapons, and its missiles should be regarded as nuclear-capable. India tested a nuclear device in 1974, Pakistan is on the nuclear threshold, and Argentina and Brazil have unsafeguarded nuclear facilities. It is the marriage of nuclear armaments with ballistic missiles that creates the most serious threat; measures to restrain nuclear proliferation will also reduce the risks posed by missile proliferation. The same reasoning holds true for chemical weapons: the negotiation of a global ban would significantly limit the dangers of missile proliferation.

The Role of Foreign Technology
Most of the ballistic missiles in the Third World are of foreign origin. Virtually all those currently operational were originally furnished by the US, the USSR or China, and even domestically manufactured third-world missiles rely on key foreign technologies. In recent years, Western European firms have become the leading suppliers of missile components and sub-systems for engines, fuel systems, guidance, fusing and heat-shielding, as well as overall missile design and manufacturing know-how. Without access to foreign technology, few developing countries could have sustained the rapid missile R&D programmes that took off in the mid-1980s.

The case of Argentina's *Condor* programme illustrates the significance of this. The *Condor* has caused grave international concern, both because it is comparatively sophisticated and because Argentina has made clear it intends to market the missile abroad. As a result of a series of investigations by journalists and government officials in the US and Europe, the links with foreign companies are unusually clearly understood.

The programme began around 1979 under the direction of the Argentine Air Force. A Swiss firm was enlisted to manage the initial R&D, including the construction of a large underground R&D facility near the industrial city of Córdoba. In the early 1980s work began on the *Condor I*, a 150-km space research vehicle which uses propulsion systems designed by SNIA-BDP of Italy, guidance technology from SAGEM of France and transporter-launchers from MAN of West Germany. Transtechnia, a subsidiary of the German aerospace firm MBB, was responsible for systems integration, testing and evaluation. The *Condor I* was displayed at the 1985 Paris Air Show and has since been tested in several modes, although it does not yet appear to be fully operational.

In 1984 British officials revealed that Argentina was developing a larger version with sufficient range to reach the Falkland Islands. In 1988 this emerged as the 800-km range *Condor II*, whose first test launch is expected soon. While the European firms involved in the *Condor* programme all claim that their work ended in 1986 with *Condor I*, the Argentine press reports that French, German, Italian and North American nationals remain active at Argentine missile R&D facilities where the *Condor II* is under development. In June 1988 Egyptian nationals were arrested in the US trying to ship illegally acquired carbon-carbon heat-shielding material out of the country. US prosecutors and defence attorneys both maintain that the operation was instigated by Egyptian Defence Minister Abu Ghazala in support of the *Condor II* programme. Egypt had joined the programme around 1984 with Iraqi financial backing, which illustrates the trend towards growing co-operation between developing countries as they pool resources to achieve common military-industrial objectives.

Arms-control Responses
The dependence on foreign technology forms the basis for most Western responses to the proliferation problem. The centrepiece of Western efforts is the Missile Technology Control Regime (MTCR). Publicly announced by the United States on 16 April 1987, this is not a treaty or a formal agreement but an informal undertaking to co-ordinate national export policies. The seven participants – the UK, Canada, West Germany, France, Italy, Japan and the US – negotiated a common list of restricted technologies relevant to the production of ballistic missiles, cruise missiles and space launch vehicles. Like the 1949 Co-ordinating Committee on Multilateral Export Controls (COCOM) or the 1974 London Nuclear Suppliers Group, the MTCR specifies export restrictions which the participating governments individually write into national law and enforce themselves.

The primary goal of the MTCR, pursued through two sets of technology controls, is to stop the proliferation of ballistic missiles capable of carrying nuclear weapons. First, there is a 'strong presumption to deny' exports of complete missile systems with ranges of over 300 km and payloads of at least 500 kg, and of major components, such as complete engines and re-entry vehicles (RV), that could be assembled into missiles. Second, there are less rigorous restrictions on production technologies that could be used in the development and manufacture of ballistic missiles. These technologies can be licensed for export so long as they are to be used exclusively for missiles of under 300-km range and 500-kg payload, or for civilian space launch programmes (which MTCR is not intended to inhibit).

There is superficial evidence that MTCR has slowed some missile programmes. None have been totally stopped, nor has any country abandoned its R&D, but countries like Brazil and India have had to postpone launch schedules and redouble their domestic research efforts. Other countries, such as Argentina and Egypt, have moved to take advantage of unlicensed, black-market technology. Israel's domestic R&D is so far advanced that it is, in effect, immune.

Implementation of the MTCR has not been smooth. Disclosures in 1987 and 1988 indicated that the French, Italian and West German governments continue to approve export licenses by applying MTCR restrictions loosely, or by connecting them to permissible activities, such as short-range missiles or civilian space launch vehicles. This has caused friction with other members, who raised the issue at the Toronto Group of Seven economic summit in early 1988 and at a special meeting of MTCR nations held in Rome on 8–9 October. On both occasions the effort was to encourage more aggressive enforcement.

By far the biggest problem for the MTCR is its failure to attract new participants. Other European governments have shown little interest in joining, either because (like Belgium, Holland and Switzerland) they prefer flexible national export policies, or because (like Sweden) they wish to avoid compromising their international non-aligned stance. Third-world exporters like Argentina and Brazil have also been invited to join, but clearly believe that missile exports are too much in their national interest to give up. Israel's participation would destroy what little legitimacy the MTCR has in many third-world eyes, but unilateral Israeli export restraint is essential to the MTCR's credibility.

The severest challenge comes from China and the USSR, which have both continued their missile exports. Of the two, Moscow has shown the greater selectiveness in sales; in 1987 it refused to sell 500-km SS-23 missiles requested by Syria, and it has been unwilling to share component technologies even with its closest regional clients, like India. Although sales of *FROG* and *Scud* continue, Soviet leaders have been willing to discuss the issue. It was on the agenda of the May 1988 Moscow summit meeting between President Reagan and General Secretary Gorbachev. This led to a US–Soviet meeting on missile proliferation in Washington on 26 September 1988 – but what, if anything, was achieved at the meeting was not publicized.

The Soviet Union is unlikely to join the MTCR, which was created as a Western initiative, but it could adopt similar export policies unilaterally. In discussions, Soviet officials have asked Washington to approve Soviet space launch services for commercial US customers as compensation for greater co-operation. Ballistic missile exports have become economically important to the Soviet Union, so it is not surprising that Soviet leaders should seek some compensation for their loss. It will be more difficult, however, for Moscow to find a substitute for the use of such exports in regional relations, as symbols of Soviet prestige and commitment.

Since the early 1980s China has become something of a rogue elephant in the arms trade, supplying arms virtually without consideration of political or security implications. Its missile exports are part of the same policy. This partly explains the DF-3 sale to Saudi Arabia and the energetic marketing of new missiles. China is also helping other countries establish their own missile industries, providing design and technical aid to Iran and, possibly, Pakistan.

Under pressure, Chinese leaders appear to be slowly modifying their position on missile exports. In meetings with US Secretary of State Shultz in July 1988, Chinese officials were unwilling to curb missile sales to the Middle East. However, when Secretary of Defense Carlucci pursued the issue during his visit to Beijing in September, Chinese Defence Minister Qin Jiwei began by protesting that Chinese missile sales were much smaller than those of other countries, but by the time Carlucci emerged from the meetings he had received at least ambiguous reassurances. And when President Bush brought up the issue in Beijing in March 1989, Prime Minister Li Peng told him that China would no longer sell ballistic missiles abroad.

There is increasing concern that export restrictions are not a sufficient response to the problem. There simply are too many potential technology suppliers, whose ranks now include other developing countries. Many of these countries are pooling their resources and borrowing technology from each other. The black market in arms that grew during the Gulf War offers another way to circumvent export restrictions.

In the long run, missile proliferation can be controlled only through measures supported by the proliferating nations themselves. With this in mind, the Reagan administration in late December 1988 proposed talks with Egypt and Israel to explore what steps might be taken by Middle East nations to limit the acquisition and use of ballistic missiles in the region. Separate talks would be held with both governments as a preliminary step towards the long-term goal of drawing all Middle East nations into a comprehensive arrangement to remove the risk of surprise attack and limit missile forces in the region. Although the Bush administration had not set out its own policies on missile proliferation by March 1989, President Bush, Secretary of State Baker and Vice-President Quayle have all spoken of the need for vigorous action to prevent the spread of ballistic missiles and chemical weapons.

Military Responses

No major initiatives for controlling missile proliferation have emerged from the developing countries themselves; regional responses to the problem have been predominantly military reactions. In classic arms-race fashion, many developing countries strive to aquire missile forces superior to those of their putative enemies, with better missiles and more destructive munitions. Iran and Iraq, Israel and Syria, North and South Korea direct their ballistic missiles against each other and view the acquisition of a new system by the other side as a challenge and a provocation. But there are important exceptions to the arms-race pattern. Where the political climate is even slightly better, the situation is different. Israel, for example, takes a relaxed view of Egyptian missile programmes, and Argentina's and Brazil's missile programmes compete not for regional domination but for export sales.

Where tensions are high, however, regional powers may be tempted to take more aggressive action against their adversary's ballistic missiles. After Saudi Arabia's DF-3 deployment became known in March 1988, there was open speculation in the Middle East about the possibility of a pre-emptive strike by Israel. Initially Israel did not discourage such talk. Several Arab governments warned that they would view any such attack as an attack on themselves, and Washington privately discouraged a military reaction. Weeks later, Israeli Chief of Staff General Dan Shomron said that the dangers of the missiles had been exaggerated and that Israel could already cope through passive measures and the threat of retaliation.

Missile proliferation has led to greater interest in Anti-Tactical-Ballistic Missile systems (ATBM). Originally envisaged as a response to short-range missiles in Europe, ATBM have won new support from advocates concerned about regional stability. In 1985, when he was in the Senate, Vice-President Quayle began to press for a US ATBM to be made available to regional friends and allies; George Bush endorsed the idea in a campaign speech in August 1988.

Obviously, ATBM technology is within the means of only a few countries. The US is modifying the *Patriot* surface-to-air missile system to give it a limited ATBM capability. Several European firms have small contracts to study ATBM architecture under US SDI funding; France and Italy are developing a surface-to-air missile with some ATBM potential (*ASTER*), the Soviet Union is developing a version of its SA-12 surface-to-air missile system, and Japan has also begun an ATBM study of its own. The most important regional effort is the Israeli *Arrow*; in July 1988 the Pentagon signed a contract with Israel Aircraft Industries to fund 80% of the programme's initial R&D budget of $US 1,160 m. Iraq also claims to have a SAM with an ATBM capability, called the *Faw*-I, but this is hard to credit.

Missile proliferation already poses a threat to regional stability and gives third-world countries the reach to hit the Soviet Union; concern has risen in the US that it could easily find itself in the same vulnerable position. In their *Report to the Forty-First President of the United States*, James Woolsey and Brent Scowcroft (before his appointment as US National Security Advisor) urged consideration of 'some limited ABM system' which 'could afford some protection of a major portion of the US against a small accidental attack or against a third-country threat such as chemically armed extended-range versions of the intermediate-range missiles now widely deployed in the Mid-East'. They caution that 'even a deployment of a limited size . . . would be a substantial defense program that would need to be assessed in the context of other major defense needs', nor is it clear that this is feasible without changing the ABM Treaty. The need for such a system is many years away, but unless some way is found to curb the spread of ballistic missiles, and their marriage to nuclear and chemical warheads, greater interest in such systems can be expected in countries that can afford them.

UN PEACE-KEEPING: FAILURES AND ASPIRATIONS

In September 1988 the Nobel Prize Committee awarded its annual peace prize to the United Nations' peace-keeping forces. While the Committee commended the UN forces for their past efforts, it clearly had more in mind the contribution the UN has been making, and is poised to make, in the present and future. In April 1988 the UN dispatched 50 members of its observer force to Afghanistan and Pakistan to monitor the withdrawal of Soviet troops in accordance with the agreement it had worked out over six years of patient effort. In August some 350 men were sent to the Gulf to provide a buffer between Iran and Iraq as they agreed a cease-fire on the basis of UN Resolution 598. The UN is now preparing a peace-keeping force for Namibia in 1989, and it has in mind, or on the drawing board, possible roles in the Western Sahara, Kampuchea and perhaps Central America.

After ten years punctuated by political failure and military misfortune, this is an extraordinary turnabout in the UN's fortunes. It is, of course, the improvement in the international atmosphere, as a result of the changing US–Soviet relationship, which has made it possible for the UN to undertake these new challenges. It will not be easy, however. Not only will considerable new money need to be found to support the new efforts (the UN at present has perhaps 10,000 troops engaged in seven peace operations at an estimated cost of $US 250 m annually; this could double in the next year) but new methods of operation and control will have to be devised to assure success.

There is, of course, a distinction to be drawn between observer missions – typically unarmed groups of experienced officers who act passively as monitors or liaison officers – and peace-keeping forces, which are larger and comprise armed military units that are often required to act more assertively on the battlefield between the opposed forces. Observers can be deployed with ease from one trouble spot to another, because they are ostensibly part of an extant organization: the UN Truce Supervisory Organization (UNTSO). Peace-keeping forces, on the other hand, are normally raised and authorized by an explicit Security Council resolution; since this requires a degree of consensus among

25

the permanent members, the deployment of such a force is a significant achievement. The last UN peace-keeping force to deploy was UNIFIL (UN Interim Force In Lebanon) in March 1978, and the force currently being assembled for operations in Namibia, UNTAG (UN Transition Advisory Group), has been under consideration since September 1978, when Resolution 435 was initially passed.

Political Failure
In the years since 1978 there has been no shortage of violence and destruction on a scale that should have warranted the attention of the United Nations. In some cases the Secretary General was unwilling, or found himself unable, to set up effective arrangements that would enhance peace. In others, regional groupings or multinational alliances eschewed his assistance, made their own arrangements to negotiate truces and cease-fires and, when these met with a degree of success, provided military forces to assist and supervise an end to hostilities.

These non-UN efforts met with a variety of success and failure. In 1976 the Arab League's Arab Deterrent Force (ADF) deployed to Lebanon, where, after an initial welcome, it failed to make much impact on the civil war and was withdrawn in 1982. In 1980 the Commonwealth Monitoring Force (CMF) – 1,500 troops from the United Kingdom, Australia, New Zealand, Kenya and Fiji – successfully superintended the cease-fire in Zimbabwe and assisted in the transfer of power. The OAU-sponsored force in Chad deployed in 1981; its 3,600 troops from Senegal, Zaire and Nigeria remained in the field only six months, and it was not deemed a success. The MFO (Multinational Force and Observers) in Sinai, an example of a well-run and effective force, was set up under the Israeli–Egyptian peace treaty, deployed in 1982 and still remains in the field. The two successive Multi-National Force (MNF) expeditions to Beirut (made up of US, French, Italian and British troops) met with contrasting fates. The first successfully carried out its mandate to evacuate the Palestinians in August 1982. The second, a more open-ended mission, finished badly with the speedy withdrawal of most contingents in 1984, after casualties in excess of 300 killed had been sustained.

There were also two significant occasions when a degree of international co-operation took place at sea: in 1984, when an international minesweeping operation cleared the Gulf of Suez, and, more recently, when a number of navies increasingly harmonized their efforts to escort commercial shipping through the Strait of Hormuz and clear Gulf waters of mines. In the latter case there was no central co-ordination of operations (although at sea there inevitably had to be some liaison), but there was clear political contact between the European participants under the aegis of the Western European Union.

It might seem that, as an institution, the UN had been something of a failure in this period. But this would be an unjust and simplistic indictment. Like any institution, the UN is only as useful as its members allow it to be. Often it was not a question of the UN failing to act, but of the international community failing to use the UN for its proper function. Although under normal circumstances peace-keeping forces are authorized by the Security Council, the conflict of interests at superpower level has been a frequent cause of stalled initiatives in this forum. In the case of the Sinai, the March 1979 treaty between Israel, Egypt and the US specifically provided for UN troops to act as the buffer-zone force in the Sinai. Although the treaty was recognized in the UN, Secretary General Waldheim needed Security Council authorization to deploy the reconstituted and retasked peace force, but the Soviet Union intimated that it would block the resolution. As a consequence, the MFO was set up outside UN auspices. A converse situation led to the deployment of the MNF to Beirut after a proposal to send a UN force was derailed by US diplomatic activity.

The US and the USSR found themselves in frequent opposition, and this lack of co-operation was a major impediment to UN peace-keeping operations. The only exception since the mid-1970s concerned the establishment of UNIFIL after the Israeli invasion of south Lebanon in March 1978. Resolution 416 was passed with twelve members voting in favour, two abstaining (USSR and Czechoslovakia), and one (China) failing to participate. Even when a peace-keeping force had been authorized, there were still fundamental differences between the permanent members as to how the force should be controlled. The USSR was unwilling to delegate the executive responsibility to the force commander or a single office within the UN secretariat; it wanted instead to be in a position to review, and if necessary veto, each change in the operational directive. The US, on the other hand, was anxious for the commanders on the ground to have freedom to react to local events. In addition to the US–Soviet rivalry which frequently stymied UN action, the parties directly involved in conflict were themselves traditionally averse to UN intervention; in these circumstances there was little the UN could do.

Weakness in the Organization
These failures were political, caused primarily by the schisms among the UN's most powerful members, and not the result of any fundamental faults in the organization. At a lower operating level, however, there were weaknesses. The deployment of newly-constituted UN multinational peace-keeping forces had not always been a tactical success, and, once they were established, the standard of operations was sometimes that of their least capable contingent. For instance, although UNIFIL was skilfully convened at a political level, its hasty and uncoordinated deployment made it vulnerable to determined attacks by both the PLO and the Israeli-supported forces under Major Haddad. There were a number of casualties during its initial establishment. Logistic supply was uncertain, and the force HQ's failure to assert itself in the early stages of deployment encouraged a lack of uniformity in the

27

conduct of its contingents; this was exacerbated by the tendency for some to look to their own national HQ, rather than the force commander, for day-to-day instructions.

Where the peace force was an instrument of a well-drafted treaty between two parties who were reconciled to its deployment, as with the UN Disengagement Observation Force (UNDOF), deployed in the Golan Heights, these military problems – endemic to any hastily convened multinational force – were not critically important. But they were important when the situation was open to doubt and the presence of the peace-keepers was likely to be challenged by militias and armed insurgents who were not party to any agreement.

The operating problems seemed to occur in three main areas. During the initial phase of the deployment there was a consistent lack of establishing procedures and an experienced military staff to apply them; then there were logistic problems caused by diversity of equipment, lack of funds and the unsettling effect of a six-monthly mandate renewal; finally, there was the variable military experience of the HQ staff members, who seldom had time to establish a common *modus operandi* before being pitched into a fast-moving military situation.

The possibility of invoking the legislation for peace enforcement and collective action against an aggressor state had fallen into abeyance since its early manifestation in the Korean War. The nature of global violence had changed, and there were political problems between the major powers in the Security Council. The Military Committee continued to meet in a purely ritualistic fashion but, in view of the long-standing disagreements between the major powers over the extent and nature of its responsibilities, was completely unable to have any influence on peace-keeping operations.

Within the Secretariat, in the Office for Operational and External Support Activities, there was an important nucleus of experts. They were able to overcome the initial organization and movement problems as well as assisting with the ongoing political task of maintaining the authority of a peace force in the field, but the military aspects of mounting and operating were still dealt with in an *ad hoc* manner. By design, UN peace-keeping forces were reactive in their concept of operation, and there was little they could do to improve conditions for their long-term success. Their peace-keeping procedures were entirely workable in a situation, such as the Golan, where the battlefield zone was strictly controlled by the main opposing forces, who had agreed to their presence. But in the Lebanon, where the 'battlefield' was occupied by a variety of armed factions, the collective will and mandate of the UN could be challenged by what amounted to small unrepresentative gangs and militias which operated outside the sanctions of the international community.

The Changes
1988 saw a turnround of these conditions, with the *rapprochement* between the super-powers being the most important single factor in this

remarkable *volte-face*. The three-way improvement of relations between Moscow, Washington and Beijing has altered the negotiating patterns in the Security Council. The Soviet Union, in particular, has reversed its attitude towards UN peace-keeping, and Gorbachev wants the USSR to play a more positive part in achieving a consensus within the Security Council. The other permanent members have already found the Soviet Union, in its new role, a more reliable and consistent partner. The United States, for its part, has relented on its refusal to pay its agreed share of the UN budget.

Even the mood in the General Assembly has changed. There is a growing sense of maturity amongst the non-aligned nations. The tougher aid policies followed by the permanent members of the Security Council have had a calming effect on the behaviour of their beneficiaries. The possibility of playing one super-power off against another has considerably diminished, and support for insurgent forces in many areas has been reduced and even removed altogether. There is less systematic anti-American rhetoric. The Reagan administration had always insisted that a realistic degree of influence and recognition must be given to the major powers, and collectively the organization is tacitly beginning to acknowledge this position.

At an operational level the situation is changing too. The USSR's previous reservations about the delegation of command has now been replaced by an up-beat policy on improving the effectiveness of peace-keeping forces. Logistically the Secretariat is better organized than ever. A more pragmatic and less political approach to logistic problems has allowed new staff with appropriate skills to be recruited and more effective supply systems to be adopted in existing forces. More importantly, Gorbachev wants a Security Council which has 'more teeth'; this implies the ability to field peace-keeping forces that are no longer restricted to a reactive posture in a buffer zone but can take problem-solving action where necessary. He seeks a more positive role for the Military Staff Committee, which may resume its proper responsibility under Article 46 for the strategic planning and preparation of the armed forces placed at the disposal of the UN.

There are a number of theatres where peace negotiations have already begun: Western Sahara, Central America and Cambodia. In each case the deployment of any peace-keeping forces, or even observer missions, would require some further progress to take place in current negotiations. But the fundamental obstacles which formerly blocked peaceful resolution of a number of long-standing disputes have been largely removed by the knock-on effects of super-power co-operation both inside and outside the Security Council.

The Central American Summit of February 1989 has provided a vehicle for agreement and a plan for the deployment of an observer mission, although at present the proposal, emanating from a regional meeting, is for a non-UN mission involving military observers from Spain and Canada and a number of civilians from West Germany. The

Maghreb summit has also yielded hopeful, but less concrete, promises for a future peace agreement between the Polisario and Morocco. There has also been progress in the Kampuchean conflict, with suggestions for a monitor force to oversee a cease-fire and election, although the number of Kampuchean insurgent forces and their peripheral supporters has complicated the negotiating process.

In addition, there are existing UN forces where the circumstances which prevailed at their initial deployment have changed, leaving the peace-keepers awkwardly maintaining an inappropriate or redundant operational mandate. For the observers in Afghanistan for instance, whence Soviet troops have withdrawn, humanitarian considerations will no doubt take precedence over the UN monitoring functions. In the Gulf, the fragile nature of the truce between Iran and Iraq and the precarious situation of the observers there has raised concerns that greater efforts to organize a formal truce agreement are needed, although there are some local discussions attempting to arrange a more durable peace. In Cyprus, the long-standing peace-keeping force has been so successful locally that it reduces the disputants' need to negotiate a realistic peace treaty, even though the search for a better solution continues. In Lebanon the vulnerable situation of the peace-keepers and the behaviour of local forces not party to the peace agreement require urgent attention. Hitherto, remedial action has been impeded by the conflicting attitudes of the super-powers, usually on issues having more to do with their opposed policies on Israel and Syria than any immediate local dispute. As these differences are reduced, the possibility of reviewing inappropriate mandates, particularly UNIFIL's role in Lebanon, may become more of a reality.

Need For New Techniques
The need for the major powers to give greater support to the activities of the UN is also strengthened by the increasing lethality of modern weapon systems and the effect of modern warfare on societies and the environment. In a theatre where military and civilian activities are intertwined, a wrong identification can destroy a passing civil aircraft and its two hundred passengers in a matter of seconds, with no time for a second look. And while the minefields laid by Syrian, Egyptian and Israeli forces in the Arab–Israeli wars are not precisely delineated, they are broadly speaking located, but there is no present technology available to clear up the indiscriminate laying of modern plastic antipersonnel mines and devices of every type in Afghanistan, Cambodia, Vietnam, Iran and Iraq.

Although the collective resolve to act is growing, the UN Charter itself may not prove equal to the circumstances, particularly where it authorizes collective action. Its Articles were largely influenced by the victorious powers in June 1945, who, after Hitler's conquests in Europe, were understandably concerned with conflicts that resulted from territorial aggression. Their legislation for collective action by 'air, sea or land' required clarity about the identity of the aggressor, a condition rarely fulfilled in the period of intense East–West competition following World War II. Furthermore, the nature of post-colonial conflict rarely involved the confrontation of regular forces along clearly drawn lines. In the war zones of Africa and south-east Asia, instead of two or three recognizably constituted and controlled state armies, the involvement of variously motivated insurgent factions reduced the possibility of the UN acting as intermediary and exacerbated the difficulties of established buffer zones and areas of separation. The identity of the aggressor became blurred and the principle of collective action became obsolete.

Currently, peace-keeping forces are authorized under the catch-all Article 29, which does not specify the use of force, and the present UN rules of engagement have been developed from a long history of allowing troops to fire only in the dire circumstances of an actual threat to their lives. Something of a legislative and attitudinal reversal may be required before the habitual peace-keeping contingents can, and do, move from policing to collective action, however desirable that might seem to the super-powers.

Even if the required legislative changes could be made, the prospects for a multinational force deployed, however carefully, in a peace enforcement role against an active insurgent force, however universally condemned, are not good. The Indian army has failed to restore normality through its operation in Sri Lanka, and the record of the second multinational force in Beirut was not an inspiring one. Nor do the super-powers have anything better than a patchy success record in low-intensity, out-of-area operations.

So far United Nations peace-keeping contingents have enjoyed a comparatively low attrition rate in areas where there have been, and still are, active insurgent forces. This is because, by following their carefully evolved techniques of interposing themselves passively between the combatant forces in the war zone, they have successfully avoided becoming a sustained target for insurgents. True, there have been repeated attacks on UN troops in the Lebanon, but these have a random character markedly different in scale and intensity from attacks by the same insurgents against Israeli forces.

A reinvigorated and politically cohesive Security Council may find it unbearably frustrating to see its carefully drafted mandates for peace-keeping deployments thwarted by small unrepresentative guerrilla forces; for instance, in Kampuchea by an intractable *Khmer Rouge* breaking away from the CGDK coalition. But a UN response that involved a role change from peaceful policing to counter-insurgency would be of doubtful legality if the legitimacy of the local government against which the insurgency was directed was uncertain; and, of course, it might not succeed where the professional armies of the major powers have failed. In the post-war period even the professionally constituted British army, arguably one of the most successful in counter-insurgency operations, had the advantage of being able to develop its tactics and procedures over a long period in theatres where it was often able to control the political, legal and social systems that could assist their success. Future UN forces will not have these advantages and, as a result, will find it safer, and probably just as effective in peace-keeping terms, to continue to operate as passive policemen. In this role they must develop an effective system of damage control against random attacks by insurgents.

Future peace forces will continue to face problems even in the ideal circumstances of a conventional buffer-zone situation between two hostile armies. The increasing sophistication of weaponry on the modern battlefield places greater demands on the peace-keeper. The debris in a recently active war zone will be dangerous, the ground dotted with indiscriminately sown mines. In addition, there may be residually active chemicals. To survive, operate and move freely, the peace-keeper will have to be better trained and more comprehensively equipped than at present.

Another area of increasing sophistication is battlefield surveillance and communications. In future operations the communication and surveillance capability of the opposing forces will sometimes exceed that of the peace-keeping force. This is already the case in the Golan, where UNDOF's night surveillance capability is limited to a few devices supplied by individual contingents, while on either side the looming antennae towers of Syria and Israel provide the opposing forces with a vastly superior all-weather reporting system. In a less well established force than UNDOF this superior capability might undermine the authority of the force commander and allow the parties to surprise and deceive his posts in the field. Because peace-keeping troops are largely chosen from developing countries, some of the contingents will have neither the training nor the technical skills to make full use of advanced surveillance equipment. Greater military participation by the major powers would solve many of these problems.

Looking ahead into the next decade, the UN's field operations will be shaped by the successful use of battlefield technology. Helicopters and light aircraft have an obvious application as battlefield transports, but their value as battlefield surveillance platforms for the peace-keeper has been ignored. Development of a UN airborne surveillance system could be considered for future peace-keeping operations.

A mainly airborne surveillance capability, backed up by observers on the ground, would also confer on the peace-keeper an authority which in his present ground-based mode he does not have. This development will place a major requirement on the Secretariat to improve its resource management capability even further and become far more air-conscious in negotiating mandates and formulating operating procedures. Selection of suitably qualified field HQ staff who are already operationally familiar with state-of-the-art surveillance techniques may also be a problem.

Another area which could alter the configuration of future peace forces, particularly observer missions, is the exploitation of information-gathering techniques. The UN is understandably nervous about the use of 'intelligence', and the concept of secrecy is quite alien to peace-keeping situations. Nevertheless, there are several well-developed technologies devoted to information gathering which are already overtly used by respectable scientific bodies, including the UN, for peaceful purposes. These include air photography, contact satellite photography and the whole range of electronic and seismic listening systems. There is no need for the UN to resort to 'spying', 'bugging' or 'snooping'; the information is readily available. What is needed is for the UN to gather it in a timely and selective manner, assess it impartially and authoritatively, and publish it as widely as possible.

UN field doctrines may be developed by other stimuli in addition to technology. The concept of a truce followed by a separation of forces, which in some theatres in the past has created a long-term division between the parties, may give way to a cease-fire followed by a process of integration of forces. This pattern was employed successfully by the CMF in Zimbabwe. And the MFO experience in the Sinai also holds useful lessons for future UN forces on command, liaison and resource management.

It is to be hoped that there will be cross-fertilization with the super-powers who (in spite of their expertise in the techniques of general war) have something to learn about low-intensity operations, and peace-keeping in particular. There is a danger that, when the UN takes to 'flexing its muscles', the mistakes of Beirut may be repeated in future peaceful interventions. There are still widespread misconceptions that peace forces can deter or cause parties to act against their will, and that large peace forces necessarily produce a better quality of cease-fire than smaller ones. Furthermore, the focus of regional conflict may have already moved from the arena of super-power influence to inter-ethnic or religious warfare, which does not easily lend itself to outside mediation. Nevertheless, the conditions for an active UN role in peace-keeping operations are better than they have been for more than a generation.

US ROLES AND RESPONSIBILITIES

Accumulating American sensitivity to change abroad, combined with economic and political pressures at home, began in 1988 to transform fundamentally the US conception of its post-war roles and responsibilities. For forty years the country's global role has been characterized principally by pre-eminence among its allies and a preoccupation with containing Soviet influence. The foundations for this role were the US political and economic ascendancy in the aftermath of World War II and the perception (shared throughout the West) that Soviet hostility to

Western ideals and values, along with Soviet military power, represented a great threat to Allied security.

In 1988 these foundations were significantly eroded by changing US perceptions of the world. Most important, American confidence in Gorbachev's sincerity in pursuing his expressed goal of peaceful coexistence increased dramatically as the Soviet leader continued to map out areas of common interest, met President Reagan twice during the year, and took some noteworthy steps both to implement reforms in the USSR and to give earnests of a reduced emphasis on Soviet military might. At the same time, Americans attached increasing significance to a range of global problems that transcend East–West competition, such as third-world debt, deterioration of the world ecosystem, and the international drug trade. More and more Americans feared that the United States' global burdens were fuelling a process of economic decline that was eroding its relative economic strength and security.

These attitudes were not wholly generated by developments during 1988; their roots stretch back many years. However, they were reinforced and reached critical mass through the presidential election campaign, in which they found widespread expression. The result was an incipient transformation of US global roles and responsibilities. How long this process will survive and how far it will go is uncertain, but it is clear that its primary themes are retrenchment and realignment.

Retrenchment . . .
Throughout 1988, pressure to rejuvenate American economic competitiveness was a driving force both in day-to-day US politics and in the presidential campaign. By the end of 1987 concerns over the country's mounting national debt of $2.6 trillion and persistent budget and trade deficits of more than $100 billion led two-thirds of Americans to believe that the US economy had become weaker relative to other nations. At the same time, Americans were increasingly beginning to consider economic power a more important determinant of international influence than military power. Moreover, this economic unease did not reflect political partisanship; it was a focal point of common concern. In the summer 1988 issue of *Foreign Affairs* former Secretaries of State Henry Kissinger and Cyrus Vance put a bipartisan imprimatur on the issue, writing that:

Foreign policy and economic policy have become increasingly interdependent . . . . Economic strength is today even more central to the way America is perceived by its friends and potential adversaries. US political leadership in the world cannot be sustained if confidence in the American economy continues to be undermined by substantial trade and budget deficits.

While concerns about American economic competitiveness did exist in 1987, they developed overwhelming political importance in 1988 as they found expression in theories of decline which resonated deeply among the American public, and in the presidential campaign, of which they became a central theme. By a margin of nearly 2:1, voters were more concerned that the new President should 'strengthen the economy' than that he should 'protect our national security interests'.

More important, the imperative of building American economic strength took on explicit national security dimensions. A March 1988 poll found that 59% of Americans felt that 'economic competitors pose a greater threat to national security than military adversaries do, because they threaten our jobs and economic security'. This sentiment – occasionally tinged with xenophobia in reaction to foreign investment in the US and the spread of technology to American adversaries or competitors – was reflected in the expansion of definitions of national security to include an economic dimension. The Reagan administration, which during its early years in office focused almost exclusively on military capabilities as a measure of national power, ranked a 'healthy and growing economy' second only to 'survival of the United States as a free and independent nation' in its definition of key national interests. This attitude was carried into the presidential campaign, where candidate Bush proclaimed that 'economic growth is now as much a matter of foreign policy as it is of monetary policy'.

US concerns about economic fatigue provide a ghostly, if inaccurate, parallel to the Soviet frustrations with the exhausted Soviet economy that are the driving force in the transformation of Soviet domestic and foreign policy. Historian Paul Kennedy brought these concerns into focus in 1988 in his best-selling book *The Rise and Fall of the Great Powers* by implying that the relative decline of the US, like the decline of previous hegemonies, was due to over-committing limited resources to the maintenance of military power. The notion of 'imperial overstretch' far more accurately encapsulated the Soviet dilemma and, as applied to the US, was fiercely rebutted by a number of Americans, but it achieved considerable currency in US policy debates. The notion also reinforced (though it did not cause) the overwhelming pressure that was developing for the US to retrench in two ways: by reducing absolute budget levels and by reappraising burden-sharing among itself and its allies.

Budget Restrictions
Concerns about economic fatigue sustained and augmented American determination to reduce the government's bloated current-account deficit, but it was reduced popular belief in the Soviet threat and rapidly growing domestic concerns that dictated the strategy of retrenchment. As recently as 1986, only 37% of American voters had believed relations between the US and the USSR were stable or improving, while 60% thought they were getting worse. By mid-1988 these proportions had changed dramatically: 94% of Americans believed US–Soviet relations were stable or getting better.

Although US public opinion was concerned to proceed cautiously in 1988, testing Soviet good faith at each turn, its optimism about the

US–Soviet relationship had undeniable budget implications. Heightened perceptions of the Soviet threat would have augured well for military strength, as they did in 1980; they might even have resigned Americans to tax increases rather than budget cuts. However, a growing belief in the sincerity of Gorbachev's soothing rhetoric, reinforced by unilateral Soviet steps, helped to reduce the political risks of budget retrenchment and made it easier to move in the direction of fiscal restraint. In 1988 the American public remained somewhat divided over the need for the Reagan military build-up, but 84% agreed there was no need to sustain it.

Another factor that compounded pressure on defence and foreign-policy spending was the widespread belief that the United States was not devoting enough of its limited resources to tackling the burgeoning domestic challenges to its own society. Just when perceptions of the external Soviet threat were lessening, and so diluting the rationale for security spending, increasing and undeniable manifestations of growing social problems at home were generating pressure for available resources to be diverted to domestic budgets. The depth of public concern over the pervasiveness of the drug culture, the ubiquity of the homeless and the growth in violent crime was reflected in the preoccupation with these subjects in public and political dialogue.

Public attention was also turning to a growing list of less dramatic, but nonetheless important, issues that were widely viewed as basic requirements for meeting the changing needs of American society. Large numbers of people believed that health care, day care and education were inadequately funded. In sharp contrast to the views they revealed on defence spending, early 1988 polls indicated that substantial majorities believed the government was spending too little on a range of domestic issues: over assistance for the poor, 68% felt this; over dealing with drug addiction, 67%; over improving the nation's health, 69%; and over halting the rising crime rate, 71%. In contrast, the same polls indicated only 5% of the public felt too little went on foreign aid, while 68% felt too much was being spent.

The sum of all these attitudes has been significant pressure on the financial basis of American globalism – the defence, foreign-aid and multilateral budgets. Throughout 1988 the Reagan administration found the Congress increasingly reluctant to sanction its efforts to hold the line on defence and foreign aid and meet American financial commitments to the UN and the Organization of American States. The political conditions underlying this reluctance have been carried forward into the new administration, sustaining pressure on the defence budget, which the Bush team intends to hold at zero growth for a year (see p. 63) and posing other difficult dilemmas. For example, the growing number of UN peace-keeping operations demands substantial funding at a time when Americans also perceive budget austerity to be in their security interests. The difficulty of reconciling these imperatives has already led the US, along with the other permanent members of the

Security Council, to call for a reduction in the size and cost of the UN peace-keeping force tasked to monitor the transition to independence in Namibia (see p. 199). How much budgetary considerations will inhibit US enthusiasm for such opportunities remains to be worked out between the Bush administration and Congress. In the short term, however, budget imperatives will certainly act as a brake on the US financial contribution to Western security.

Burden-sharing
A related manifestation of changing American attitudes to security, and one that also has potentially long-term implications, is the prominence of the burden-sharing issue. Two factors lay at the root of public concern about the relationship between the resources which the US devoted to the common defence and those contributed by its allies. The first was the greater importance now ascribed to economic competitiveness, as opposed to military power, and the widespread perception that US economic competitiveness was in decline. The enormous pressures on American budgets inevitably stimulated a reappraisal of defence commitments – in 1988 both Senator Sam Nunn and National Security Advisor Brent Scowcroft estimated that $300–400 bn would have to be cut from the five-year defence programme – and naturally America's largest defence commitments, in Europe and in Asia, received close scrutiny. This focus was reinforced by a growing resentment of the fact that the United States' principal economic competitors were its allies in Europe and Asia. At a time when the US was afflicted with a huge trade deficit, Americans believed it was spending a disproportionate amount to defend such allies. The implications of these trends were powerful. By May 1988 polls indicated that 86% of the American public thought that their country 'may seriously damage [its] economy by spending too much to defend other countries'.

Determining the exact burden that any country actually does contribute to an alliance is an inexact and contentious business at best. It is difficult to assign dollar values to many of the costs borne by US allies in the name of common defence – such as conscription, wear and tear due to front-line training, or infrastructure contributions. In absolute dollar terms, however, the US seems to have been bearing more than half of the cost of defending Europe, and it has spent more on defence than all the members of NATO and Japan together. A Pentagon assessment of allied efforts, released in the spring of 1988, concluded that the US was paying more than its fair share of the costs of helping to defend NATO and Japan. Fairly or not, Americans saw gross inequities in the distribution of the defence burden.

The force of this perception was evident in the actions taken throughout 1988 to address the burden-sharing issue. In May, President Reagan sent Deputy Secretary of Defense Howard Taft IV on a campaign through Western Europe and Asia to encourage the allies to spend more. In June, Secretary of Defense Carlucci echoed this appeal in Japan. And during the latter half of the year NATO's Defence Planning Committee worked to assess burdens within the Alliance in an effort to come to grips with the burden-sharing problem (see pp. 85–6). Throughout the year the Reagan administration's approach was to stave off US defence budget cuts by citing the intangible contributions the allies make and by calling upon allies to raise their defence budgets. However, European NATO nations point to their record of steady defence budget growth (in contrast to the 'stop-go' approach of the US), to the substantial budget increases annually being made by some, and to the political constraints that work against pushing through abnormal defence budget increases, especially at a time when public opinion has decided that the Soviet threat has been receding swiftly.

To a large degree, the initiative to eliminate disparities between US and allied investment in the common defence resides with Congress, which in early 1988 convened a Defense Burdensharing Panel under the auspices of Rep. Patricia Schroeder. It is not yet clear what action Congress will take in response to the final report of the Panel. However, there is no doubt that – whatever US or NATO initiatives are taken in the future – so long as allied economies are perceived as competing with the US economy, a positive determination not to tolerate what is perceived as defence 'free-loading' will be fundamental to American attitudes to burden-sharing. The challenge for the US and its allies is to manage amicably American pressure for greater equity in burden-sharing. This challenge and the friction it creates may be eased in the coming years by a lightening of the common defence burden as a result of arms reductions and by any easing of the problems created by the twin US deficits. Equally, however, the friction could be compounded by any sharpening of economic competition arising out of protectionist moves, whether in a single European market or in North America. Similarly, a breakdown of multilateral trade mechanisms, most notably the General Agreement on Trade and Tariffs (GATT), and a move towards regional trading blocs would exacerbate the burden-sharing debate and threaten Alliance cohesion.

American retrenchment – in the short term with budget cuts, and over the longer term via burden-sharing changes – would imply a retreat from the hegemony characteristic of the United States' alliance role in the post-war era. However, it must not be mistaken for resurgent isolationism, and US political leaders will have to work hard to restrain the more emotional appeals for retrenchment that give this impression. Instead, it should be recognized for what it is: a restructuring of alliance burdens to reflect more accurately the ability to pay. For their part, Americans must recognize that a process of retrenchment that relieves them of unwanted financial burdens would also necessarily relieve them of some of the great influence to which they have become accustomed. Encouragement of a European pillar in NATO must be accompanied by tolerance for a greater European voice. Similarly, demands for US allies in Asia (notably Japan and South Korea) to bear a greater share of the defence burden must be accompanied by a recognition that they will want a greater voice as well. This transition will be particularly difficult to manage because there will be disagreements over the definition of the threat – which is increasingly less clear – and hence over what the total burden should be. At the same time, the community of interest between America and its European and Asian allies will also become less clear-cut, as attention shifts from diminishing East–West competition to economic competition between the industrialized regions of the world. These are problems worth having – in that they are born of the economic and military success of post-war US alliance strategy – but they could prove enormously disruptive if poorly managed.

. . . and Realignment

The pressures for retrenchment created by changing American perceptions of the world were of immediate consequence in budgetary and political terms. The pressures for the realignment of US policy priorities had implications that were both more nebulous and at the same time potentially more profound. During the 1988 presidential campaign George Bush proclaimed that the post-war era was over and a 'revolutionary' era had begun. However, he failed to communicate clearly what the characteristics of that 'revolutionary' era are; the sense of transition was stronger than the sense of destination. If it is clear that many Americans perceived the post-war era to be ending (as did many of their country's allies), it is not yet clear that they have any real vision of the prospects for the new era and any bright new world it might offer, nor yet of what America's roles and responsibilities in it might be. Nevertheless, some basic elements are visible.

The overwhelming force in the realignment of US foreign policy is the increasingly benign American view of the Soviet Union. Many have come to believe that the basis of East–West relations is shifting rapidly from confrontation and containment to co-operation. More than 40 years ago George Kennan had set out a process of 'mellowing' the Soviet Union as an objective of the containment strategy that became the foundation of American post-war globalism. During 1988 more accommodating Soviet rhetoric and actions gave the appearance of such 'mellowing' and reinforced the trend away from preoccupation with the Soviet threat. During the summer, polls indicated that more than seven out of ten Americans endorsed US–Soviet co-operation to combat environmental pollution, the illicit drug trade and terrorism; to expand cultural exchanges; to resolve conflicts in the Middle East and other regional trouble spots; and to eliminate most nuclear weapons by the year 2000. In combination with other American attitudes in 1988, this trend created pressure for US realignment in two dimensions.

America Turning Inward

For the short term, and perhaps for the long, American views of the world in 1988 established the basis for reassessing the way in which US resources were allocated between domestic and foreign policies. Not only were domestic problems growing in intensity, but the reduced perception of the external threat increased their relative importance. In his call for a 'kinder, gentler' nation, and in his desire to become the 'education' President, Bush recognized the growing desire of the American public to tackle a host of domestic problems that had simmered unattended through the Reagan presidency. The extent to which President Bush's rhetoric can be translated into domestic change is limited by the budget crunch – at least in the short term – but there is a clear intention to devote the funds which are available to the demanding domestic agenda. In his budget for 1990, Bush announced that funds which the Reagan administration had allocated to increasing defence spending by 2% in real terms would be diverted into a number of social programmes, including education, the fight against drug addiction and homelessness, and cleaning up the environment. To be sure, he called for small increases above inflation for defence in the years following 1990, but the increases allocated to social spending represent such a small down-payment on a 'kinder, gentler America' that it will be very difficult to direct resources back to defence after just one year. For the immediate future the policy focus has shifted from challenges abroad (which played such a role in stimulating the Reagan revolution but are now perceived to be diminishing) to challenges at home. To the extent that resources are redirected from foreign policy to domestic policy, the 'revolutionary era' that candidate Bush proclaimed in 1988, if it does not bring a revolution in American society, will at least bring about significant change.

Beyond the Cold War
While the balance between domestic-policy and foreign-policy priorities may be shifting, the United States retains a firm commitment to a global role. But this role is also undergoing realignment, as the conditions which underpinned the country's post-war foreign policy continue to change. For much of the post-war era US foreign policy has been characterized by a tension between moralism and the expedients of containment. As the requirements of containment diminish, the guiding principles of foreign policy are reverting from expedience to ideals more fundamental to American democracy. Americans, and the Bush administration, are committed to sustaining the 'peace through strength' formula championed by the Reagan administration and seen by many Americans as having been critical to breaking the East–West political and military deadlock. However, other principles – such as commitment to democracy, human rights and free markets – are becoming increasingly influential in foreign-policy decision-making. This is not to say that such principles have not been a major influence on American foreign policy, nor that the US has now abandoned the objective of containment, but, if the reconciliation between East and West continues, US foreign policy can move from being based almost

wholly on containment towards a basis in which these principles play a larger and more significant role. Signs of this evolution already exist in a presidential transition otherwise notable for the political continuity it represents. During his Senate confirmation hearings in January 1989, Secretary of State Baker asserted that 'through a realistic approach [we can] write a new chapter of American leadership for a rapidly-changing world', and called for a broadening of the Soviet–American dialogue to include discussions on co-operation to resolve problems with the international drug trade, terrorism and the environment.

Potentially, this evolution has profound implications for the orientation of American foreign policy. The increasing weight of universal principles in the framework guiding that policy will give US bilateral relations a stature increasingly independent of US relations with the Soviet Union. If the principles of democratization and commitment to human rights and free markets are not distorted by, or subordinated to, the need to contain a Soviet 'threat', the US would be freed from the need to be the 'world's policeman'. It will be able to see the problems of the world's impoverished nations – their critical debt burdens, fragile political processes, and related human-rights violations – in their own terms, rather than through an East–West prism. Whether these trends will be confirmed and whether they will lead the US to give greater weight and aid to multilateral initiatives – including a rejuvenated UN – remains to be seen, but the odds in favour are better in a post-containment world than they have ever been.

The trend towards realignment of US foreign-policy priorities, both *vis-à-vis* domestic priorities and in terms of the principles that guide it, does not signify a swing in American foreign policy so much as an evolution. Like fiscal retrenchment, realignment represents a maturing of America's global role in the light of changing US perceptions of the world. As Secretary of State Baker stressed in his Senate confirmation hearings, the realities that underlie those changing perceptions 'will not permit a blind isolationism or a reckless unilateralism', a point he underscored with his determined pragmatism and calls for a new bipartisanship. Should bipartisanship be re-established in the coming years on the basis of a more balanced US contribution to world security, increasingly derived from principles other than simple opposition to the Soviet Union, 1988 will truly have been a watershed year in American foreign policy.

Arms Control

As with so much else in 1988, the arms-control process entered a transition phase in a broad range of negotiations. On the one hand, steady progress was made in implementing the INF Treaty on intermediate-range ground-based missiles, in negotiations to reduce strategic offensive nuclear forces, in developing a mandate for negotiations on conventional forces in Europe, in trying to strengthen existing limits and add impetus to the existing negotiations on chemical weapons, and in developing new verification procedures for the two unratified treaties on nuclear testing. A dramatic matching of deeds to words by the Soviet Union offered the prospect of many more advances in arms control. On the other hand, the initially cautious attitude taken by the Bush administration, exemplified by its intensive review of military and arms-control policy, combined with questions about Soviet readiness in the short term to make further deep cuts in conventional forces either unilaterally or on a negotiated basis, and the oft-expressed doubts about how many arms-control balls the super-powers could keep in the air at once, made it hard to see with any certainty where and how fast progress could actually be made.

Implementing the INF Treaty

The INF Treaty, signed at the Washington summit in December 1987 and completed by the exchange of instruments of ratification at the Moscow summit the following May, entered into force on 1 June 1988. The overall implementation has been received with general satisfaction on both sides, but both Washington and Moscow have raised a number of compliance issues, most of which appear to have been little more than oversights. Perhaps most serious, and controversial, was the possibility that the United States had failed to declare 145 ground-launched cruise missiles (GLCM) in the Memorandum of Understanding. This possibility was revealed when the US Navy awarded two contracts, totalling $462 million, for converting GLCM to sea-launched variants. It was uncertain, however, whether the missiles involved were completed versions of the GLCM or whether the conversion process was to use components of previously unassembled missiles. In either case, the issue raised serious compliance concerns which have yet to be resolved.

Despite these concerns, the INF Treaty has provided useful experience for arms control in general. It has furnished positive proof of a Soviet willingness to undertake deep, significant, asymmetric and closely verified cuts in its armed forces – proof that usefully underlines the possibilities for negotiations on conventional forces. Its implementation has further familiarized both parties with the procedures for on-site inspections – procedures that will be crucial if the US and USSR agree to reduce their respective strategic nuclear forces.

Nuclear and Space Talks

The optimism that infused the Nuclear and Space Talks in Geneva after the Washington summit in December 1987 soon faded, as negotiations to reduce strategic offensive weapons and examine the future of strategic defensive systems came to grips with the magnitude of the task. No treaties were signed at the Moscow summit in mid-1988, nor had the negotiators been able to surmount the main obstacles, notably the issues of sea-launched cruise missiles (SLCM) and strategic defences. The framework that had been negotiated by December 1987 still remained the basis for an agreement. (For details, see *Strategic Survey 1987–1988*, pp. 40–43.)

Throughout 1988, the negotiations in Geneva focused on five main areas: air-launched cruise missiles (ALCM), mobile missiles, SLCM, strategic defences, and verification. In each of these areas important details were agreed, but significant differences remained in all of them. As the talks recessed in late 1988, the two sides had been able to agree on 350 pages of a Joint Draft Text for a START treaty, though much of the language was still tentative.

Air-launched Cruise Missiles

Perhaps the most significant progress in the negotiations was made over air-launched cruise missiles. In long sessions during the Moscow summit US and Soviet chief negotiators Paul Nitze and Marshal Akhromeyev set out the areas of agreement and disagreement. The former included the following:

– All existing long-range ALCM will be considered nuclear-capable, and future conventional ALCM must be distinguishable from nuclear variants;
– Heavy bombers carrying ALCM must be distinguishable from those that carry gravity bombs and short-range attack missiles (SRAM);
– Only those heavy bombers equipped to carry ALCM may carry them, and such bombers must not be deployed at bases where non-ALCM-carrying bombers are deployed;
– The number of ALCM counted will be calculated by multiplying the number of each type of ALCM-carrying heavy bomber by the number of warheads attributed to that type and totalling the results.

Nonetheless a number of significant issues remained unresolved. The first concerned the methods for distinguishing nuclear ALCM from future conventional ones, and for distinguishing ALCM-carrying bombers from those that carry gravity bombs and SRAM. Second, there was the definition of 'long-range' in relation to ALCM. The United States wanted to define treaty-limited ALCM as those systems with ranges in excess of 1,500 kilometres, because it wanted to keep open the option of deploying a longer-range tactical air-to-surface missile. The Soviet

Union insisted on using the SALT II definition, which put the critical range limit at 600 km. Reagan administration officials had indicated privately that they might be willing to compromise on a 1,000-km limit if all other ALCM-related issues were solved.

Finally, there was the question of how many warheads to attribute to each ALCM-carrying heavy bomber. The US position was that, since ALCM are slow-flying missiles which could not be used in a pre-emptive attack, their deployment should not weigh as heavily against the agreed limit of 6,000 accountable warheads as other, more destabilizing systems. As a result, it proposed that ten warheads be attributed to each ALCM-carrying bomber. Because this number understates the US potential but overstates the current capability of the Soviet *Bear* bomber, the US has also indicated that it might be willing to accept a lower attribution number for Soviet ALCM-carriers that similarly understates their full potential. The USSR has rejected this, arguing that the attributed number should reflect the maximum capability of each bomber: i.e., 12 warheads for the B-52G, 20 for the B-52H, 22 for the B-1B, and 8 for the *Bear*. Neither side has so far been able to suggest an acceptable compromise.

Mobile Missiles
Progress was also achieved with regard to mobile missiles. The US position remained that mobile ICBM should be banned unless an effective verification regime can be agreed upon. The Soviet Union, which has already deployed two mobile missiles – the single warhead, road-mobile SS-25 and the 10-warhead, rail-mobile SS-24 – rejected the American proposal, suggesting instead a limit of 800 mobile missiles with a total of no more than 1,600 warheads. Despite the American position, Nitze and Akhromeyev did agree in Moscow to a number of procedures which would enable compliance with agreed limits on mobile missile deployments to be monitored.

The critical mechanism for ensuring effective verification of mobile missile deployments is the concept of restricted deployment bases and garrisons. Deployment within these restricted areas, and exit and entry patterns from them, would be governed by specific rules, including a numerical limit on the number of missiles and launchers deployed in each area; provision for specific measures (such as opening garages) to enhance observation by national technical means (NTM); and numerical restrictions on, and notifications of, the movement of mobile missiles from the restricted deployment areas.

A number of important issues, however, remained unresolved. These included the size of the restricted deployment areas, which the United States sought to limit to 25 km^2 and the Soviet Union to 100 km^2. Exactly which production facilities associated with the mobile missile force should be subject to permanent portal perimeter monitoring also remained in dispute. In addition, the US sought to ban the deployment of liquid-fuelled rockets on mobile launchers and favoured placing tags or tamper-resistant seals on accountable stages of the missiles and on mobile launchers. Finally, and from a verification point of view most critically, there was the issue of how to verify the absence of a 'covert' missile force. Because each side would retain a large number of non-deployed missiles, as spares and for testing and training purposes, it would be difficult to ensure that these could not be used as a potential means of breaking out of the treaty limits. Both sides committed themselves to negotiate limits on the number of non-deployed missiles, but neither the numerical limits nor strict verification procedures were agreed.

Sea-launched Cruise Missiles
With the ALCM and mobile missile issues seemingly on the way to resolution, the focus of attention shifted increasingly to those areas where significant disagreement persisted. Prime among these was the question of sea-launched cruise missiles. In December 1987 both sides agreed that long-range, nuclear SLCM should be limited by the START treaty, though such limits would fall outside the ceilings of 1,600 launchers and 6,000 accountable warheads. In view of the difficulty of verifying the distinction between conventional and nuclear SLCM, the Soviet Union proposed that all SLCM should be limited to 1,000, and that their deployment aboard specific classes of ships and submarines should be restricted. This proposal was rejected by the United States, which argued that a treaty limiting strategic offensive nuclear arms should not affect the deployment of non-nuclear weapons.

In March 1988 the Soviet Union proposed a verification package which addressed some of the US concerns but did not resolve the issue. It included permanent, on-site inspection of cruise missile production sites and controls on transporting the missiles to deployment areas. Verification could be enhanced if the missiles were to have tags affixed at the production sites. Second, procedures would include permanent inspection at naval bases and other facilities where warheads are married to the missiles, thus improving verification of the total deployment limits, and inspection of the procedures for loading the missiles aboard naval vessels. Finally, short-notice challenge inspections would be allowed aboard ships and submarines entering or leaving ports.

The US remained sceptical of the prospects for effective verification of SLCM limits because of the small size of the weapons and the ease with which they could be stored on large ships in violation of a treaty. This opposition is reinforced by an unwillingness to abandon the US policy of neither confirming nor denying the presence of nuclear weapons aboard its naval vessels. In view of this policy, Paul Nitze suggested in early April 1988 that the US should propose the banning not just of nuclear SLCM but of all naval nuclear weapons (except sea-launched ballistic missiles); accepting such a ban would obviate the need for the 'neither confirm nor deny' policy.

Nitze's radical proposal did not win support within the Administration and was never presented to the Soviet Union. Both civilian and military officials in the Pentagon insisted that SLCM were critical to extended deterrence as a result of the removal of the INF missiles. While the logic of this position might be debatable, the fact that this remained the US position meant that the two sides had made no real progress on the SLCM issue since the Reykjavik summit in October 1986, when Marshal Akhromeyev first made it clear that strict and verifiable limits on SLCM had to be an integral part of any START agreement. In view of the difficulty in reconciling the super-powers' differences over SLCM, it is possible that the issue could be put 'on the shelf' (as the question of MIRV was in negotiating SALT I) while START is agreed. Even if the Soviet Union were willing to agree to this, the US might find – as it did with MIRV – that it was creating a new vulnerability for itself.

Strategic Defences

The issue of strategic defences shared a similar fate to that of SLCM. The disagreements that had divided the two sides at the beginning of 1988 were still there at the end. These included, first, the link between strategic defences and reductions in offensive weapons. The United States insisted that the merits (and hence the acceptability) of offensive reductions should stand on their own, and that the two issues should therefore not be linked. Yet it seemed to link progress on START explicitly to Soviet actions in the field of strategic defences, by insisting that the Krasnoyarsk radar violation of the ABM Treaty be resolved before a START agreement could be signed. The strength of US adherence to this stipulation, of course, was not tested, since conclusion of an agreement never became a remote possibility.

Krasnoyarsk dominated the ABM Treaty review conference which was held in late August 1988. The US had threatened to declare the radar a 'material breach' of the ABM Treaty – a declaration that, under international law, would have justified a proportionate American response, including abrogating the Treaty. While the US never did make this declaration, it continued to insist that both the radar transmitter and its receiver had to be dismantled.

The Soviet Union, which halted construction of the radar in the autumn of 1987, offered to dismantle its 'equipment' and to turn it into an international space research centre. Since an inspection of the radars by US Congressmen in early 1988 failed to detect any equipment other than the receiver and transmitter, the meaning of the Soviet offer remained unclear. In any event, the US position that it would not sign a START treaty unless the Soviet Union was again in full compliance with the ABM Treaty meant that the Krasnoyarsk radar had to be destroyed in its entirety before a treaty could be signed.

The USSR did link the issue of strategic defences to the prospects of START in another way. It insisted that reductions in strategic forces should be conditional on full compliance with the ABM Treaty 'as signed' – meaning in accordance with the traditional interpretation of the Treaty (see *Strategic Survey 1987–1988*, p. 46) that the US Administration, but not the Congress, has challenged.

Negotiations on this issue thus remained in a stalemate. The compromise that was seemingly reached at the Washington summit, including a yet-to-be-agreed commitment by each side not to withdraw from the ABM Treaty, was enmeshed in disagreements over details. Four issues, in particular, held up further agreement. The first, and least important, was the length of the non-withdrawal period. The Soviet Union proposed a period of ten years, and the US seven. A compromise of eight or nine years seemed likely, if only because there was no prospect of an early US decision to proceed with full-scale engineering development of a strategic defence system.

The US has also insisted that the agreement to a non-withdrawal period should include a clause that would allow the parties to withdraw from the non-withdrawal commitment if supreme national interests were jeopardized, or if the other side committed a material breach of the ABM Treaty. A 'supreme national interests' clause is probably required before the US Senate would ratify the treaty, but the USSR has refused to accept such a clause. This raises the third issue of disagreement, which concerned each side's intentions at the end of the non-withdrawal period. The Soviet Union argued that both sides should then continue to comply with the ABM Treaty. The US, on the other hand, argued that each side should be free to deploy defences, if it so desired. With a 'supreme national interests' clause and a non-withdrawal period, the ABM Treaty would change from one of unlimited duration into one with a limited duration, i.e. the length of the non-withdrawal period.

A final source of disagreement concerned the kinds of space-based testing of strategic defence systems that would be allowed during the non-withdrawal period. Disagreement on this issue reflected the dichotomy between the traditional and the broad interpretations of the ABM Treaty's terms. In order to reassure the Soviet Union that space testing of strategic defences was not the beginning of a deployment programme, the US proposed in early 1988 to limit such testing to specific orbital test ranges. The USSR rejected this. In October 1988 the US tried again, this time proposing that the number of satellites used at any one time in tests of strategic defence systems should be limited to 15. Each side would commit itself to notifying the other of the tests shortly after the satellites were launched, and would similarly inform the other side if the satellites changed orbit or were about to re-enter the atmosphere. The limit would only apply to satellites designed to intercept missiles and warheads, not to sensors. Not only was this proposal rejected by the USSR, it was also heavily criticized in the US. The strategic defence issue thus continued to plague negotiations in Geneva, although there are some tentative indications that the USSR may be considering adjusting its position.

Verification

At the Washington summit both sides had made specific agreements regarding on-site inspection and other verification provisions that went beyond those agreed in the INF Treaty (see *Strategic Survey 1987–1988*, pp. 43–4), and further specifics were agreed during the year. The sheer magnitude of the task of verifying such an ambitious agreement as the emerging START treaty was always certain to cause concern. Indeed, in December 1988 the US Central Intelligence Agency reportedly submitted a 600-page report which concluded that monitoring Soviet compliance with the terms of a START treaty would pose 'severe problems' for US intelligence capabilities. Three areas, in particular, were singled out: counting mobile missiles; verifying limits and distinguishing between conventional and nuclear cruise missiles; and monitoring the declared number of re-entry vehicles (RV) on ballistic missiles. The report concluded that it could take up to two years to find solutions to these problems. Personnel requirements and costs would be immense; in late December 1988, CIA Director William Webster said that at least 2,500 facilities throughout the USSR would have to be inspected to monitor Soviet compliance.

In September 1988 Soviet Foreign Minister Shevardnadze proposed that the US and the USSR sign an interim agreement that would prohibit the testing of existing ballistic missiles with more warheads than would eventually be deployed on these missiles; the specific limits would be those declared at the Washington summit. Under the formula previously agreed, however, both sides reserved the right, upon notification and assuming effective verification, to increase the number of RV on a ballistic missile if they so desired. The Soviet proposal would instead have frozen the number of warheads, a position the US rejected, partly because it wanteded to continue testing the *Trident* II missile with more warheads (10 or 12) than it intended to deploy.

Another verification issue concerned the scope of challenge inspections at suspect sites. In October 1988 the United States proposed that each side should have the right of challenge inspections at designated sites, including installations 'associated with' the production of rocket motors for solid-fuel missiles. In addition, each side could request inspection of an undeclared site, but the other side could refuse this if it could explain its reasons and take actions that would alleviate concerns about non-compliance. In the end, the US settled for considerably less than the 'anywhere, anytime' challenge inspections that it had championed not long ago in various arms-control negotiations.

There are clearly many issues that have still to be resolved. What has been agreed so far on ALCM – and indeed in START generally – provides an incentive for both super-powers to improve their bomber capacity, with or without ALCM. The seemingly intractable nature of the SLCM issue is a particularly hard hurdle to surmount.

The Bush administration has embarked on an in-depth review of its strategic policy to see where and how it can reach accommodation with the Soviet Union. This much-needed pause will give each side some time for reflection and should allow both to match the direction of arms control with the wider aims of strategic policy. The American review is likely to focus on what kind of strategic forces the United States would desire, given arms-control and budgetary constraints. Only after these decisions have been made can the future direction of START and its eventual completion become clear.

Conventional Arms Control in Europe
1989 ushered in a new chapter in the long history of efforts to control conventional arms in Europe. On 2 February the fruitless 15-year NATO–Warsaw Pact negotiations on Mutual and Balanced Force Reductions (MBFR) in Central Europe ended at their 493rd plenary. They were replaced on 9 March by new negotiations in Vienna, covering the whole of Europe from the Atlantic to the Urals (ATTU) and termed the 'Negotiations on Conventional Armed Forces in Europe' (CFE), which includes all Alliance and Warsaw Pact countries and will attempt to draw down force size through negotiated structural arms control. Simultaneously, a parallel negotiation, the second 35-state Conference on Confidence- and Security-Building Measures (CSBM), will meet to address operational arms control and seek further to enhance transparency and mutual confidence by building on the Stockholm agreements of 1986.

Although autonomous, the CFE negotiations will proceed 'within the framework' of the 35-state Conference on Security and Co-operation in Europe (CSCE), and the CFE negotiators will periodically exchange views and information with the European neutral and non-aligned states. This arrangement reflects deep-seated differences among the participating states about the future elaboration of European security and co-operation; although the neutral and non-aligned states themselves are not at the moment willing to subject their armed forces to CFE limits, they are seeking a more direct input to the negotiations. France insists on tying CFE to the broader CSCE process to avoid a purely 'bloc-to-bloc' framework.

A number of factors have raised hopes that the unfortunate experience of MBFR will not be repeated. These include the two sides' gradual convergence since 1987 on the scope, principles and objectives of the talks; the similar elements of both alliances' opening positions; the unprecedented publication by the Warsaw Pact of its own, relatively detailed, force comparisons; and the announced unilateral reduction of forces including 12,000 tanks in the ATTU zone – seven times what NATO initially sought at MBFR – undertaken by the Soviet Union, Poland, Hungary, East Germany, Bulgaria and Czechoslovakia. The improving political climate also gives cause for guarded optimism. But the magnitude of the task ahead must not be underestimated, for serious differences have still to be resolved before the level of the post-World-War-II military confrontation can be substantially reduced.

Negotiations on Conventional Armed Forces in Europe
The CFE mandate, adopted on 10 January after almost two years of negotiations, is far more specific than that for MBFR. While the latter committed the participating states to work towards 'the general objective' of contributing 'to a more stable relationship and to the strengthening of peace and security in Europe', the CFE mandate defines the objectives as establishing a stable and secure balance of conventional armed forces at lower levels, eliminating disparities; and, as a matter of priority, eliminating the capability to launch surprise attacks and initiate large-scale offensive action. These objectives are to be achieved by 'reductions, limitations, redeployment provisions, equal ceilings and related measures, among others', and they are to be achieved 'in a way which precludes circumvention'.

Nuclear weapons, naval forces and chemical weapons will not be included in the negotiations, but dual-capable weapons are not excluded. This compromise reflects Western determination that nuclear weapons should not figure as such in CFE, and Eastern determination that dual-capable systems should not automatically be excluded solely on account of their nuclear capability.

Compliance will be verified by on-site inspection and exchange of information. The modalities of inspection and the detail and order of data exchange will be agreed at the talks themselves, but both sides appear eager to avoid getting bogged down in a numbers dispute about in-place forces, focusing rather on verification of residual levels.

Both sides published data before the talks began; NATO in November 1988 and the Warsaw Pact in January 1989. But both made clear that their figures were not immutable and did not prejudge the size of the disparities to be reduced by the CFE negotiations. These disclaimers are reassuring, since the counting rules, the area and the precise categories under consideration differed between the two sides' presentations, making direct comparisons difficult. (It simply is not possible to compare NATO and Warsaw Pact counting rules on artillery, for example.) However, the Warsaw Pact clearly admitted superiority in tanks, artillery, infantry combat vehicles and armoured personnel carriers, while suggesting that NATO had advantages in anti-tank systems, combat helicopters and strike aircraft. Eastern references to naval forces, where Pact figures showed NATO superiority, also indicated an oft-repeated determination that naval forces could not be discounted in the overall security picture – a position the Alliance rejects because of geostrategic asymmetries, and which the Pact has not actually insisted upon within the CFE mandate.

The opening positions were presented in outline form on the first day of the conference. British Foreign Minister Sir Geoffrey Howe presented the Alliance position, developed over two-and-a-half years of laborious and frequently acrimonious discussion but not, in fact, finalized until the day before the presentation. It reflected the degree of political compromise that had proved necessary, given the French view on the relationship between CFE and CSCE, the sensitivity of the flank countries to 'central regionitis' and other national concerns involving zones and particular categories of forces.

The West proposed a collective limit on the total number of tanks (40,000), armoured troop carriers (56,000) and artillery pieces (33,000) in Europe, with each alliance entitled to 50% of those totals (20,000 tanks, 16,500 artillery, and 28,000 armoured troop carriers, of which no more than 12,000 could be armoured infantry fighting vehicles). According to NATO's own data, this would mean Warsaw Pact reductions of over 31,500 tanks and 26,900 artillery launchers, and NATO reductions of 2,224 tanks and 828 artillery launchers – amounting to roughly 60% of current Pact and 10% of current Alliance strength. A point that will require clarification concerns the distinction between equipment in active units and that in storage. Alliance data includes a specific figure for stored equipment for its own forces, but not for the Warsaw Pact.

To prevent any one country dominating others by force of arms, no state could deploy more than 30% of these overall limits within the ATTU zone, meaning a maximum of 12,000 tanks, 10,000 artillery pieces and 16,800 armoured troop carriers for any one state. This would affect only the USSR, which would be required to remove over 25,000 tanks and 23,000 artillery pieces from the area. To influence the location of forces, active forces that can be stationed outside national territory are restricted to 3,200 tanks, 1,700 artillery pieces and 6,000 armoured troop carriers – a restraint that again would fall largely on the Soviet Union.

Within the Atlantic-to-Urals area, overall ceilings are adopted on weapons in active units, and three sub-zones have been created. In the smallest of these, comprising the former MBFR zone (for NATO, the territory of West Germany and the Benelux countries; for the Pact, that of East Germany, Poland and Czechoslovakia) tanks would be limited to 8,000 for each side, artillery to 4,500, and armoured troop carriers to 11,000, with temporary exceptions allowed for pre-notified exercises. Although the approach presupposes sub-limits for the other regions, these are left unspecified.

Each year, holdings of these treaty-limited items and of personnel in combat and combat support units would be notified, disaggregated down to battalion level. To 'buttress' force-level reductions stabilizing measures would be negotiated, including measures of transparency, notification and constraint applied to the deployment, movement, storage and levels of readiness of conventional armed forces. In the longer term, the Alliance would also be willing to contemplate other steps, such as further reductions and the restructuring of armed forces to reduce offensive capabilities and enhance defensive capabilities.

For the Warsaw Pact, Soviet Foreign Minister Shevardnadze proposed a three-stage reduction, drawing on the Pact position outlined in July 1988. In the first phase, lasting two to three years, asymmetries would be eliminated in troop numbers and five categories of armament: attack combat aircraft, tanks, combat helicopters, combat armoured vehicles and armoured personnel carriers, and artillery. These would be reduced to quantities some 10–15% below the lowest level currently possessed by either alliance. In addition, a zone along the line of alliance contact would be created in which military activities would be limited and the most destabilizing weapons withdrawn, reduced or otherwise limited. In a second phase, both sides would reduce by another 25% – approximately 500,000 troops, together with their equipment and a further reduction in other types of armaments. A third phase envisages the armed forces of both sides being given a strictly defensive character, and ceilings would be negotiated on all other categories of arms.

Although the CFE mandate explicitly rules out negotiations on nuclear and naval forces, Shevardnadze made three direct references to nuclear weapons, indicating a Soviet determination that these could not be ignored: he proposed that tactical nuclear weapons be removed from the line-of-contact zone established in the first phase; suggested that separate negotiations be started on reducing and eventually eliminating tactical nuclear weapons from Europe; and charged that nuclear modernization 'can destroy the fragile trust that has just begun to emerge in Europe'. He also referred to the developing threat posed by SLCM and suggested limiting the 'destabilizing functions and capabilities of naval forces'. Apart from his proposed withdrawal of tactical nuclear weapons from the line-of-contact zone, Shevardnadze did not explicitly link nuclear weapons or naval forces to a CFE agreement. But he gave notice that the 'scope of eventual agreements will to some extent be effected by, among others, the factor of naval arms', and 'the question of modernizing tactical nuclear arms, if such plans are translated into practical actions'.

It is difficult to predict the future course of the negotiations. At the outset there is apparent agreement on limiting three major categories of ground combat forces, Warsaw Pact willingness to undertake vastly asymmetrical reductions (even if based on its own data), acceptance of mandatory on-site inspections, and a desire to avoid a paralysing MBFR-type data dispute. On the question of data, an important first step will require that both sides establish some common language and definitions of the categories being discussed, rather than agreeing on precise numbers. At the same time, however, the two sides differ over what additional categories of forces the negotiations should cover, the Soviet link with naval and nuclear forces, how deep reductions could proceed after the elimination of disparities and restructuring, and the issue of a demilitarized zone along the line of contact. Moreover, for NATO, the negotiations raised two fundamental strategic issues: how parity in conventional forces would affect the need for nuclear weapons (and – equally, if not more importantly – public support for the nuclear component of NATO strategy), and how reduced force levels would affect the strategy of forward defence and the Alliance's evolving operational concepts. Much remains to be done, but an important step has been taken in the right direction.

Confidence and Security-Building Measures

A second, and complementary, forum that also began on 9 March 1989 in Vienna was the second 35-state Conference on Confidence-and Security-Building Measures (CSBM). It is tasked to 'build upon and expand the results' of the 1986 Stockholm CDE document, whose provisions have by all accounts been successfully implemented. By the end of 1988, 83 military activities (33 NATO, 46 Warsaw Pact and 4 non-aligned) had been notified as required by the CSBM regime, and invited observers had attended 35 of them. Moreover, 18 challenge inspections had taken place without reported problems (five each by the US and the USSR, two each by the UK and East Germany, and one each by Bulgaria, West Germany, Turkey and Poland).

For NATO, which tabled the first proposal on 9 March, the next CDE should concentrate on more detailed and comprehensive information exchange, and especially that concerning military organization, manpower, equipment and major conventional-weapon deployment programmes subject to pre-planned inspection of normal peace-time unit locations. NATO will also seek to lower the threshold for military activities requiring observation to 13,000 troops, increase inspections, enhance methods of observation (including aerial survey) and access for accredited military personnel, create dedicated communication links, and exchange views on military policy. The last provision includes a seminar on military doctrine and discussions on annual defence spending, force training and the number and pattern of notified military activities.

If NATO has its way, constraints on military activities, which many delegations at Stockholm felt should form a part of 'security-building' measures, will not be negotiated in CSBM but may possibly evolve as 'stabilizing measures' in the CFE process. It is unclear, however, whether any such measures would precede, accompany, or follow agreements on structural limits.

The Warsaw Pact position, tabled at Vienna on 9 March, shares some elements of the NATO proposals. It favours regular exchange of information on the numbers, structure and deployment of all forces down to the level of brigade and regiment (lower than NATO's divisional level), plus other measures to allow the discussion of military policy and the exchange of official visits. The Pact also favours lower thresholds for notification and observation of ground forces activity and for improving observation (including aerial survey).

The proposals contain measures which go far beyond those advocated by NATO, however. Under 'Constraining Measures' they call for the limiting of military activity to 40,000 troops only, including occasions when separate but notifiable and concurrent activities occur in one state, and when unrelated exercises take place in close proximity to one another. This measure would preclude NATO's annual *Autumn Forge*

53

series, the component exercises of which collectively exceed 200,000 men. There are detailed proposals for the notification and observation of air force exercises, which would be limited in size, and naval exercises, which would be limited in size, frequency, duration and area. A final set of measures returns to the CFE proposal of zones in which special limits on force levels and activity would be enforced.

Although there are thus wide differences between NATO and Warsaw Pact positions on constraint, some moderation of NATO's stance is not inconceivable, given Norwegian and Turkish concerns about Soviet naval activity and West German public opposition to large-scale NATO exercises (which caused the Federal Republic to halve the number of its exercises and the US to postpone until 1990 its main annual reinforcement exercise, *Reforger*). There is therefore a reasonable prospect that the CSBM talks may achieve results sooner than CFE and may achieve militarily significant effects by reducing the risks of sudden, unexplained departures from the military norm. Sensibly, there are no deadlines for either negotiations. But the next follow-up meeting of the Conference on Security and Co-operation in Europe, the parent forum of both negotiations, is scheduled to convene in Helsinki in 1992, and this could be a logical target date for the achievement of initial agreements.

Chemical Weapons
While negotiations on chemical weapons continued in the Conference on Disarmament in Geneva, the most significant developments involving such weapons occurred outside this forum. After their use in the Gulf War, and particularly when it was confirmed that Iraq had used poison gas against its own Kurdish population, the issue of chemical weapons took centre stage. The vivid television images of the effects of the use of these weapons on innocent civilians that were broadcast around the globe could not but result in widespread official and public expressions of concern. The US Congress took the lead in condemning the Iraqi action and called for specific sanctions. The Administration, while similarly condemning the use of chemical weapons, opposed sanctions so as to avoid appearing to tilt towards Iran at a time when cease-fire negotiations in the Gulf were reaching a critical stage.

Instead, the Administration used a speech by President Reagan to the UN General Assembly to call for an international conference to restore confidence in the 1925 Geneva Protocol that prohibits the use of chemical weapons in war. Ironically, the development that most directly led to the call for such a conference – the Iraqi use of these weapons against its own population – was not strictly a contravention of the Protocol, even if it did perhaps violate other international agreements and customs. The idea of a conference was nevertheless endorsed by a large group of nations, including France, which, as the original depository of the Protocol, offered to host the conference in Paris in January 1989.

In addition to suggesting an international conference, the Reagan administration also began to call public attention to the impending spread of chemical weapons around the globe. In a series of speeches and Congressional testimonies, CIA Director William Webster and others pointed out that these weapons were proliferating at an increasing rate in a variety of countries in unstable regions, including Syria, Iraq, Iran and, most ominously, Libya. The issue came to a head just before the Paris conference convened. A number of Administration officials, including President Reagan himself, raised the possibility of military action against what was alleged to be a chemical weapons factory at Rabata in Libya. The President's statement, made in a prime-time television interview, was soon followed by newspaper stories in *The New York Times* accusing firms in a variety of Western countries of directly supplying chemical materials and expertise to Libya. The specific naming of a West German concern, Imhausen-Chemie, caused quite a political storm in Germany. Bonn first denied the various reports, then accused the American media of spreading false rumours, and finally revealed that West German intelligence had known for some time that German companies were directly involved in exporting materials that would enable chemical weapons to be produced at the Libyan factory.

The 149 nations that gathered in Paris debated the chemical-weapons issue for five days and finally signed a consensus declaration. Among the more notable aspects of the conference and the declaration were the lack of any explicit mention of the events that had directly led to the conference in the first place: Iraq's flagrant use of poison gas against Iran in the Gulf War. The US similarly failed to get agreement on how to deal with future violations of the Protocol, and it was also disappointed in its efforts to strengthen the UN Secretary General's investigatory powers in cases where a violation was suspected. The US and other countries did, however, succeed in blocking an attempt by Arab states to link the prospects for chemical disarmament with Israel's alleged nuclear programme.

The final declaration, endorsed by all 149 participants, contained some positive features, including a call to all countries to adhere to the Geneva Protocol's provisions and to join it if they had not already done so. In addition, the declaration endorsed the Conference on Disarmament's efforts to ban chemical weapons. This was particularly important, for the Paris participants thereby committed themselves to supporting a treaty that would ban not only the use but also the possession of chemical weapons.

The overall implications of the conference were mixed. On the one hand, the proceedings might have harmed current efforts to negotiate a chemical-weapons ban in Geneva by strengthening some countries' belief that such weapons might have useful military functions. On the other hand, the conference in general, and the final declaration in particular, did give new impetus to efforts to achieve a complete and global ban on chemical weapons. Given these results, the future outlook for the chemical weapons negotiations are equally mixed. Even though, as a result of significant Soviet concessions (see *Strategic Survey 1987–*

1988, pp. 61–2), the design of an acceptable verification regime no longer poses the obstacle to a treaty that it once did, the proliferation of chemical weapons to troubled regions creates a new impediment to achieving a chemical-weapons ban. How to ensure that all actual and potential proliferators assent to a ban is an issue that will be exceedingly difficult to resolve. On the other hand, not only is there a renewed global interest in, and commitment to, a treaty, but there is a new US President who is personally committed to eliminating 'this terrible scourge' from the face of the earth. This offers reason to hope that such a ban might in fact be achieved in the years ahead.

Nuclear Testing

Since July 1986, representatives of the US and the USSR have met on a number of occasions for expert-level discussions on the entire range of issues relating to nuclear testing. The primary US objective in these meetings has been to negotiate agreements for effective verification of the Threshold Test Ban Treaty (TTBT), which limits the explosive yields of underground nuclear tests to 150 kilotons, and the Peaceful Nuclear Explosion Treaty (PNET), which places a similar limit on peaceful nuclear explosions. The treaties were signed in 1974 and 1976 respectively, but the United States has yet to ratify either, because it believes that effective monitoring of Soviet compliance with these testing limits requires additional verification procedures.

The American objectives in the talks are informed by a conviction that a Comprehensive Nuclear Test Ban Treaty (CTBT) – achievement of which was a goal of all US Presidents from Eisenhower to Carter – is currently undesirable, and by a belief that further nuclear testing restrictions are undesirable so long as the TTBT limit cannot be verified effectively. This view stems from repeated US allegations that the Soviet Union has violated the 150-KT testing limits: allegations that have been challenged by a variety of US officials, including the Congressional Office of Technology Assessment and nuclear test monitoring experts at the Lawrence Livermore National Laboratory. The Soviet long-term objective is to achieve a comprehensive ban on nuclear testing, although in the short term Moscow has been willing to seek arrangements to ensure effective verification of the two unratified treaties.

On 17 September 1987 the nuclear testing discussions reached a new level, when Secretary Shultz and Foreign Minister Shevardnadze announced that both sides would begin full-scale, stage-by-stage negotiations on nuclear testing. They agreed that as a first step they would develop effective verification measures for the TTBT and PNET, later proceeding to negotiate further intermediate limitations, ultimately leading to the cessation of all nuclear tests, 'as part of an effective disarmament process'. Negotiations opened on 9 November 1987 and led to an agreement, announced one month later during the Washington summit, to conduct joint verification experiments (JVE) at the Semipalatinsk and Nevada nuclear test sites designed to provide each side with an opportunity to measure the explosive yield of nuclear tests using their preferred measurement techniques.

The US has maintained that the traditional seismic measurements favoured by the USSR would be insufficient to monitor the yields of nuclear tests. Instead, the US has argued that its proposed CORRTEX method (continuous reflectometry for radius versus time experiments), involving a long electronic cable lowered to within a few feet of the buried warhead, is more accurate. The yield of the test is measured by the rate at which the cable is crushed in the explosion.

Tests using the CORRTEX method as well as seismic measurements were completed at Nevada on 14 August 1988 and at Semipalatinsk on 14 September. They were apparently inconclusive. Some reports suggested that the CORRTEX method was less accurate than the US had previously maintained and that the seismic sensors estimated the explosive yields within a similar margin of error; others maintained that the CORRTEX method was extremely accurate. Subsequent examination of the testing and measurement data failed to determine which method was more accurate and, hence, to be preferred.

As the testing negotiations recessed in December 1988, the two sides were no further along than they had been a year before. The United States continued to insist that the CORRTEX method should be adopted, a position that would ensure virtually permanent on-site inspections by both sides at each other's test sites. The Soviet Union maintained that the JVE had clearly shown that, with a few inspections, the US could learn enough about the test sites to monitor the yields of nuclear tests accurately with traditional seismic sensors.

While the negotiations are certain to resume, no date has been set, because the Bush administration wants to conduct its review of all arms-control negotiations first. The prospects for resolving outstanding issues are, however, uncertain. Moreover, President Bush apparently shares the Reagan administration's belief that a CTBT is undesirable as long as nuclear weapons exist. If maintained, this position makes an early end to nuclear testing highly unlikely.

The Super-powers

THE UNITED STATES: AFTER THE ELECTION

Although George Bush's election to the Presidency in November 1988 promised an unusual degree of continuity in American foreign and domestic policy, it nonetheless marked the end of an era. Ronald Reagan had presided over the return to a more self-confident American leadership in world affairs, a number of foreign-policy triumphs, and a remarkable period of economic growth and prosperity. President Bush will have to try to match the successes of the Reagan administration, while contending with its failures, the most formidable being a federal budget deficit that will limit his policy options across the board. Moreover, the new President will have to contend with a nimble adversary in Soviet President Mikhail Gorbachev, who has not only embarked upon a course of change in the USSR which promises a radical revision of the geopolitical scene, but has also demonstrated a particular dexterity in exploiting the differences of opinion that always exist within the Western Alliance. And, finally, President Bush will have to survive and prosper politically without his predecessor's unique rapport with much of the US public.

The Reagan Record
No President leaves office with an unblemished record in foreign and domestic policy; Ronald Reagan's is arguably more mixed than many. There were a number of significant accomplishments accompanied by unhappy disappointments and some outright failures. Drawing up a careful balance sheet is difficult and perhaps best left to future historians; what can be said even now, however, is that, along with his successes, Reagan failed to achieve some of his most cherished policy objectives, and that he has left some difficult problems for the country and his successor. One area in which there is certain to be change, and perhaps improvement, is the day-to-day management of the policy-making apparatus. Whatever questions there may be about other aspects of his stewardship, here there are none: Reagan set new standards of carelessness.

The centrepiece of his foreign-policy platform was a commitment to reverse what many saw as a dangerous deterioration in the global balance of power. The Soviet Union had added appreciably to its strategic nuclear capabilities during the 1970s and, late in the decade, had begun to deploy large numbers of intermediate-range nuclear missiles capable of reaching Western Europe and the Far East. In addition, the 1970s had seen Soviet gains in many important parts of the world: Vietnam, Angola, South Yemen, Nicaragua, the Horn of Africa and Afghanistan.

At the same time, US forces had at best stood still, and were constrained by inhibitions on their use.

The Reagan administration's response to these developments was to embark on the biggest peace-time military build-up in history and, through the Reagan doctrine, to challenge the Soviet Union and its proxies aggressively in regional contests. In both areas it achieved some notable successes. Its ambitious programme for modernizing US offensive strategic forces, along with its promotion of the Strategic Defense Initiative, gave Soviet leaders a powerful incentive to negotiate seriously on strategic arms limitations; the framework for a Strategic Arms Reduction Treaty that would make impressive cuts in the super-powers' strategic arsenals was in place by the end of Reagan's second term. His administration's steady implementation of NATO's dual-track decision on INF deployments and arms-control negotiations laid the groundwork for the 1987 INF Treaty, which will eliminate two classes of nuclear missiles from US and Soviet inventories. NATO weathered the 1982–3 storm over INF deployments, which was fuelled by both West European nuclear angst and Soviet machinations, and emerged from the crisis stronger than it had been.

As far as the Third World was concerned, Reagan proudly claimed as he was leaving office that Soviet expansion and adventurism had been stemmed in the 1980s and that no new state had fallen into the Soviet orbit during his time in office. In fact, Moscow took the unprecedented step of withdrawing its forces from Afghanistan in the face of staunch *Mujaheddin* resistance that was stiffened by US arms shipments; the last Soviet detachment evacuated Afghanistan on 15 February 1989. The Reagan administration can also take considerable credit for the 1988 agreement on the withdrawal of Cuban and South African forces from Angola and independence for Namibia. Reagan's decision to invade Grenada in 1983 headed off what some thought was another Nicaragua in the making. In addition, however belatedly, the Administration supported democratic reform in the Philippines and in South America, with significant success. Finally, its active naval policy in the Gulf arguably played a role in Iran's decision in July 1988 to accept a cease-fire in the eight-year old Gulf war.

At the end of their watch, Administration officials were claiming that the ideological tide had turned in the 1980s. Both the People's Republic of China and the Soviet Union were turning away from rigidly planned economies. Political and economic reforms of various kinds were being pursued throughout much of the socialist camp. The viability of the socialist economic model was being called into question with increasing frequency in many parts of the Third World. And democracy was making important advances in many countries.

This is not to say that the Reagan administration's conduct of US foreign and defence policy was impeccable. Critics charged that the President's blind commitment to the SDI programme undermined the 'grand compromise' on offensive and defensive forces that was at the heart of the prospective START treaty. The fourth Reagan–Gorbachev summit in Moscow in May/June 1988 did not produce the START breakthrough that many hoped for, and the START negotiations subsequently stalled. Reagan and Gorbachev had to content themselves at the summit with exchanging ratification instruments for the INF Treaty, which had been approved by the US Senate only at the last minute, after months of deliberation over the acceptability of its terms and verification provisions. In addition, the two leaders were able to sign a handful of minor agreements on ballistic missile testing, monitoring of nuclear tests, co-operative ventures in space research, and cultural exchanges. However, Reagan refused to sign a Soviet-drafted statement that committed the two sides to 'peaceful co-existence', and he irritated his hosts by forcefully pushing his human-rights agenda in his speech at Moscow State University and in his meetings with dissidents and *refuseniks*. Gorbachev lamented 'lost opportunities' at his post-summit news conference and blamed Reagan's 'propaganda gambits' for the summit's failures.

The Moscow summit, though, dramatized how much Soviet–American relations had improved during the decade and how remarkably Reagan's views of the USSR had changed in eight years. When Reagan came to office his opposition to the Soviet Union had deep ideological as well as geopolitical roots. At his first press conference he stated his belief that Soviet leaders reserved 'the right to commit any crime, to lie, to cheat' in pursuit of their objectives. He later called the Soviet Union 'the focus of evil in the modern world', and he urged the West to embark on a 'crusade' against 'the evil empire'. Not surprisingly, US–Soviet relations were frosty during his first term, a condition which was exacerbated by the USSR's continuing action in Afghanistan, its policy over Poland, the KAL-007 incident, rapid turnover in the Soviet leadership, and Moscow's decision to walk out of the INF and START negotiations once the US began to deploy INF missiles of its own in Europe. In Reagan's second term, super-power relations began to improve, as the nuclear arms-control talks resumed, stability returned to the Kremlin, and a series of Reagan–Gorbachev summits got under way. Even so, it was surprising to hear Reagan say in Moscow that Soviet emigration policy was the work of faceless 'bureaucrats'; he implied that bad policy was simply the inevitable by-product of big government, rather than the intended policy of a particular kind of government. According to this line of thinking, Reagan and Gorbachev were kindred spirits on a bipartisan crusade against bureaucratic excesses, rather than the leaders of two fundamentally different political and economic systems. Reagan's eagerness to dismiss his own critique of the Soviet system as belonging to 'another time and another era' showed the President at his worst: an essentially simple man too easily caught up in the pageantry of super-power summits, uncomprehending of the complexity and pace of events, and swayed by personalities.

Reagan's record on Alliance relations was mixed as well. The other allies were taken aback by the Administration's SDI programme and his goal of making nuclear weapons 'impotent and obsolete'. They were stunned by his willingness to enter into discussions on general nuclear disarmament at the Reykjavik summit. These episodes convinced many West Europeans that Reagan did not have even a rudimentary appreciation of the fundamentals of NATO strategy and the role that nuclear weapons played within it. His handling of the INF negotiations also raised questions. The Administration's reaction to the Soviet Union's 'second zero' proposal seemed unnecessarily hasty, bruising relations with West Germany in the short run and sharpening German misapprehensions about 'singularity' that are still affecting the debate over modernizing short-range nuclear forces.

By the same token, the Administration's policies towards regional conflicts did not produce an unbroken string of successes. One of Reagan's main foreign-policy objectives was to overthrow the *Sandinista* regime in Nicaragua, but he failed to muster the support in Congress he needed for an extended military campaign spearheaded by the *Contras*; Congress has frozen $16.3 million in military aid for them since 1986. Nor did the Administration succeed in unseating Panamanian strongman Manuel Noriega in 1988, after failing to extradite him to the US to face drug-trafficking charges. In the Middle East, its policy was marred by the terrorist truck-bombing of the US peacekeeping force in Lebanon in 1983, which killed 241 Marines; this tragic incident highlighted the fact that Reagan's Middle East policy was both poorly conceived and poorly executed. The decision to escort ships through the Persian Gulf was successful on the whole, but not without costs: the US destroyer *Stark* was hit by an Iraqi missile in 1987, and in June 1988 the US cruiser *Vincennes* mistakenly shot down an Iranian civil airliner, killing all on board.

The biggest foreign-policy fiasco, of course, was the Iran/*Contra* affair, in which members of the National Security Council felt at liberty to arrange the sale of arms to Iran in exchange for Iranian efforts to free American hostages held in Lebanon; the proceeds of the sales were then diverted to the Nicaraguan *Contras*, thus circumventing Congressional restraints on US support for them. Few would have guessed in January 1981 that an Administration headed by Ronald Reagan would one day sell arms in exchange for hostages. Although Reagan's popularity at home sank as the facts came out, it ultimately recovered (in fact, he left office with an approval rating of 64%, an all-time high for retiring Presidents). The legal side of the case continued to unfold in 1989, as the most serious charges against Col. North, the NSC staff member at the centre of the affair, were dropped; he still faced others, however, and it was possible that Reagan himself would be called to testify at North's trial.

Finally, the Administration's record in domestic and economic policy was also a mixed bag. It was certainly true that while Reagan was in office inflation dropped from double digits to 4.4%; that interest rates dropped from double digits to 8.2%; that unemployment dropped to a 14-year low of 5.3%; and that the post-recession economy had a remarkable run of 75 straight months of growth. It was also true that much of the credit has to go to Paul Volker, the former head of the Federal Reserve, and to good fortune: oil prices collapsed in the 1980s, which dampened inflation and spurred economic growth. This economic record was also fuelled by massive deficit spending. The 1980 presidential candidate who campaigned on a promise to balance the federal budget by 1984 ended his second term having increased the national debt by 170% to $2.6 trillion and left office struggling to get the projected budget deficit down to $150 bn. The trade deficit also soared, to a record $170 bn in 1987, and was still $137 bn in 1988. During the Reagan presidency, the world's leading creditor nation became the world's leading debtor.

Challenges for Bush
Although Bush took office with the country at peace, the economy strong, and no major foreign or domestic crises in sight, he nonetheless faced several major challenges. The first was to overcome the bitter resentment felt by many Democrats over an election campaign which they believed had featured brutal, if effective, attacks on Democratic nominee Michael Dukakis' patriotism, liberalism and commitment to law and order. Dukakis came out of the primaries in June with a 17-point lead in the public opinion polls, but it quickly evaporated once the Bush campaign went on the offensive. Bush's very strong performance at the Republican convention in August was tarnished only slightly by the controversy that surrounded his selection of the 41-year-old junior Senator from Indiana, Dan Quayle, to be his running mate. Dukakis failed to fend off the Republicans' attack or mount an effective counter-attack, and his lukewarm performance in the two Presidential debates sealed his fate. Although he bounced back in the campaign's final weeks, when he embraced his liberal heritage and adopted a more open persona, the surge came too late. Bush captured 54% of the popular vote and 426 of the 538 electoral college votes in an election for which barely 50% of the voters turned out. Although the victory was decisive, Bush's coat tails were not long enough to swing even the Senate over to the Republican party, as Reagan had done in 1980; instead, the Democrats consolidated their control over both Houses of Congress.

One of the ironies of the campaign was that Bush went into it with the image of a 'wimp', but emerged with a reputation for being combative. Pundits predicted that there would be no honeymoon with Congress and that relations with the Democrats would be testy at best. After the election the new President moved quickly to effect a reconciliation with Capitol Hill, and his selections of James Baker as Secretary of State and Brent Scowcroft as National Security Advisor were well-received; Baker's repeated call for a return to a bipartisan foreign policy and his emphasis on Congressional participation in the making of foreign policy were especially welcome. Bush's Inaugural Address continued in this 'kinder, gentler' vein and, until his nomination of John Tower as Secretary of Defense came unstuck, it granted him his honeymoon after all.

Struggling with the Defence Budget

One of Bush's most difficult challenges will be to reduce the federal deficit while maintaining a robust defence posture, and yet to fulfil the pledges he made throughout the campaign that he would not raise taxes. The Gramm-Rudman-Hollings budget bill obligated the President to reduce the Fiscal Year 1990 budget deficit to $100 bn, but as Bush entered office the projected deficit for 1990 was $127 bn. As a first step, Bush resubmitted Reagan's final budget to Congress in early February 1989; however, his proposed defence budget contained only an inflation adjustment and no real growth. This and other spending cuts might enable the President and Congress to meet the $100-bn target for 1990, but the mandated target of $64 bn for 1991 will, in all probability, force Bush to face up to the issue of increasing revenue. Although the President continues to insist that he will not raise taxes, it is doubtful that Congress will let him off this hook easily.

Managing the defence budget will be especially tricky. The 1990–94 Five Year Defence Plan, put together by Reagan's military planners, was based on the assumption that defence spending would increase by 2% per year after inflation; Bush's revised spending plan assumed a 1–2% real growth rate for 1991 and 1992. It will be hard for the new team to reconcile the military's existing five-year plan with budgetary realities even if it gets these annual increases, and it is far from guaranteed that it will. One problem that Bush's budget experts will have to face is the 'bow-wave effect' created by all the new programmes started during happier fiscal times; these will require higher appropriations levels as they move into the more expensive production phase of the acquisition cycle. Another problem is the 'stern-wave effect' created by the operating and maintenance costs of many programmes. These structural budgetary pressures will inevitably force the Bush administration to stretch out many programmes and cancel others. Its efforts to get on top of the fiscal situation were hampered by the fact that the Senate refused confirmation of Tower, after several weeks of deliberation.

Although Bush stressed the importance of procurement reform in the wake of the insider information scandal that rocked the Pentagon in mid-1988, that is no panacea. Overhauling the procurement process will not generate enough savings to evade hard decisions about which programmes must be cut, and, in any event, few are optimistic about the prospects for meaningful reform. By the same token, closing military bases in the US will not significantly ease matters, although it will help. The bipartisan commission on military bases, which reported to Reagan in late December, recommended that activities at dozens of bases should be streamlined and that many bases should simply be closed.

Implementing these recommendations, which Congress and the new Administration are almost certain to do, would eliminate a great deal of waste from the defence budget, but it would not provide an easy way out of the fiscal dilemma.

Budgetary constraints will force a review of the US strategic force modernization programme. On current fiscal projections, Bush will not be able to push the B-2 bomber into production and build a mobile ICBM at the same time. Pressure is mounting to slow the B-2 by at least two years and defer production until its flight-testing programme has been completed and evaluated. The bomber is already moving into production, however, even though flight testing has yet to begin, and the programme is quickly becoming irreversible. The Air Force acknowledged in November 1988 that the B-2's unit cost had grown to $520 m, which put procurement costs for the 132-bomber fleet at over $68 bn. Not surprisingly, many have begun to ask whether the new aircraft is needed.

The Air Force had long argued that the B-2 was needed for search-and-destroy missions against the USSR's growing set of mobile targets, which the B-1B could not cope with, but in late 1988 it dropped this argument and admitted that even the B-2 would have problems performing this mission. The aircraft's strategic rationale, therefore, reverted to the need for a credible penetrating bomber. However, the case against the B-2 was weakened by the B-1B's continuing technical problems. The Air Force acknowledged in mid-1988 that the B-1B's defensive avionics system had structural flaws that would probably prevent it meeting its original performance specifications. As a result, few advocate cancelling the B-2 outright; slowing the programme and waiting to see how the B-1B and the B-2 turn out now strikes many as the most prudent course of action.

Slowing the B-2 down would also free budgetary resources in the short term for production of a mobile ICBM. In early 1989 the new Administration had to choose between the rail-based MX and the road-mobile *Midgetman*. Although the Air Force had pushed the less expensive 10-warhead MX for years, Brent Scowcroft (the new National Security Advisor), Sam Nunn (chairman of the Senate Armed Services Committee) and Les Aspin (chairman of the House Armed Services Committee) had long favoured the more mobile, single-warhead *Midgetman*. Scaling back the B-2 programme would enable them to pursue the *Midgetman* instead of the MX.

These issues led Bush and Scowcroft to conduct a review of US strategic force structure plans in the first few weeks of the Administration. Since this included a review of the START negotiations, strategic arms-control negotiations with the USSR were placed on hold while the Bush team deliberated over US strategic policy. Many believed that the new administration's predisposition to deploy a mobile ICBM and its less dogmatic approach to strategic defences would help remove some of the obstacles to a START treaty.

Bush also had to contend with the impending negotiations on conventional forces in Europe, as well as a range of NATO force-structure issues, the most prominent of which was the question of short-range nuclear force modernization. The burden-sharing issue, which had become especially contentious during 1988, would also have to be addressed by the new team as it tried to chart a course for NATO force-structure and arms-control policy. Secretary of State Baker made a whirlwind 14-nation trip to Western Europe in mid-February to set the stage for these deliberations.

Outstanding Questions

Although peace was breaking out in many parts of the world as Bush came to office, he still had to contend with a number of thorny regional problems. The USSR completed its withdrawal from Afghanistan during his first few weeks in the Oval office, but the war had not ended, and decisions on how and how much to continue to aid the *Mujaheddin* remained to be made. The Reagan administration's December decision to enter into face-to-face discussions with the PLO thrust the US into a more active role in the Middle East negotiations and, for better or worse, put this issue high on Bush's and Baker's foreign-policy agenda. And the previous administration's efforts to draw attention to Libyan chemical-weapons activity will undoubtedly be pursued vigorously by its successor; military confrontations between the US and Libya, such as the January 1989 incident in which US Navy F-14s shot down two Libyan MiGs over the Mediterranean, are always a possibility. US policy towards Central America was complicated by the election in El Salvador and constrained by Congressional reluctance to see greater US involvement in the region.

Finally, President Bush will be challenged to match Soviet President Gorbachev's statesmanship and gamesmanship. Gorbachev's speech to the UN General Assembly on 7 December 1988 sketched a vision of international relations that many found compellingly attractive. Bush has yet to outline his vision of world affairs and the role the US should play within it. He has assembled an able team of pragmatic thinkers and effective policy-makers, and he himself is known for his pragmatism and wealth of experience as a member of the foreign-policy establishment. Whether this team of experienced pragmatists can also make the great conceptual leap forward remains to be seen. Managing this conceptual transition may well be President Bush's greatest challenge.

THE USSR: CHANGE AND UNCERTAINTY

As one observer remarked in 1988, the question about Mikhail Gorbachev and his reform drive was no longer 'does he mean it?', but rather 'will he get away with it?' Almost more pertinent and urgent is the question of what the 'it' will ultimately mean, both for the Soviet Union and the rest of the world. Although there had been an almost breathtaking departure for new shores in 1988, in both domestic and foreign policy, it remained quite uncertain where the new shores were, whether they would ever be reached and – perhaps most importantly – what would happen if they were not reached.

Mikhail Gorbachev decided, or was forced, to attack issues head-on, in spite of (or, indeed, because of) mounting signs of crisis. He was rewarded with considerable tactical success, but his dilemma remained that the successes provoked as many, if not more, new questions as they provided answers. The shape of the future remained uncertain, perhaps precisely because of the pragmatic approach of the USSR's dynamic leader. As that leader never tires of saying, there is a revolution under way in the Soviet Union today, and, as history makes clear, the outcome of revolution is almost by definition unclear. Nor can the outside world have high expectations of influencing events significantly. Accepting this as a reality, and acting accordingly, may be the single most difficult challenge for a West as hopeful as it is impatient.

Mounting Problems
At the end of 1987 and the beginning of 1988 Mikhail Gorbachev was confronted with a growing list of complex interdependent problems. His position had been visibly shaken by the Yeltsin affair, which had emboldened his opponents in the leadership while damaging his own credibility. Economic results had been more than discouraging during 1987. If the economic programme, which he had initiated, was to bear fruit it clearly was going to take considerable time: much more than the impatient General Secretary had anticipated, and perhaps more than was available. Not only was there no improvement in the supply of food or other basic commodities to the Soviet population, but the situation actually deteriorated further, making it all the more difficult for the leadership to create a solid social base for its reform policy. Polls indicated that a majority of the population – disillusioned by too many broken promises in the past, bewildered by the disappearance of old benchmarks and by the uncertainty of the new, and worried about the sweeping nature of the economic (and political) changes envisaged for the future – has adopted a wait-and-see attitude.

To transform this scarcely hidden scepticism into outright support would be a daunting task under the best of circumstances. In an environment of passive resistance by a bureaucracy that fears the loss of its own privileges, the task resembled an effort to square a circle. If *perestroika* stagnated, *glasnost* had been picking up steam. Yet the result was ambiguous. The circulation of publications profiting from the increased freedom of speech mushroomed, though what could be printed (predominantly bad news and disturbing disclosures about the past) was hardly the raw material for generating enthusiasm and optimism. *Glasnost* brought new freedoms – but those freedoms were claimed, first of all, by the national minorities. Ethnic unrest on the periphery of the Soviet Union became widespread and explosive.

There was a surging momentum in foreign policy, highlighted by US–Soviet summit meetings in Washington, Moscow and New York, and a continuing and broadening dialogue between the United States and Moscow. This was amplified by a further improvement in Soviet–West European ties as well as important changes in Sino-Soviet relations. Yet courageous decisions, such as the withdrawal from Afghanistan, turned out to be difficult ones as well. More significantly, the Soviet Union was unable (or unwilling in an American election year) to offer any further concessions in arms control – until the surprise announcement in December 1988 of a cut in its conventional forces.

The timing of this decision may have been due to the arrival of a new US Administration, but the roots went deeper. The Soviet economy continued to stumble, and a new allocation of resources was becoming more and more necessary. If the USSR is to hope for more economic and technological aid from the West, the change in the international political atmosphere must be maintained. Hence, even if the Soviet military leadership opposed giving up further ground, the political leadership apparently felt it had to face down its resistance. Unless overcome, that resistance, combined with the opposition of the bureaucracy and the apathy of the Soviet population, would soon ring the death knell for Gorbachev's policies. There emerged a profound dilemma: without further foreign-policy successes, the USSR would be unable to win the time needed for reform, and opposition would grow at home; without a rapid breaking of that opposition, further foreign-policy initiatives might be impossible, and the time gained from previous foreign-policy changes would be useless.

Characteristically, these sobering realities seem to have increased Gorbachev's resolve to forge ahead. Through a combination of tactical skill, the will to run risks and the ruthless exploitation of opportunities, he succeeded in completely changing the picture during 1988.

Consolidating Power
Gorbachev's first moves were defensive ones. Caught on the hop by the development of the Yeltsin affair, which burst open at the October 1987 Central Committee plenum, he personally appeared at a meeting of the Moscow city Party committee that resulted in Yeltsin's removal as Moscow Party chief. The language used in the meeting was extremely harsh. Not surprisingly, Yeltsin was dropped from the Politburo at the next Central Committee plenum in February 1988, although he remained active, vocal and available to Western media, indicating the change between the Stalinist 1930s and the present.

At the same time, Gorbachev appeared to be reducing his objectives for a special Party Conference, to be held in Moscow between 28 June and 1 July. The purpose of that conference, the first such gathering since 1941, was to 'further the revolutionary restructuring and to make it irreversible', as Gorbachev said. It had been anticipated that this would entail a purge of the Central Committee (up to 15% of its members can be replaced by a Party Conference). Yet if Gorbachev had originally aimed for such a purge (and there is evidence that he did), he now buried the idea. Instead he used the Yeltsin affair to seize the middle ground, condemning both conservative resistance to reform and over-zealous advocates (like Yeltsin), while stubbornly pushing for further change. The February Central Committee plenary not only brought Yeltsin's demotion, but also the appointment of two new candidate members of the Politburo, G. P. Razumovski (a long-serving close associate of Gorbachev) and D. Masluykov (named head of the Central Planning Organization in place of N.V. Talyzin, now Politburo candidate member in charge of CMEA affairs).

The conservative challenge was far from defeated, however. This became obvious in March when, while Gorbachev was abroad on a visit to Yugoslavia, the newspaper *Sovetskaya Rossiya* published a long letter that was a frontal assault on Gorbachev's policies of *glasnost* and democratization. Allegedly written by Nina Andreeva, a chemistry teacher from Leningrad, it had undoubtedly been heavily edited in the Central Committee apparatus, most likely under Yegor Ligachev's supervision. It took *Pravda* three weeks to respond and strongly condemn the letter; that a power struggle was going on behind the closed walls of the Kremlin can be safely assumed. In April there were rumours that Ligachev, who appears not to have sufficiently covered his move, had been formally censured by the Politburo for his behaviour in the affair and might be dismissed. Though Gorbachev himself disclaimed these rumours, the result was to weaken Ligachev's position while demonstrating to Gorbachev the extent of the resistance to his course. This resistance was again illustrated during the selection process for delegates to the nineteenth Party Conference. Although Gorbachev succeeded in sending many of his supporters to the conference, some of the most prominent were not elected, and it was fair to assume that traditional forces would form the majority of the 5,000 delegates.

The main task of the conference was to debate the Ten Theses adopted by a Central Committee plenum on 23 May 1988. While they reconfirmed the Communist Party's monopoly of power, and, in many respects, did not go as far as many of the reformers would have liked, they still made very interesting reading. *Inter alia* they proposed strengthening the role of the governmental councils (soviets) at all levels, advocated clearer separation of functions between Party and Government, asked for multi-candidate elections for state and Party officials to be limited at all levels, called for the tenure of Party officials to be limited to ten years (extendable only in extraordinary circumstances, and by a three-quarters majority vote of the electing body, to fifteen years), pushed for further legal reforms, and strongly attacked foreign policy under Brezhnev.

When Gorbachev opened the Party Conference he went beyond the Ten Theses, in particular adding an entirely new point to the agenda by proposing the complete reshaping of the Supreme Soviet. He recommended that the current Supreme Soviet be replaced by a new Congress of People's Deputies (of 2,250 members), representing the population, the Union's constituent parts and the country's 'social organizations'. This would elect a smaller Supreme Soviet of the USSR (roughly 450 members), which would meet regularly (with up to six months of sessions in a year) and would have real legislative power. (The present Supreme Soviet meets in full twice a year for brief sessions, rubber-stamping decisions made by the Party Central Committee or the Council of Ministers.) The new Supreme Soviet in turn would elect a 'Chairman of the Supreme Soviet of the USSR' (or President) with substantial powers in both foreign and domestic policy. Though Gorbachev did not spell it out, it was clear he felt this was a position the General Secretary of the CPSU would hold. Gorbachev was thus establishing a new position for himself, and one whose authority and power would be significantly upgraded, to the point of provoking expressions of disquiet from some of his own supporters, such as Andrei Sakharov, over what they saw as a potentially dangerous concentration of powers in the hands of a single man.

The proposal took the conference by surprise, and it was hardly questioned in the ensuing debate. But there was considerable debate on other matters. For four days conservatives and reformers clashed publicly on the podium in a way that has no parallel in Soviet history. The whole conference was broadcast live on television, with the culminating moment a heated exchange between Yeltsin (in his role as a delegate to the conference) and Ligachev. When Gorbachev declared the conference closed soon afterwards, he had been rewarded by having nearly all his proposals practically unánimously adopted (they were later confirmed by a Central Committee plenum in July). His objectives at the conference appear to have been threefold: to lay the ground for a further increase in his power base by establishing a strengthened Presidency (to which he is expected to be elected in the spring of 1989); to portray himself as a moderate and reasonable man arbitrating the sharp clashes of the two wings of the Party; and to shake the population out of its apathy, and win its support, by broadcasting the whole show into every Soviet home.

The conservative forces mounted renewed efforts to regain some of the ground they had lost. This was particularly true of Ligachev, who, in a speech in Gorky in August, attempted to resurrect the role of class struggle in foreign policy. This led to an unprecedented public debate about foreign policy, during which Ligachev's position was sharply attacked by Aleksandr Yakovlev, another Politburo member close to Gorbachev. Ligachev's prestige was clearly slipping. The situation came to a head on 30 September, when Gorbachev, exploiting a short absence from Moscow by Ligachev, hastily convened a surprise Central Committee plenum that altered the power relationship in the Politburo. Andrei Gromyko was sent gracefully into retirement (the following day an extraordinary session of the Supreme Soviet elected Gorbachev to succeed him as Chairman of its Presidium). Another full member of the Politburo (M. Solomentsev) and two candidate members (V. Dolgikh and P. Demichev) were sacked (as was Anatoly Dobrynin as Secretary of the Central Committee, though he appears to have been retained as foreign-policy adviser to Gorbachev). Viktor Chebrikov was removed as head of the KGB, but made a Secretary of the Central Committee in charge of the KGB and MVD. Ligachev lost both his ideological portfolio (which went to a newly appointed full member of the Politburo, V.A. Medvedev) and his informal position as 'Second General Secretary' (a function which nobody apparently now performs) and was awarded instead the agricultural portfolio in the Secretariat – a doubtful prize, given the parlous state of agriculture in the USSR. Aleksandra Biryukova (the first woman to reach such heights since Furtseva in 1960) and Anatoly Lukyanov gave up their positions as Secretaries and became candidate members of the Politburo. Both are said to be close to Gorbachev.

At the same time, the structure of the Secretariat of the Central Committee was profoundly changed when its former 22 departments were regrouped into six new commissions (Party structure and cadre policy, ideology, social and economic policy, agriculture, international policy, and legal policy), each headed by a member of the Politburo. The move was widely read as indicating that Gorbachev planned to streamline the entire Party bureaucracy. A similar step had already been taken with regard to the government apparatus.

Through these moves Gorbachev has not simply strengthened his position, nor merely again combined the positions of General Secretary and acting President of the USSR (as all his predecessors had also done). He has completely changed the Soviet political landscape and opened a new stage in his battle to modernize the country.

First, while Gorbachev's personal power has grown, that of the three traditional pillars of the Soviet system – the Party, the armed forces, and the internal security forces – has been simultaneously weakened. The Defence Minister today is only a candidate member of the Politburo. No new Marshals are being appointed, and when the Chief of Staff resigned (nominally on health grounds but, significantly, at the same time as the announcement of a unilateral arms-control move by Gorbachev in December) he was replaced by a young General promoted over the heads of many more senior officers. A powerful Party figure, Chebrikov, has been removed as chairman of the KGB, and his successor, a more purely professional man, no longer holds a seat on the Politburo. Ligachev's demotion and the abolition of the informal position of a 'Second General Secretary' was accompanied by the distribution of top Party positions among several people, some of whom are not even members of the Politburo. None of them can henceforth claim to speak for the Party as a whole, as Ligachev frequently did before the September shake-up.

Secondly, the new Presidency which Gorbachev will acquire in the spring will be very different from the old. Not only will it have new and stronger powers; it will also acquire some of the prestige of a Presidency elected (even if only indirectly) by popular vote. The populist element, always present in Gorbachev's leadership style, will be enhanced – at least psychologically. As a consequence, the General Secretary will clearly no longer only be *primus inter pares* in the Politburo, he will be aiming at a power base which extends beyond that body.

Thirdly, having accumulated further power in his own hands, Gorbachev will now also be forced to accept personal responsibility for the success or failure of his drive for reform. There will be hardly anyone left to shoulder the blame (except the unfortunate Ligachev, where the agricultural sector is concerned) should things go wrong – and they could go wrong all too easily. Even more than before, the new realities created by Gorbachev have acquired the aspect of a colossal gamble; he seems to believe that he can impose his will successfully, if he can only concentrate enough power into his own hands.

Whether the outcome of the Congress of Deputies election held on 26 March 1989 will help or hinder is still unclear. Leaving aside that voters were not in every case given a real choice, Western observers reported that, at least where they monitored them, the elections themselves were run fairly and efficiently. The partisans of reform can take pleasure in that. But the results may not be as happy for the Party apparatus. Boris Yeltsin, the Party's *bête noire*, gained 89% of the vote in Moscow despite all its efforts to prevent his election. In some key constituencies (notably Kiev and Leningrad), the voters, angry at having no choice, crossed the names of unopposed Party stalwarts from the ballot papers and left them with less than 50% of the vote. Over two dozen Party leaders, including a candidate member of the Politburo, found themselves embarrassed in this way. For the most part, these leaders appear to have been opponents of reform, and to that extent the voters have registered a firm *Da* to reforms, and to Gorbachev.

The Challenges

Gorbachev's success or failure will have to be measured in three areas: the economy, and particularly the visible improvement of the population's standard of living; his handling of defence policy, which not only is crucial for foreign-policy prospects but also involves a sector that devours much of the USSR's scarce resources; and the urgent, and now explosive, nationalities problem. Each of them represents a formidable challenge.

The Economy

On the surface, the Soviet economy seems to have done considerably better in 1988 than in 1987. In the first three-quarters of the year national income grew by 4.7% (compared with a target of 4.3%, and the 2.3% achieved in 1987). According to Soviet claims, industrial output during the same period was up by 4.3% (target 4.5%, 3.6% achieved in 1987). Labour productivity was said to have increased by 5.2% (4.2%, 2.5%). The harvest turned out to be acceptable, and energy production continued to increase across the board.

The figures, however, may capture only part of the reality. 1987 was a particularly bad year, and impressive growth in the succeeding year was thus much easier to achieve. Much more worrying are the puzzles hidden behind the most recent set of statistics. Soviet light industry was said to have grown in the first half of 1988 by an impressive 5.5%; yet none of the various industries that are grouped under this heading increased physical output by this amount. Consequently, the growth appears to have been in prices, rather than in production *per se*. The same may be suspected of other areas of the economy. The new law on state enterprises, as well as the new law on corporations (passed after considerable difficulties in May and already being qualified in December) can indeed be expected to encourage price increases and to foster hidden inflation, which may run as high as 7%. This calls the published 1988 results seriously into question.

A prudent approach to Soviet data also seems to be warranted because of another fact: having boasted of constant budget surpluses in the past, the USSR admitted in November that there was a deficit in the 1989 budget plan of 36.2 bn roubles ($US 59 bn at official exchange rates) or 7.3% of public spending. Gorbachev himself soon added the revelation that there had been deficits throughout the 1980s. Western experts estimate that the cumulative deficit may have risen from some 20 bn roubles in 1980 to 95 bn roubles in 1987, and perhaps to as much as 120 bn roubles in 1988. Whatever the precise figure, it makes it even clearer that putting the Soviet economy back on an even keel will be a gargantuan task. Indeed, according to some Soviet accounts, the state of the economy is considerably worse than the most pessimistic Western assessments.

The Soviet Union, already struggling with a deteriorating foreign trade situation (at best exports stagnated in dollar terms in 1988, while imports rose sharply), will continue to require a massive influx from the West for years to come: capital (Soviet borrowing has continued its steep rise), technology (industrial espionage has been increased in the Gorbachev years), and managerial know-how through joint venture arrangements (more than 2,500 are now under discussion, and the rules governing them have been made gradually more attractive). These harsh economic realities go a long way to explaining Gorbachev's interest in improving East–West relations.

Another aspect of the Soviet economy may be even more crucially relevant to Gorbachev and his reform plans. The General Secretary is clearly trying to gain enough popular support for his policies to overcome the resistance of the bureaucracy; yet, without a visible improvement in the living conditions of the average Soviet citizen, it will be impossible to attain that support. The frustration that is piling up over living standards was dramatized when Gorbachev visited Siberia in September. He was not only confronted with angry crowds, he was literally dragged into empty stores to witness the situation for himself. While this episode may have been staged to make a point, there is no doubt that basic supplies of consumer goods have actually declined since Gorbachev came to power. Individual savings (an indicator of unsatisfied demand) have continued to soar and have now reached close to 300 bn roubles. Whether Gorbachev can improve this situation will clearly be an important yardstick by which he – and his ideas – will be measured by the Soviet population.

Defence Policy

An obvious way out would be to cut defence spending (currently consuming at least 17% of the Soviet GNP). Gorbachev himself seems to be contemplating precisely this. Talking of the economic situation of the country in January 1989, he bluntly stated that the problems would be 'so acute that we will have to look at our spending on defence. Preliminary studies show that we can cut it without lowering the level of security and the country's ability to defend itself.' It was, therefore, only logical for Gorbachev, during his impressive speech at the UN General Assembly, to announce a reduction of Soviet armed forces by some 500,000 men (about 10% of the total), 10,000 tanks and much other equipment. The move – which will reduce, but by no means eliminate, Soviet conventional superiority in Europe – was obviously designed to enhance the prospect for success in the forthcoming negotiations between NATO and the Warsaw Pact on conventional force reductions in Europe. And on the success of the negotiations is likely to rest a further improvement in East–West relations within which the flow of Western capital and technology to the USSR can be fostered. On 19 January 1989, at a meeting with members of the Trilateral Commission, Gorbachev announced that the defence budget was to be reduced by 14.2% and spending on military hardware by 19.5%, but, in the absence of reliable data on Soviet defence budgets, the true significance of these figures is uncertain.

There have been indications that Gorbachev had been pushing for unilateral Soviet force reductions for quite some time. He had undoubtedly met stiff resistance from the Soviet military, which had not only publicly ruled out this option but declared it fundamentally dangerous for Soviet national security. Simultaneously with Gorbachev's UN announcement in December, Chief of Staff Marshal Akhromeyev resigned, ostensibly on health grounds. That the General Secretary went ahead in the face of clear military opposition can be read as a sign of his improved power situation after the 30 September shake-up. His preparations to face the problems that such a move must create can be seen by the appointment of a young and relatively junior officer, Col.-Gen. Moiseyev, as Chief of Staff over the heads of many of his seniors.

Other foreign-policy moves, above all the withdrawal from Afghanistan, may have been greeted with silent relief by the armed forces. Yet some of the information released in the process – for example, film from Soviet archives showing the summary execution of Afghan villagers by Soviet soldiers (which was officially provided to a British television team) and revelations about the Red Army's role in mass executions in the Baltic states in 1940 – cannot be expected to cause enthusiasm in the armed forces, and may well have been intended to undermine their position. In essence, Gorbachev seems determined to insist on a true subordination of the military to civilian and Party control. He will, however, have to come up with genuine successes in arms control and foreign policy to justify that approach. His dilemma is that what the military (and conservative forces in general) consider 'success' in this area is likely to be utterly incompatible with what the West considers as its own minimum security requirements. Domestic policy requirements may push the General Secretary to pursue his foreign and arms-control offensive more vigorously in the two crucial years leading up to the next Party Congress in early 1991.

Nationalities
Scarcely less complex is the situation in the third crucial area – the nationality problem. Ethnic unrest, which had already surfaced in Kazakhstan in December 1986 and manifested itself in mass rallies in the Baltic Republics and demonstrations by the Crimean Tartars in Moscow in 1987, took on a new dimension in February 1988, when the Armenian problem exploded. The ostensible reason – the Armenian demand for the return of the largely Armenian-populated enclave of Nagorno-Karabakh from Azerbaijan to Armenia – was but the tip of the iceberg. When the disturbances continued throughout the year (with some mass demonstrations reaching up to a million participants) and found an echo in ever more far-reaching demands for autonomy in the Baltic Republics, it became all too apparent that the USSR, the last remaining undivided colonial empire, was facing an unprecedented challenge to its very cohesion.

The situation was not ameliorated by prompt moves from Moscow, nor by attempts to sweep the problem under the rug (when the central government for constitutional reasons simply refused any change in the status of Nagorno-Karabakh), nor by the shock of the devastating earthquake which hit Armenia in early December, claiming 25,000 lives and leaving hundreds of thousands homeless. Indeed, the earthquake highlighted the inadequacies of Soviet organization to cope, in contrast to prompt Western assistance. Ethnic unrest continued in Armenia; less visibly, but no less dangerously, other nationalist movements grew in turn in the Baltic Republics, Azerbaijan, Georgia and Moldavia.

Demands did not abate, but escalated. Estonia even formally demanded a veto power over legislation adopted by the Supreme Soviet, and new legislation on national languages passed by the Baltic

Republics will have a discriminatory effect on the sizeable Russian populations there. The only mitigating factor in 1988 was that large-scale unrest had not affected the largest non-Russian Republic, the Ukraine. But that may not be far away.

While Gorbachev clearly recognizes the importance of the problem, equally clearly he has no new, neat answer to it. With regard to Armenia and Azerbaijan he has attempted a solution that bears a remarkable resemblance to the one the British government has been trying for years in Northern Ireland: he sent in troops to keep the peace and put the disputed territory of Nagorno-Karabakh under direct rule of the central government. It has also been announced that a forthcoming meeting of the Central Committee will be devoted to the nationalities problem. Gorbachev demonstrated his increasing irritation and anger at the obduracy of ethnic feeling when he lost his temper at the end of his visit to catastrophe-stricken Armenia and summarily blamed the unrest on conservative and criminal elements.

Neither Gorbachev's anger nor the measures taken so far will make the problem go away. On the contrary, it will in all likelihood turn out to present one of the litmus tests of how far democracy can go in the USSR and how serious Gorbachev truly is in his proclaimed objective of listening to the needs and demands of Soviet citizens. In all probability, it will also provide rich material for argument for those who advocate a sharp return to repressive methods. It was thus not surprising to hear Gorbachev declare in January 1989 that 'some people are increasingly nostalgic for the good old days. Conversations are heard that the country needs a "firm hand". Some propose using the sad experience of 1937' (the height of Stalin's purges). He was certainly right when he added that this would be 'unacceptable'. Without *glasnost* the General Secretary will not be able to rally popular support for his programme, nor will that programme succeed without such support. Equally, heavy-handed internal repression would destroy, at a stroke, Gorbachev's achievements with the West in building a picture of a responsible and normal Soviet Union with which all nations 'can do business'. This, however, leaves completely unanswered the question of how long there can be *glasnost* without a solution of the nationalities problem. Most worrying of all, it does nothing to answer the question of how the ethnic unrest can be solved.

Looking Ahead

In 1988 the Gorbachev revolution entered a new, and perhaps decisive, stage. Gorbachev is now much more fully in charge, but as a result he bears an even greater degree of responsibility. He has managed to check, but not yet fully defeat, the conservative forces which he has been blaming for having delayed his reform programme. Open opposition and challenges have been replaced with grumbling beneath the surface. This does not necessarily make Gorbachev's situation any less dangerous, however, particularly if he is not able to show concrete results before the next Party Congress.

The problems facing Gorbachev have not decreased; if anything they have continued to grow. The chances that his reforms will succeed have consequently not improved, even though they may well be the only available solution to the USSR's problems. To provide useful answers, the reforms will probably have to go farther and faster. Gorbachev may be willing to contemplate precisely this, but whether the country can absorb that increase in scope and speed, or the system tolerate it, remains a much more open question. Gorbachev is running the clear risk that he is creating enemies much faster than he is winning popular support. Yet the alternatives to his course might be disastrous, not only for his personal position but for the USSR as well.

Equally worrying must be the fact that the remedies Gorbachev proposes contain a growing number of contradictions. How can the Soviet economy be seriously reformed without touching the pricing system? Yet how can that pricing system be altered without causing a popular uproar? How is the push for more legal security and cautious democratization compatible with the sort of enlightened dictatorship the General Secretary appears to want? Where will he find a social base for *perestroika* if the reform is perceived by the people to be more a threat than a blessing? How can there be open political debate if it cannot include the most burning contemporary issue: the role of the Communist Party within the system? How many Armenias can *glasnost* and the USSR (and the Soviet hold on Eastern Europe) afford? Above all, how can *perestroika* and moves towards a market economy be reconciled with fundamental and ultimate Party control?

It appears likely that Gorbachev will seek success where he can get it, particularly in foreign policy. The chance combination of a Soviet leader interested in moving vigorously forward in foreign policy and a degree of continuity between US administrations not seen in modern times promises a further intensification of the East–West dialogue. Whether this confluence will yield positive results depends more on internal developments in the USSR than on the West. Yet managing its relationship wisely with a Soviet Union in upheaval for some time to come will remain a formidable challenge for the West. How it is managed will be crucial, not least because it is only over the course of the next few years, if Gorbachev remains in charge, that the dynamic Soviet leader's objectives will become clear.

Europe

WESTERN EUROPE FACING A NEW CHALLENGE

NATO entered its fortieth year, the longest-standing multinational alliance in history and the cornerstone of a prosperous Western Europe, justifiably satisfied by its success in containing post-war Soviet expansionism and eliciting signs of greater liberty for Eastern Europe. Yet the Alliance's hour of triumph brought signs of political exhaustion, with many uncertainties about the future of Western strategy and divisions of opinion about the best basis for future security. This was only one of the paradoxes that emerged in Europe in 1988.

Moscow's policy reversals in arms control, human rights, regional conflicts and economic dogma, combined with the Communist leaders' admission of historical errors – the virtual surrender of the Soviet Union in many areas of the East–West struggle – paradoxically bred in much of Europe a 'Gorbymania' that eclipsed any sense of vindication. This sentiment mixed fascination with Mikhail Gorbachev's courage and appeal, a sense of prospective relief from the threat posed by the Warsaw Pact, and enthusiasm at the novel prospects being thrown open in the East.

Beyond this psychological swing, Western security policy started to adjust to the prospect of an environment of changing political and military realities. As 1988 wore on, even conservative European policy-makers were won over to the view that they were not dealing with another Nikita Khrushchev, whose propensity for bold and daring ventures in domestic reform seemed almost organically linked to bluster or hostile moves against the West. Gorbachev, by contrast, seemed to require accommodation with the West – and seemed to know it. But that posed policy dilemmas of a new kind. Could Western leaders sustain Alliance cohesion during a long period of military build-down? How would European stability evolve in the face of sharply reduced military threats and ideological pressure from the East? What was the West European vision of the future political and security landscape of their continent?

Accumulating Problems

Even as the West pocketed Soviet concessions on human rights in Vienna, and as Soviet military intimidation subsided, European consensus started to crumble, momentarily at least, on East–West issues: military spending, arms control, credits and strategic trade, diplomatic tactics to be adopted towards the Gorbachev administration. While there was no agreement on exactly how to deal with Gorbachev, there was a broad consensus in Europe that it was in the West's interest for his reforms to succeed (if only because it would make the Soviet Union less

Soviet). This contrasted with opinion in the United States, where the desirability of helping Gorbachev was still debatable.

In addition, potentially disruptive dynamics gained momentum in most European nations. Governments faced mounting difficulties in sustaining support for defence in a phase when burden-shedding, not burden-sharing, was almost irresistibly appealing to ˙most voters. Resentment grew, particularly in West Germany, against military training manoeuvres, such as low-level flying. Broad disaffection spread against the doctrine of nuclear deterrence, with the resurgence of an anti-nuclear malaise that had never fallen completely dormant. The eagerness for more funds for social spending, partly to offset fears of social Darwinism as the EC reduces internal barriers to competition, added rigidity to the burden-sharing argument. Europeans were particularly determined not to pay more for defence if they thought the need arose mainly from mismanagement of the US economy. The prospect of an integrated post-1992 Western Europe brought with it fears of greater American use of industrial protectionism in defence, under the guise of national security. All these reactions gained strength in every European country, but most of the trends were strongest in West Germany.

Paradoxically, in comparison to previous periods of Alliance stress over how far to invest in detente, the strains were not exclusively between the US and its European allies but were equally strong between Europeans. If the Soviet threat was going to be reduced merely to the unavoidable problem of living with a neighbouring super-power, Europe would theoretically find it easier to assure its own defence. The possibility of a partial US military withdrawal from Europe in the 1990s, perhaps in response to major cuts in Soviet forward forces, had a dampening effect on the much-discussed moves to forge a 'European Pillar' of NATO, lest it be interpreted by Congress as a licence to leave. One of the simpler solutions to US concerns over burden-sharing would, after all, be to 'bring home the boys'. As a result, European governments began to put more emphasis on the compatibility of their own closer defence co-operation and NATO's work.

But in Europe itself divergences over how to respond to the change in the Soviet bloc could eventually undermine the recent momentum towards the full economic integration of the Common Market. That danger was usually referred to as 'the German problem', meaning that some thought West Germany might become a less reliable European ally and NATO anchor because leaders in Bonn saw national opportunities in the liberalizing Warsaw Pact. European developments might be subtly diluted by the prospects of an enhanced role for West Germany, based on its status as the most effective Western power in the search for a more independent Eastern Europe. While Western leaders encouraged a vigorous West German role in Eastern Europe (partly to stimulate their economies and partly to buy off any excessive fervour while these nations quietly and gradually loosened the Soviet grip), there was also concern that West European integration might coalesce too slowly to contain West Germany's involvement in the East. The ensuing lack of West European cohesion could compromise the outlook for a new transatlantic bargain.

While the present leaders of Western Europe would never consciously trade American protection for Soviet goodwill, the potential for a crisis in Western ranks was increased by the rise of commercial rivalries, mainly associated with the still-unclear outcome of the process leading to 1992, simultaneously with the decline of the Soviet threat that had made military unity a higher priority than transatlantic trade disputes. Many would have preferred Mr Gorbachev to wait a year or two longer before starting to change life, so that the West would have time to transform its world to be ready for him.

If Europe had reached a watershed in relations with both its superpower ally and its super-power adversary, the Atlantic Alliance still appeared to be the best tool for encouraging a peaceful evolution in Europe. But NATO itself, despite its success in deploying and then destroying intermediate-range nuclear missiles and its success as a bulwark against Soviet military intimidation, often seemed to perform inadequately in trying to cement Western capabilities and focus Western aspirations in a period of new opportunities in the East and new problems in the West. Many people felt that the basic problem facing NATO was to renew the confidence of Allied governments and public opinion in its purposes and effectiveness.

Support was growing for an overhaul of the Alliance. In this view the West needed at the very least to re-equip itself doctrinally to deal with a contained Soviet Union and regalvanize public opinion in each Alliance country behind a Western security pact to underpin a broader solidarity. Nowhere would European seriousness be more necessary. After all, the North Atlantic Treaty, the most profound and important departure in US history from the nation's wariness of foreign entanglements, resulted not from US intentions but mainly from the initiative and drive of the British foreign secretary, Ernest Bevin. Similarly, it took the drive and initiative of a number of West European politicians to ensure the adoption in 1967 of the Harmel Report (*Future Tasks of the Alliance*) which helped ensure the political relevance of the Alliance during the Brezhnev years. The lack of a political road-map of this kind is a growing liability for an Alliance whose *raison d'être* is increasingly questioned. The absence of in-depth, sustained inter-allied discussion on NATO's role, notably *vis-à-vis* Eastern Europe, encourages perceptions of political disorientation.

Pivotal Germany

The dominant security issues in Europe were most intense in West Germany, NATO's key front-line nation. The ally most dependent on NATO solidarity, it was also the nation with the biggest investment, political and economic, emotional and historical, in improving access to the East.

EUROPE

As European NATO's major bastion of conventional forces, West Germany was also the first to want relief from the annoying syndrome of military near-saturation. Political pressures against short-range nuclear arms welled up across the political spectrum. The public mood grew unhappy with the performance of the armed forces, German and Allied, and particularly with air forces, which were associated in the public mind with a string of disastrous crashes. The coalition government – led by Christian Democrat Chancellor Helmut Kohl, but in which Foreign Minister Hans-Dietrich Genscher, a Liberal, seemed to control security policy – cited West Germany's exceptional record as a staunch Alliance member, but Bonn seemed to be out in front of most other Western governments in believing that significant efforts should be made to help the Gorbachev reforms in the hope of making them irreversible. For most of the opposition and much of the governing coalition, the idea seemed to prevail that future security could be based on arms control first and on defence second. By refusing to dwell on the risks, critics said, Genscher was feeding a mood of euphoria in West Germany, sometimes at the expense of a sound security policy, which needed to adjust slowly, so as to ensure that Soviet military capabilities were indeed transformed. Convinced that Western security was not now in jeopardy, Genscher sought to raise the political profile of his electorally vulnerable Liberal party by portraying himself as the guardian of West German interests in a coalition in which the Chancellor and his majority Christian Democrats might be too deferential to the US and other allies.

The Bonn government was also experiencing the first turbulence of having to take the political responsibility of a more independent national line. The outcry over laxity in allowing German firms to co-operate on third-world weaponry, including nuclear and chemical warheads and missile technology, was a chastening experience. Beyond that, West Germany was sensitive to the prospects of the new European order that would certainly emerge if arms-control negotiations decisively restructured Soviet power.

The salient security issue in West Germany was whether and when to replace ageing *Lance* missile launchers as part of a NATO package to restructure its short-range nuclear forces (SNF) in Europe after the INF Treaty had come into effect. The oscillations of Chancellor Kohl and the ambiguities of Mr Genscher illustrated the style of German political leadership, its responsiveness to domestic political developments and the reasons why Allied governments were often frustrated with German policy. In March 1988, after the INF Treaty was agreed, NATO held its first summit since 1982 to signal its support for the Treaty and to consider accelerating its planned modernization, including a follow-on for *Lance*, due to be withdrawn in the mid-1990s. Kohl, anxious to postpone another deployment battle, enlisted the help of French President Mitterrand to prevent the summit from insisting on a *Lance* decision. The result was a non-decision. Kohl claimed the summit's final communiqué meant that *Lance* was a 'subject for the first third of the 1990s', a date conveniently after West German parliamentary elections in 1990, which the Christian Democrat-led coalition was favoured to win. Over the ensuing months, Kohl was won round to the view that it was tactically wiser to agree to modernization quickly in 1989, thus putting the issue behind him and tying Foreign Minister Genscher and his Liberal Party to the decision, and to the coalition, beyond the 1990 elections. Kohl announced his plans privately to US leaders in Washington and also to Mrs Thatcher and President Mitterrand, with the result that French Foreign Minister Roland Dumas ceased his calls for the deferment of an early modernization decision, including a land-based follow-on to *Lance*. But when Mr Kohl's party was badly upset in elections in Berlin a few weeks later, he publicly reverted to the view that any decision should be postponed.

In the domestic context, *Lance* modernization was opposed by a majority covering a much broader political spectrum than had opposed the deployment of *Pershing* II and cruise missiles in West Germany in the early 1980s. The left-wing opposition mounted a campaign to eliminate all remaining nuclear weapons on German soil. Ironically, even some conservatives in Mr Kohl's own party also opposed the modernization of ground-launched systems. They argued that the Alliance should not be allowed to confine its nuclear arsenal to weapons whose ranges meant that in wartime they would be fired or targeted on the soil of West and East Germany only.

This mood was fuelled by a campaign – initially led by the Soviet Union, but with East Germany later playing the more active role – for the removal of short-range nuclear forces described as 'only designed to kill Germans'. In January 1988 Soviet Foreign Minister Eduard Shevardnadze, paying the highest-level visit to Bonn since the deployment of *Pershing* II, warned that nuclear modernization would 'scuttle all that has been achieved in arms control so far'. This message, was pressed on Kohl when he made his long-sought visit to Moscow in October to see Gorbachev. Throughout 1988 the theme of denuclearization received strong East German support, and it was reinforced in January 1989, when Shevardnadze announced the withdrawal of Soviet SNF systems organic to the six armoured divisions that the USSR had pledged to withdraw, and called for a freeze on further modernization.

The Alliance was split several ways over modernization. The US and the UK believed that NATO should upgrade its arms quickly in order to demonstrate that modernization was a matter of routine. They opposed new negotiations on short-range nuclear forces because of fears that the anti-nuclear momentum, fuelled by Soviet diplomacy, might create overwhelming political pressure to eliminate US nuclear weapons from West Germany. Such a development would involve a serious risk of seeing the United States, under a policy of 'no nukes, no troops', withdraw its conventional forces. In addition, it would fuel long-term hostility to the nuclear deterrents of France and the United Kingdom. Italy, the Netherlands and Belgium advocated East–West negotiations on SNF in order to eliminate the Soviet advantage in this category of weapons (missiles with ranges under 500 kilometres). Compared to NATO's 124 *Lance* launchers, 88 of them in West Germany, the Soviet Union has an estimated 1,360 launchers west of the Urals.

Lance modernization coloured perspectives on a larger issue: would nuclear deterrence continue to reassure West Europeans that they were secure and was military stability – and perhaps peaceful political evolution in Europe – assured by some mix of nuclear and conventional forces? West German public opinion appeared hardest hit by doubts about nuclear deterrence, partly because the post-INF atmosphere, after strong public debate, had left West Germans with high expectations of follow-on nuclear disarmament agreements, covering, *inter alia*, the short-range systems on German soil.

French and British (and indeed some West German) officials argued vigorously that the disappearance of nuclear weapons could destabilize European peace because of the permanent problem of a neighbouring Soviet super-power. Manfred Wörner, in the 1988 Alastair Buchan Memorial Lecture, said that some recent Soviet pronouncements appeared to reveal 'acceptance of the doctrine that a nuclear war is not winnable by either side [and thus] suggest a possible doctrinal consensus. It would be very odd if the Alliance were to jeopardize its policy of deterrence just at a time when there are prospects of making the Soviet leadership understand the importance of its contribution to maintaining the sort of stability in Europe which is the necessary condition for peaceful change'.

Facing The Challenge
A cascade of conciliatory statements from Gorbachev set the tone for the year, starting with the announcement of the Soviet withdrawal from Afghanistan. His United Nations speech in December 1988 offered the vision of a co-operative USSR, not an adversarial one. The Soviet Union would be supportive of the work of the UN, which had already lifted European hopes of seeing more international conciliation by its contribution to the truce in the Gulf War and the agreement over Namibia. European desires for international co-operation on other forms of security – for example, economic security from the debt crisis, and environmental security from global ecological threats – were assuaged by Soviet new thinking. Above all, Gorbachev signalled his acceptance of the idea that the relationship between the USSR and Eastern Europe was open to some change; and he stated that the Warsaw Pact would restructure itself to become purely defensive. In December he announced significant cuts in Soviet forward-deployed forces, cuts that would blunt the Warsaw Pact's ability to launch a surprise offensive. Later came fresh announcements of unilateral cuts in non-Soviet Warsaw Pact forces, and the provision, for the first time ever, of Pact

data about its own conventional forces. Taken together, these steps indicated Soviet interest in a new security system in Europe, with far fewer forces and more latitude for European nations, both East and West.

European reactions varied from euphoric to cautious, but even Mrs Thatcher pronounced the Cold War to be over, suggesting that no European leader felt that it would be possible to restore the Communist threat. West Germany sought to capitalize on every possible military cut and industrial opening during what might, after all, prove only a limited window of opportunity to advance detente before another crisis froze the situation again. Bonn made a kind of Pascalian wager: if it lasts, we will be vindicated; if Gorbachev fails, we will still have gained as much as possible. Therefore, there was also a tendency to act as if anticipated change had already actually occurred in Eastern Europe and the Soviet Union, and many strains in the Alliance could be traced to West Germany's new assertiveness in pursuing this Eastern policy. During *Ostpolitik* in the 1970s, it had sought to tighten its links to the West simultaneously with its opening to the East, to show Moscow that there were limits to its ability to make concessions. This time, Bonn was more inclined to try carrying its European partners along, winning them over to German views.

Tensions were sharpest with the UK, which seemed to resent the West German challenge to its authority in the Alliance. Despite (or because of) its hard-nosed attitude towards the Soviet Union, London was treated as an uncircumventable player by Moscow. The UK thus firmly established its own niche in the *Ostpolitik* process. France chose a policy of trying to accompany West Germany, partly as a continuation of Franco-German co-operation in reconstructing post-war Europe, partly in order to position itself to exercise restraint if it felt West Germany was becoming unreliable. Paris took pains to hew out an identifiable French line, and to be seen as playing a leading role in the diplomatic arena, notwithstanding its active efforts to develop connections with East European states. In addition, French leaders felt that public opinion would not support Western defence indefinitely if it judged that leaders had failed to explore adequately every opportunity for accommodation. Italy and Spain, the Netherlands and the Nordic nations largely shared the German interest in quick progress, but there were hints of nervousness that Bonn might go too far, and thus jeopardize the cohesion of the post-1992 Common Market and even transatlantic solidarity.

West Germany was anxious to encourage developing trends in Eastern Europe, and through investments and trade (and advocacy of East European countries' interests in the councils of the European Community) it was actively waging a diplomatic campaign in the area where Germany had had strong pre-war influence. Its goals were to raise hopes of better conditions and to control inflammable expectations that might derail a process of cautious change. With scant means beyond its political prestige, France copied this policy of trying, in an official's words, to 'encourage the East Europeans to creep out of Yalta' over the next decade. The idea was that East European nations could reassure the Soviet Union on security issues, while reorienting their economies largely towards the West. Italy, indirectly helped by the Pope's Polish heritage, sought a similar approach. If Gorbachev was offering a 'common European house', most West Europeans found it easier to envisage Middle Europeans as co-tenants than Russians. There is 'no symmetry between the Soviet Union and the West European countries', a French official said, adding: 'Even if it were deSovietized, Russia would still, by its scale, pose problems for Europe'. This French suspicion of Russia, he implied, contrasted with wishful thinking in West Germany.

But European governments were agreed that trade was a mutual interest. Credits, at commercial rates, were forthcoming: $1.7 bn from West Germany, $775 m from Italy, $2.1 bn from the UK. Debate was starting about how to formulate a common line on sensitive trade issues, including the control of strategic goods.

The common denominator in Western thinking was well articulated in Manfred Wörner's 1988 Alastair Buchan lecture: our aim, he said, must be to reassure Gorbachev that the West will not interfere with, and where possible will assist, the process of reforms he has launched in the Soviet Union. But, beyond that, he continued, our goal 'should be to ensure that the Soviet reforms lead to a major degree of military self-restraint. A crucial question is whether or not Soviet military capabilities, after a period of change and reform, will still remain a key determinant of the European political order'.

This goal seemed closer as preparations were completed for talks on cutting conventional forces in Europe. Soviet propaganda before the talks suggested big concessions in terms of cuts in tanks, artillery and armoured fighting vehicles, though these would be conditional upon Western concessions on strike aircraft and perhaps naval forces. Soviet pressure for measures to address theatre nuclear weapons was also clearly on the cards, but the extent of any linkage to conventional ground force reductions, at least in the initial stages, was unclear. Big Soviet reductions and intrusive verification, coupled with expanded confidence-building measures, offered the prospect of Soviet fulfilment of Gorbachev's promises to operate a smaller, cheaper, less menacing Soviet military force.

In these negotiations the European Allies played close to an equal role with the United States. In preparing both the East–West mandate for the conventional stability talks and NATO's opening proposal, European nations had the chance to air their national interests (for example, Norway's fears about amphibious forces, Turkey's concern about air power and the determination of both flank countries not to be separated from the central front of the Alliance in disarmament planning any more than in military strategy). France, playing a full role in NATO for this purpose, won assent for its constant position that, contrary to intuitive reasoning, equal ceilings in conventional forces do not in themselves guarantee stability. NATO proved able to accommodate national interests, but at the cost of delay in reaching a consensus and perhaps a loss of reaction time in comparison to Gorbachev's light-footed ability to make sudden concessions and demands during talks. To many, however, the exercise suggested that NATO's political flexibility was improving.

Facing up to Burden-Sharing

Quite apart from its promise of reducing security tensions, the prospect of possible deep force reductions offered eventual relief for military budgets and hopes of reversing a trend of worsening Alliance tension over burden-sharing issues. There was a risk, of course, that burden-sharing could prove politically divisive among the Allies, particularly if some countries appeared to be moving prematurely to drop responsibilities.

The other new factor in the burden-sharing dispute was the economic climate, notably fears in the United States that it was declining economically while the European countries were undergoing a renascence as significant trade competitors. All the traditional arguments for cutting US commitments in Europe had re-emerged: the European economy could afford to pay more, individual European nations (notably Denmark, Spain and Belgium) were failing to pay enough, and the United States needed help to maintain non-NATO commitments that served European interests as well.

The Reagan administration, anxious to head off Congressional complaints and, if possible, to make burden-sharing an issue among all Alliance nations, encouraged a NATO exercise to find a new approach to the question. The resultant study, *Enhancing Alliance Collective Security*, published by NATO's Defence Planning Committee in early December 1988, took into account European arguments, particularly the view that spending figures alone neglect the unquantifiable, invisible contributions and burdens of some Allies. Europeans reject the most commonly used indicator of defence spending, the military budget as a share of gross domestic product, because it includes non-NATO commitments, of which the United States has by far the largest share. The study took into account relevant non-military economic spending (such as some forms of aid), the value (and hidden costs) of conscript armies, and the Allies' relative constancy in military spending in contrast to the fluctuating US levels.

West Germany gained more recognition for its unmatched burden-bearing in non-financial areas, such as its unique density of military personnel and bases, the dual capabilities of its highways, the nuisance of military exercises (with damages regularly exceeding $30 m per year), the frequency of low flying, its conscript army (especially the extension of military service for draftees from 15 to 18 months, due to start in summer 1989). Acceding to Bonn's arguments that public opinion needed relief from an 'annoyance syndrome', Allied nations curbed low flying (despite the fact that the capability to fly under Warsaw Pact radar is a key element of Western air power) and limited manoeuvres, even putting the 1989 *Reforger* exercise back into 1990 and scaling down this, the Alliance's biggest annual exercise, which involves reinforcements flown from the United States. Aerobatic flying was banned after two Italian jets crashed into spectators at an air show, injuring 350 and killing 70. There were 22 NATO aircraft crashes in West Germany during 1988. West German officials called the cutbacks temporary, but did not say how long they would last. Part of the sensitivity of this issue lies in the question of sovereignty, that is, the rights of the stationing powers to make the decisions.

Co-operation or Competition?
In Europe, as in the US, leaders sought to emphasize the potential for getting more defence for less money, primarily through better co-operation on new weapons. But the outlook for major change was unclear. European defence industries were concentrating nationally; transnational teaming was developing more slowly. Many industrialists were pessimistic about overcoming national barriers to defence procurement, even in the context of 1992. NATO's Independent European Programme Group made some progress towards establishing greater transparency in the bidding process for defence procurement, while moving slowly towards creating the conditions for European-scale technological defence co-operation. There was some debate about whether Europe should ensure protection for its military industries, risking a US backlash. The EC's mishandling of the issue of tariffs on US arms exports caused avoidable, and intense, irritation between the US and Western Europe.

There was little support during 1988 for the Western European Union (WEU), after several years in which it had been loudly encouraged by West European leaders. It seems at least conceivable that, faced with the prospect of a US force draw-down as a result of burden-sharing fatigue or precipitate arms-control activity, the European view swung, as it had in the past, from one of seeking to do more to one of fearing that enhanced Euro-capability would merely reinforce any American propensity to do less. Much more continues to happen in terms of European defence integration inside NATO, or on a bilateral basis, than in the WEU. In any case, developments seemed to occur as bilateral or multilateral steps, rather than collective leaps.

Probably the most revealing shift was the open disenchantment of France's President Mitterrand about the short-term prospects for stronger European defence by European nations. His views, long obscured by his policy of letting cabinet ministers speak without contradiction or confirmation, emerged in what appeared to be a largely extemporaneous lecture on French security policy at the Institute for Higher Defence Studies. In it he dismissed the prospects for a European pillar until after Europe had achieved economic unity in 1992 and then consolidated a European political structure. He was scathing about the gap between European rhetoric and European realities on this issue. In particular, he has been discouraged by the obstacles to forging greater industrial co-operation on weapons projects, particularly with West Germany. He singled out the UK Prime Minister for her obstinacy about national independence within a more closely-knit Europe, but in fact his views, for different reasons, seemed to have moved close to hers. France's Defence Minister Jean-Pierre Chevenement was still able to talk about the French independent nuclear deterrent, together with the British nuclear force, eventually forming the embryo of a European deterrent covering Europe's 'vital interests', which would be defined politically as the need arose.

The WEU reflected this stretching-out of the Europeans' time-scale in working towards their own defence. Spain and Portugal were formally admitted to the organization, but it seemed to have lost the momentum it had developed during the previous year. It served instead as a forum for decisions, such as the dispatch of a Gulf armada, that governments wished to take for their own reasons. The WEU was also deprived of any new momentum resulting from Franco-German military co-operation, which has taken a higher institutional profile. The joint Defence Council received parliamentary approval in December 1988, and a secretariat was established in February 1989. Even the European Fighter Aircraft project, acclaimed as the proof of European industry's ability to provide a second pillar, seemed to be troubled by rivalries in the four-nation consortium, notably over whether to choose a European-developed radar or a Europeanized version of an American design.

In contrast, much seemed to be happening in NATO. New French moves towards a more active role in NATO military planning were highlighted by a decision to participate in the development of NATO's future Air Command and Control System (ACCS). (French participation in ACCS planning had been shelved during the period of power-sharing in Paris that ended when the Socialists regained a working majority in parliament in May.) Despite the unpopularity of nuclear weapons, Denmark's surprise election produced a face-saving compromise in which the government 'assumed' that NATO warships complied with Danish rules against nuclear arms, but did not ask the Allies to break their policy of 'no confirmation, no denial'. Italy agreed to take the F-16 squadron (the US 401st) that had been compelled to leave Spain. Greece's hostility to NATO seemed likely to diminish as a result of the ruling Socialist Party's difficulties. And the British Labour Party was in the throes of an overdue debate on defence, with every indication that its leadership was seeking to move away from an electorally unrewarding unilateralist stance.

With many Europeans feeling hopeful that new Soviet approaches would lead inevitably to a loosening of the future political relationships in Europe, there were signs that NATO recognized a need to discuss its future political role, if it was to recapture support in member nations and prove its capability to play a positive role in shaping a transition from the axioms which had governed the post-war world. If it did not, there was a possibility that it would not survive its latest challenge: the winds of change blowing from the East.

THE WINDS OF CHANGE IN EASTERN EUROPE

Eastern Europe continues to be heavily affected by Mikhail Gorbachev's efforts to reform both Soviet domestic life and Soviet foreign relations. There was mixed and extraordinary movement within the Eastern bloc in the course of 1988, as some governments began to accept the implications of his preachings on reform, while others saw these as threatening stability or regime survival, and opposition to the possibilities of reform began to cohere. As a result, the Warsaw Pact currently appears to be evolving into two political alliances in one: a reforming *troika* made up of the Soviet Union, Poland and Hungary, and a triad of opposing states (East Germany, Czechoslovakia and Romania) which reject most of the new policies. Bulgaria, which claims to accept the need for reform in principle, is doing nothing about it in practice, and thus sits somewhere outside both groups. The range of variation within the bloc is expanding rapidly, with no leadership quite certain of where it is heading.

If they can, the reformers are hoping to control the changes they have set in motion, so as to avoid destabilizing their own positions, but even their caution cannot rule out the possibility that they are unleashing forces that will be difficult to control. Further movement towards economic and political change in Eastern Europe is unquestionably still tethered to the success or failure of the process of reform in the Soviet Union, and it is not yet clear whether Gorbachev will succeed in what he is attempting. While his goals for the Soviet Union are reasonably clear, he has not yet devoted a great deal of attention to Eastern Europe. One result has been the diversified and unsettled state of development in the region, with hopes, disappointments and fears chasing each other across the political spectrum.

The Lack of a Blueprint
Gorbachev's appeal remains quite strong in Eastern Europe, but some of his policies also led to serious disappointments in 1988. The allure of his reforms is evident on three levels: in international relations, within the socialist community in Eastern Europe, and in the domestic response to Gorbachev. At the international level, his continuing campaign of relaxation towards the West is clearly popular with East European publics. It is generally seen as a positive step, particularly after the fears raised by the Soviet campaign against the Western INF deployment in the early 1980s and the chill in relations that followed. Detente is perceived to be in the national interests of most of these

countries, because it both lessens the threat of conflict and offers a promise of economic benefit. Further relaxation of tensions and improvement in political relations is expected to lead to increased trade with the West and to greater access to Western capital, technology and know-how. Considering the desperate state of many Eastern-bloc economies, Western economic ties have never been more crucial.

The economic advantages of better East–West relations are augmented by the possible lessening of the defence burden on members of the Eastern bloc. Gorbachev's December announcement of unilateral withdrawals of some Soviet forces from Eastern Europe may not drastically reduce their support payments, but it is a beginning. More importantly, the Soviet reduction set the stage for reductions in military forces and budgets in 1989 by all the Warsaw Pact countries except Romania. Both developments stand in sharp contrast to earlier Soviet efforts to achieve increased defence spending in the Warsaw Pact, and further conventional cuts through negotiations hold the possibility of domestic savings.

Gorbachev also raised hopes in Eastern Europe in 1989 through his comments about relations between socialist states. Soviet statements and writings have increasingly stressed that no single model of socialism exists. Instead, repeated stress has been laid upon the need for each state to find its own path to socialism in light of its unique history and current situation. During his visit to Yugoslavia in March 1988 Gorbachev went even further, stressing the importance of each respecting the 'autonomy' of different socialist parties and governments, regardless of ideological differences. Though this was far from an unambiguous repudiation of the 'Brezhnev Doctrine', it did raise questions about Moscow's continued support for that doctrine. Taken together, these changes in the Soviet stand on uniformity within the bloc raise the possibility that something closer to equality could develop in relations between the USSR and Eastern Europe.

On the level of domestic response, Gorbachev's personal appeal in Eastern Europe is manifest. In 1988, as in 1987, opposition figures such as Lech Walesa cited Gorbachev and his policies as providing backing for the changes they were urging in Eastern Europe. (Indeed, in the Polish case, high-ranking figures in the Soviet Communist Party have made comments which suggest that independent trade unions in Poland might be acceptable to Moscow.)

However, there is also disappointment with Gorbachev's policies in Eastern Europe – particularly in Poland, after his trip there. Gorbachev's support for Jaruzelski caused discontent among the population, which does not see the General as a legitimate ruler. It is hardly surprising that Gorbachev should strongly support Jaruzelski in the light of Poland's importance to the Soviet Union, the good personal relationship between the two leaders and the especially difficult internal situation that Jaruzelski faces. It is equally unsurprising that the Polish population, which looks on Soviet reforms as validating the need for changes at home, should be disappointed that Gorbachev did not actively push for internal reforms in Poland. During his visit, Gorbachev also hedged when asked directly whether the Brezhnev Doctrine was still applicable, saying only that a response to this question was under consideration. His caution contrasted sharply with the forthright statements made during his earlier visit to Yugoslavia. But it is understandable; it reflects the USSR's interest in continued stability in Eastern Europe. Disintegration or revolution in the Eastern bloc would have obvious consequences for Gorbachev's own position if his policies should lead to such destabilization. Yet his willingness to support leaders who baulk at the sort of changes he promotes cannot have helped his popularity in the Eastern bloc, since it implies that the desired changes will not be forthcoming at his behest very soon. And, as in the Soviet Union, domestic support will be necessary if and when reforms do begin.

To compound this popular disappointment, developments in the USSR have enhanced elite fears in various East European countries that Gorbachev's position as Soviet leader is not yet secure, and that he might even be removed in the near future. This doubt has two consequences. It makes East European leaders interested in serious efforts to reform their own systems more cautious. If Gorbachev is removed, his successor could well be more conservative, and reformists must worry that they could go too far too fast, and so find themselves out of line with new, post-Gorbachev policies. Then, the perceived tenuousness of Gorbachev's position tends to encourage those who do not favour the reforms he advocates. With this perception paramount, they feel they can afford to sit things out on the fence, however uncomfortable this may be. Both responses slow any reform measures that are attempted in Eastern Europe.

Gorbachev's reforms have also created a substantial anti-reform element in some East European countries, most clearly in East Germany and Czechoslovakia. Concern about the changes in the Soviet Union has existed since the new policies began, but more cohesive opposition has appeared only recently. The anti-reformists are worried by Gorbachev's policies, both their substance and their speed, and also by the more recent steps towards reform that have been taken in some countries, such as Hungary. Doubts about the implementation of new reforms touch on very sensitive issues for the socialist community: whether the changes are moves towards less socialism; and the concern of individuals about their continued grip on leadership if the changes continue. Two aspects of the reform process – the questioning of the past that has arisen in the Soviet Union and *glasnost* itself, with the demand it creates for openness and publicity – appear to be causes of major concern. These two concerns intertwine, since, if history is to be re-examined, both the legitimacy of the present leadership in many of these countries and the right of the Communist Party to rule could come into question. East Gemany has serious concerns about both. The Communist Party still worries about its ability to maintain any sense of authority or legitimacy if real choices were available to the population, since the example of a democratic alternative exists next door in West Germany. East Germany has therefore been unwilling to implement any meaningful version of internal *glasnost*. In November East Germany banned an issue of the Soviet journal *Sputnik* because of an article containing 'distorted' views of the historical role of the German Communist Party – something which is unacceptable to the current leadership. And the regime has refused to allow a number of recent Soviet films to be shown in cinemas. (Ironically, its population continues to be the best informed in the bloc, due to its access to West German television).

For Czechoslovakia, *glasnost* and historical questions converge on 1968 and the leadership's sense that it is tainted in the eyes of the population by its involvement in the dismantling of the Prague Spring. Indeed, until the most recent changes in November, many of the Party leaders had been those who were put into power after the Soviet-led invasion. In addition, a real alternative to the current leadership exists, for (however unlikely his reinstatement might be) Dubcek is still alive. This concern about the past and current regime legitimacy exists also in Hungary and Poland, since both Jaruzelski's and Kadar's governments were associated with the repression of popular movements. However, in neither country has this fear led to the opposition to reform seen in East Germany and Czechoslovakia, perhaps because Poland's and Hungary's internal problems are far greater than those of the other two countries. Poland's net external debt was $US 39 bn at the end of 1988 (up from $36 bn at end of 1987), its rate of inflation was 70% and, while the IMF was demanding wage reductions averaging 10%, the government's typical concession to striking workers was wage increases of 60%. Hungary's debt at the end of 1988 was $US 16.6 bn, its rate of inflation was 17%, real wages dropped 8.5% during the year, and outside economists now believe that as many as 2 million (20% of the population) are living below the poverty line.

Political Developments
The most significant political development during 1988 was the reappearance of pluralism as a serious issue in these two countries. While both are struggling with the implications, there are important differences between them. In Hungary, the government raised the issue before a viable nationwide opposition had emerged; in Poland the opposition had existed for many years and has now forced the government to recognize it as a legitimate player on the political stage.

In January 1989 the Hungarian Parliament became the first in the Warsaw Pact to legalize the basis for a multi-party system. Development of a new system and the formation of opposition parties are still in the early stages, and members of the current leadership have expressed very different views on whether moving to a multi-party sys-

91

tem is either possible or desirable. Prime Minister Karoly Grosz himself has pointed out that allowing other parties the right to form implies that at some time in the future the sole right of the Hungarian Socialist Workers' Party (HSWP) to rule could be brought into question, and this is still an unacceptable idea. Gorbachev characterized such a system as 'rubbish' when asked for his reaction to the possibility of the USSR following Hungary, yet he has endorsed the Hungarian moves. The Hungarian government has tried to skirt the danger by advocating the legalization of earlier parties (such as the old Peasant's Party or Populist Party), which may have difficulty establishing their legitimacy as truly independent. But it may not have the chance to choose its own alternatives. A new social democratic party, claiming historical ties with the one that existed in Hungary before 1948, was formed in January 1989. Such a party could be particularly threatening to the HSWP, since it, too, could claim to represent the interests of the workers.

Two other developments in Hungary strike at very sensitive nerves within the socialist community. In apparently stormy meetings in February 1989, the Central Committee came up with a mixed reappraisal of the 1956 revolution, acknowledging for the first time that it had been, at least initially, a popular revolution. The government also drafted a new constitution which omitted any references to the 'leading role' of the Communist Party in governing. These moves raise questions about the very definition of socialism and the HSWP's right to rule. Yet, surprisingly, Moscow approved Hungary's independent course shortly after these steps were taken.

The spectacular re-emergence of Solidarity in Poland has led to the second example of a recognition of pluralism by an East European government. Solidarity, and its leader, gained strength again in the wake of the renewed round of strikes in May and August. With the enormous economic problems facing the country and hints that the Soviet government might be willing to countenance some legal status for Solidarity, the Polish government could no longer stall on this issue. In January 1989 it announced that it was willing to legalize Solidarity as a trade union, and began 'round-table' negotiations with Solidarity's leaders to work out details for its legalization and the new power-sharing arrangements that this would entail. The negotiations have proved both acrimonious and momentous. In early March 1989 the Party announced that the two sides had agreed on three major changes in the Parliamentary structure: the formation of a new upper chamber, whose members would be chosen in free elections; the creation of a six-year presidency, over which the Party will have control (at least initially); and an agreement on the division of power within the existing *Sejm*, with 65% of the seats reserved for the Communist Party and the remaining 35% open to the opposition. The implication of this series of moves is that Poland will, for all practical purposes, have a politically recognized opposition during 1989, though Solidarity's status as a political 'party' has not been clarified. (Poland's multi-party system may thus become active before Hungary's does.) The agreement between the government and Solidarity appears to be based, at least partly, on the assumption that the political reforms will be accompanied by significant Western assistance in the area of credits. It remains to be seen whether this assumption may not lead to misunderstanding between Poland and the West.

In another significant development, the first signs of the beginnings of a generational change in leadership are at last beginning to appear in Eastern Europe. This process began late in 1987, with the replacement of Husak in Czechoslovakia, followed in 1988 by the replacement of Kadar in Hungary. The actions of the new Hungarian leader, Karoly Grosz, have shown that some of the new generation may be willing to act decisively to deal with the problems faced by the Eastern bloc. His shake-up of the Politburo led to a continuing series of surprises in terms of the broad range of issues the Hungarian leadership is now willing to consider. Hungary is currently in the forefront of economic reform and privatization, and is far ahead of Gorbachev in legalizing a multi-party system before its next elections.

Yet the accession to power of younger men has been no guarantee that a change in attitude will follow. Indeed, the appointment of Milos Jakes to replace Gustav Husak in Czechoslovakia appears to be almost a stalling manoeuvre, rather than a change in view. Though younger than his predecessor, Jakes is still one of those who came into the leadership after the Soviet invasion in 1968 and is known to be a firm opponent of reform. He solidified this reputation in November 1988 by presiding over the removal of Lubomir Strougal, one of the few Czech Politburo members with some claim to support at least a modified reform effort.

There were no major leadership changes in the other countries of the region (beyond some cosmetic changes in Bulgaria). This again underscores one of the problems with implementing in Eastern Europe reforms like those in the Soviet Union. To emphasize the need for serious change, Gorbachev laid the blame for the disastrous state of affairs that he inherited on the previous Soviet leadership – but the leaders of the East European countries (apart from those of Poland and now Hungary) were in place throughout much of Brezhnev's reign. For such leaders to condemn the past is therefore to condemn themselves. The reappraisal of the 1956 revolution that has been allowed in Hungary only after the change in leadership, and only after bitter debate, underscores the sensitivity of this point.

A fascinating incident that throws light on questions of leadership change and reform apparently occurred in Romania in early 1989. In January 1989 six prominent members of the Communist Party reportedly sent a letter to President Ceausescu, strongly criticizing his repression of the Romanian people and his distortion of socialism. The group's ability to influence Ceausescu's policies is not large, and Ceausescu retaliated. The son of one of the signatories was arrested in mid-March and accused of spying for a 'foreign power' for the last fifteen years, and steps against the others may follow. Yet, the existence of opposition to Ceaucescu within the Communist Party may provide Gorbachev with a means of pressing the Romanian leader to relax his intransigent stand in both foreign and domestic policy.

The changed atmosphere created by Gorbachev's 'new thinking' has also led to an expansion of efforts to develop contacts with the West. Several countries in Eastern Europe have expressed increased interest in ties across the East–West frontier. The East German Party continued its contacts with the Social Democratic Party in West Germany, holding a second conference on nuclear-free zones in Central Europe in June. And all six Balkan states attended a conference held in Yugoslavia in February (the first time that Albania had agreed to participate in such a meeting). The goals of the meeting were strictly limited – in the event, it concentrated on economic co-operation – yet the countries involved were able to avoid the kind of acrimonious disputes over borders and minorities that had kept such a group from convening earlier. Indeed, one of the meeting's successes was to discuss even limited issues, for this makes further such meetings possible. Hungary has worked out a special trade agreement with the EC, and Poland is trying to do the same. While there is no obvious common thread among these moves, they do reflect the greater latitude available to East Europeans, since Gorbachev began reshaping the USSR, to find solutions to the problems they face.

Just as the East European states are now freer to express themselves with regard to West Europe, they can now openly express their antagonism to each other. This has clearly been seen in the incidents of open conflict between them in 1988. Most notable was the tension that developed between Hungary and Romania over the latter's treatment of its Hungarian minority. A stream of ethnic Hungarian refugees from Romania began to appear in Hungary early in the year, and matters came to a head when Romania announced a plan to raze up to half its rural villages and resettle the inhabitants in large agro-industrial complexes, allegedly in order to streamline the country's agriculture. Hungary protested, arguing that this move was intended to destroy the ethnic identity of Romania's Hungarian population. That conflict should exist between these two countries is hardly remarkable, considering their historical antagonisms. But such an open argument between two fraternal socialist allies in Europe is quite new.

Throughout Eastern Europe other conflicts have arisen recently over issues such as cross-border trade. But the more fundamental differences are over the nature of the political reforms being implemented or discussed. These differences have increased tension within the region – a tension which will be hard to overcome, given the evolution of pro- and anti-reform countries. The reform and anti-reform camps in Eastern Europe are now openly criticizing the actions of other governments within the alliance, playing out a debate which mirrors the internal arguments within the Soviet Union. This does not bode well for future calm in a region where potential conflicts exist between almost all states.

Yugoslavia In Extremis

The disintegration of governmental control in Yugoslavia in 1988 presents a grim warning to the rest of Eastern Europe and the Soviet Union of the worst-case dangers that some of these countries could face. The unique governmental organization inherited from Tito unquestionably made it more difficult for Yugoslavia to cope with its economic problems, but the rising inflation and massive foreign debt that underlie them are endemic to other socialist states as well. The nationalist tension that has arisen in their wake must give Gorbachev nightmares as an example of how much worse the present ethnic unrest in the Soviet Union could become.

The economic situation in Yugoslavia, already parlous at the end of the 1970s, was desperate by the beginning of 1988. The government had ignored the problems resulting from the oil shocks of the 1970s and its growing foreign debt, and continued essentially unregulated and massive borrowing from the West in the early 1980s to offset its own low level of production. By 1988 this debt had reached $US 20 bn and seemed likely to spiral even further out of control. Unemployment rose to 15%, while the inflation rate zoomed up above 150%. The government finally had to face the unpalatable facts, and in April 1988 it announced drastic austerity measures to comply with IMF requirements for receiving emergency loans. It also pledged to reduce the inflation rate to 90–95% by the end of the year.

This announcement was greeted by two forms of protest, which have continued ever since. Government efforts to alleviate the economic crisis stimulated strikes over wages and food shortages, and these quickly grew to levels which, though tiny by Western standards, had never been seen in Yugoslavia during its entire post-war history; demonstrations in Belgrade in June involved around 5,000 workers. The concern aroused by the scale of these wage protests stands in ironic contrast to the 500,000-strong demonstrations over nationalist issues which were to appear within the year.

The first round of ethnic tension in 1988 arose in Slovenia, which, as the richest and most liberal of Yugoslavia's component republics, felt hardest hit by the government's proposed austerity measures. The Slovenian leadership, under Milan Kucan, protested by calling for a vote of no-confidence in the central government, and this led to a deferral of the austerity measures while Prime Minister Branko Mikulic reshuffled his cabinet in early May. During this period both the central leadership and other republic leaders heavily criticized the Slovenian leadership for the greater liberalization of the press and toleration of political opposition allowed in Slovenia. Kucan's conflict with the central authorities was exacerbated by rumours that the army had planned a coup against the Slovenian government, and the subsequent arrest of

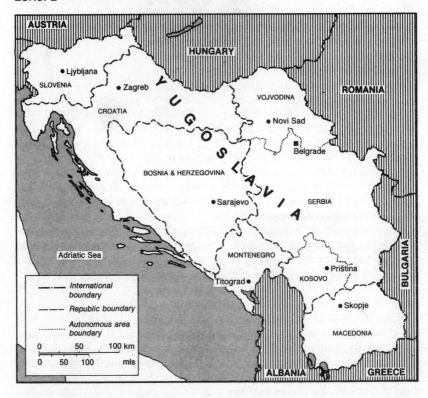

the journalists who reported this story generated more protests from the Slovenian population.

By mid-July the display of Slovenian nationalism was completely overshadowed by the emergence of Serbia's efforts to expand its control over the country. Serbians are the largest ethnic group in the country, making up almost half its population. Led by the charismatic rabble-rouser Slobodan Milosevic, the Serbian leadership has resurrected the issue of its right to govern Kosovo and Vojvodina, two regions which were historically part of Serbia. Control of them was removed from Serbia under the constitution Tito created in 1974, which was intended to grant greater power to the republics (and to these two new 'Autonomous Provinces'), so as to reduce the risk of Serbian domination of the country. Though the Serbian movement began as a protest against the ethnic Albanian majority's alleged mistreatment of the Serbian minority in Kosovo, this appeared to be an attempt by Milosevic to swing the power balance in Yugoslavia in Serbia's favour, since Serbian predominance over these two areas would upset the equilibrium that Tito had created in the republic.

The combination of this rapid explosion of Serbian nationalism and Milosevic's criticism of the government's economic policies led not only to a second reshuffling of Mikulic's cabinet in July but also to a third wave of ethnic protest, with Albanian nationalism reacting to Serbia's moves. Serbian rallies were attracting crowds of over 100,000 by the end of September, and the surge of opposing ethnic Albanian protests led to fears of an impending civil war. Though the government managed to regain at least the appearance of central control in the autumn, by calling up army reservists and uniting the other republics in criticism of Milosevic's inflammatory nationalism, the success of these measures was short-lived. Mikulic caved in to Serbian pressure in November and fired the ethnic Albanian leaders of the Kosovo government. This pressure – coupled with fresh strikes, continued inflation of 250%, opposition from the republics to the new economic reforms, and a refusal of the Parliament to approve his budget – led Mikulic and his entire cabinet to resign on 30 December 1988.

The simmering Albanian resentment at Serbian nationalism, intensified by government's concessions, exploded in an outbreak of miners' strikes in February 1989 protesting the dismissal of Kosovo's leadership. The central government managed to negotiate an end to the general strike which developed, but the Serbian backlash over its agreement to remove three of Kosovo's leaders who were perceived to favour Serbian interests was so fierce that the government again retreated, renouncing this deal almost immediately. A new crackdown in Kosovo resulted, with the imposition of a curfew and the detention of twenty Albanian leaders. Two ethnic Albanians were killed by Serbian nationalists as well, in the first bloodshed during the protests.

The central government's latest capitulation aroused vociferous protests in the other Yugoslav republics. Both Slovenia and Croatia condemned it; the emergence of the dangerous Serbian leader Milosevic and greater Serbian power over the central government clearly makes the leadership of the other Yugoslav states nervous. One Bosnian official noted that 'Mr Milosevic is the first Communist leader since Stalin to resort to arrests as a means of solving disputes with his political opponents'. Milosevic has ridden the wave of nationalism to a position of immense power, creating his own personality cult, but in the process he has unveiled the dangers inherent in rampant nationalism throughout much of Eastern Europe.

Adding to these ethnic problems, new developments from both the Left and the Right threatened the central government in early 1989. Slovenia's progression towards a more democratic system continued with the formation of three independent opposition parties, while the Yugoslav Army made clear its willingness to use force to support the existing constitution in the face of continued ethnic tension and to keep the country from splitting apart. Meanwhile, Yugoslavia's economic condition has only worsened; inflation is now closer to 300%, the foreign debt remains at $US 20 bn, and the new central government seems paralysed and unable to respond to the immense internal problems which it must resolve.

The new prime minister, Ante Markovic, appointed in mid-January 1989, may offer some hope to the country, since he is considered a fairly liberal reformer. He has stressed the importance of giving economic concerns priority over nationalist tensions, and has pledged to move towards a much freer market as the only solution to the country's economic dilemma. Whether this can be done, or will prove a sufficient response, remains to be seen. The country's ethnic problems are not likely to be so easily set aside (in late March 1989 more riots in Kosovo resulted in more deaths), and the government's ability to resolve without further bloodshed the bitter conflicts that have resurfaced between its republics seems seriously in doubt. The army's clear opposition to the disintegration of the state as a unit may keep the country together for a while, but, if it is forced to take control, Yugoslav unity will have been achieved at a high price indeed.

NORTHERN IRELAND: TROUBLED STILL

History is often said to be a curse for the Irish, a people who seem unable to forget the past but are perfectly ready to repeat it anyway. The failure of Tudor monarchs to consolidate Ireland into their realm bequeathed to it a near-permanent state of uncertainty down to our own time. Over the years it has experienced periods of being disenfranchised, but not silenced; oppressed, but not enslaved; persecuted in religion, but not recusant; impoverished, but not degraded; conciliated from time to time, but ever unforgiving. For twenty years past, the United Kingdom has once again been required to commit units of its army on active service to keep the peace across the Irish Sea, this time in the province of Northern Ireland. Casualties continue to mount – not merely policemen, soldiers and terrorists of both Republican and so-called 'loyalist' persuasions, but bystanders: men, women and children caught in the crossfire.

In the opening months of 1989 evidence was available that another campaign of violence by the Irish Republican Army (IRA) was in preparation. Between December 1988 and the following March, caches of some 385 pounds of Semtex high explosive, manufactured in Czechoslovakia and presumably supplied via Libya, fell into the hands of British authorities, together with what appeared to be a target list of prominent individuals in the UK. Intensive police searches were under way for two covert IRA teams who, it was believed, were planning a large-scale bombing campaign in mainland Britain. With a fine sense of irony, the IRA in Ulster pursued its campaign, nominally aimed at the unification of Ireland, via renewed attempts to cut the principal rail link between the North and the South. Its murder of three civilian bystanders in Coagh, none with any connection with the security forces, was, it was claimed, yet another 'mistake', inconsistent with announced

IRA policy of not striking civilian targets. Far from being reassuring, such admission of error only reawakened fears that IRA's leadership was no longer fully in control of its operational cadres. In a country with a taste for ritually commemorating events of as long ago as the Battle of the Boyne in 1690, there was general expectation that the IRA was preparing a major campaign of violence for the summer of 1989 to mark the twentieth anniversary of the deployment of British troops to the province.

The Seeds of the Uprising
Although the historical roots of the problem of Ireland are to be found in the distant past, the conditions for the present disturbances were a result of the 1921 peace treaty between London and the self-styled 'Provisional Government of Ireland', which ended the first successful urban guerrilla war of the twentieth century. The Tudor monarchy and its successors had won all the battles; the indigenous Irish had finally won the war. Or, in the view of many Republican veterans, half-won. For the treaty established dominion status for a partitioned Ireland with separate 'home rule' parliaments, the Dail in Dublin and Stormont in Belfast, and required an oath of allegiance by all elected officials to the crown. The British government might have been ready to bargain away the North, but this possibility was foreclosed by the bitter refusal of its Protestant population to be cut adrift from the United Kingdom to become a submerged minority in a country whose religion it detested, whose culture it did not share, and whose Republican traditions it expressly repudiated.

With partition as its reward, the Irish Republican Army, which had borne the brunt of the struggle for independence, felt betrayed and fought on to reject the treaty. In the harsh civil war which followed, the new government in Dublin asserted itself as the source of order and hounded the IRA practically out of existence. The population of the South had had enough of violence, and would give no political support to those for whom violence was an essential ingredient of policy. The Dail elections of July 1922 returned only 26 anti-treaty Republicans out of 128 seats; the Public Safety Act of 1931 made the IRA illegal, and the 1939 Offences Against the State Act introduced internment, which the Dublin government used to imprison 400 Republican activists during World War II to prevent their connivance with Nazi Germany. *Fianna Fail* (Warriors of Destiny), became the repository of Republican traditions, and *Sinn Fein* (Ourselves Alone – the IRA's political front) saw its vote in the South sink from a token 5% in 1957 to a humiliating 3% in 1961. In the North, an effective police force, entirely controlled by the Protestant majority (about 62%, against 34% Catholic), successfully reduced such IRA presence as there was to little more than a furtive social association.

This is not to say, of course, that the IRA abandoned violence after its defeat in the civil war. In 1939, for example, some 127 bombs were set off in England, including one in Coventry which killed five civilians. The early 1950s saw a number of IRA raids or ambushes against military targets to acquire weapons. Starting in 1956, a 'border campaign' of military sorties from the Republic (so called since 1937, when it had quietly shed dominion status without a shot being fired) into the North involved some 500 incidents which left 6 members of the Royal Ulster Constabulary (RUC) and 8 IRA members dead before it was abandoned in 1962. Tragic or dramatic as they were, however, these episodes represented little more than gestures, with little real political significance.

Such abortive violence accomplished little, except to add another unhappy irony to a history already well supplied with paradox. It served to confirm Ulster Unionists in their siege mentality and stoke their fears of a threat to the existence of their state. Yet the failure of the border campaign to stir Catholics in the North (or even generate much political excitement in the South) had the effect of undermining the IRA's commitment to physical force, one of its most sacred principles. Under Cathal Goulding and the Marxist Roy Johnston, the IRA leadership in Dublin began to talk of a political – that is, socialist – solution to the perennial 'Irish problem', appealing across sectarian lines to build a working-class movement in which the unity of Ireland would be identified more with proletarian liberation than with the satisfaction of nationalist honour. At this point, in the words of one observer, the IRA at the top 'was thinking and behaving like a small, conventional left-wing political party' – so much so that the more old fashioned IRA cadres, like the radical Sean MacStiofain (the English-born John Stephenson), were uncomfortable with the movement's politicization and distressed by its flirtation with non-Irish, anti-Catholic elements such as Marxists and Communists.

As the 1960s opened it appeared that most of the Irish, Northern and Southern, had learned to accept the *status quo* inherited from the treaty of 1921, even if many of them did not much like it. As events were to prove, however, dangerous elements remained in this seemingly stable state of affairs. A younger generation, both in the Republic and in Ulster, were learning about the past as if it were literature, rather than history, and coming to think of politics as an exercise in vindicating old claims, rather than a means to compose differences. Moreover, a lively memory for grievances was not a Republican and Catholic monopoly: Ulster Protestants could recall how close they had come to a fate worse than devolution. If continuing acts of Republican violence do not in hindsight seem to have been a realistic threat, they were certainly enough to constitute a persisting menace. The explosive mixture in Northern Ireland, predating gelignite and Semtex, was a deep-seated sectarian disorder: triumphalism wedded to fear on the Protestant side; among the Catholics, impotence paired with deep resentment at finding themselves second-class citizens in what they saw as their own country.

Although the Protestants of Ulster regard themselves as a different people from the indigenous Catholics, they do not think of themselves as any less Irish, and can look back on a history of settlement in Northern Ireland at least as long as that of white Europeans in North America. For the most part, however, they are descendants of English and Scottish settlers who, like their counterparts in North America, came to occupy other peoples' lands in a foreign country on the authority of the English crown. Unlike the English landowners of the south, the Ulster settlers were Protestant Dissenters, rather than Anglo-Catholic, in religion, and middle-class and enterprising, rather than aristocratic, in class. They regarded themselves more as an embattled brotherhood than a charmed ascendancy, and flourished as the latter faded away. In contrast to the largely agricultural South, moreover, Ulster became an urban industrial centre with major shipbuilding interests. Even now, with the highest unemployment rate in the UK, its general level of prosperity is above that of the Republic. The Ulster Protestant identification with the UK has never weakened down the centuries: it was forged, perhaps, with the Battle of the Boyne and the relief of Londonderry by William of Orange, but it has been renewed in the twentieth century, with the casualties of the Somme and of major bombing during World War II – in one night alone, Belfast lost more than 1,000 civilians.

Because of their electoral majority in Northern Ireland, Protestants have always commanded, even monopolized, political power there; and, because of the history of sectarian rivalry, they used such political power to secure their own advantage. The mentality of clannishness is not unique to Ireland, South or North, and 'taking care of one's own' is a lively political principle in most societies, particularly those with deep ethnic or religious divisions. At one time such political tribalism may have represented a rough but acceptable method of political compromise. But with the growth of the welfare state, better organization of public services and the advent of a new and better educated generation, the partisan use of political power came to be seen as incompatible with the requirements of a modern democracy. In this, of course, Northern Ireland was only one more example of a ground swell of popular demand for change in the old order that characterized the 1960s generally, the impact of which was felt across the world from Berkeley, via Paris, to Prague. Catholics experienced discrimination at many levels, from access to university education and selection for official posts, through the allocation of housing, down to the most petty concerns of everyday life. Gerrymandering diluted their minority even further. Worst of all, they came to regard the Royal Ulster Constabulary, which had only a 10% Catholic membership, and the Special Constabulary (particularly the armed 'B Specials', with no Catholic membership) as hostile and sectarian forces.

The Return to Violence
The Northern Ireland Civil Rights Association (NICRA) grew out of discussions within the Wolfe Tone Societies, a republican group whose

Dublin branch was dominated by the IRA leadership. During the disturbances of the 1960s, and even today, many Ulster Unionist politicians maintain that the civil-rights movement was a front of the IRA, or, at the least, was 'infiltrated' by it. (In this respect, they resemble President Johnson, who could not be convinced that foreign manipulation was not at least partly responsible for the anti-Vietnam war movement in the United States. Such invocation of the power of 'subversion' was a common response in the 1960s to the otherwise inexplicable phenomena of student riots and urban disorders.) The fact, in this case, seems to be that the IRA leadership welcomed the civil-rights movement but certainly did not control it; while four members of the original NICRA steering committee were Republicans, ten were not, and civil-rights leaders, particularly in the North, often took pains to avoid giving the authorities a pretext for claiming that the campaign for civil rights masked a threat to the state.

As might have been expected, however, the campaign of marches and demonstrations that began in 1968 on behalf of civil rights in the North set off a train of events which soon degenerated into a species of urban civil war: hatred and mistrust between the two communities reinforced each other and fed a continuing spiral of violence. Provocation by demonstrators led to over-reaction by the police. Civil Rights Associations mushroomed, crowds increased and became more unruly, Protestant attitudes hardened, and public order deteriorated. Three days of rioting in Londonderry, starting on 12 August 1969, were matched by five days of riots in Belfast; together they proved a turning point. The police feared an IRA-inspired insurrection, the Catholics a Protestant pogrom, and incidents of mayhem, arson and police use and misuse of force provided grist enough for both mills of misinterpretation. Whatever remaining confidence Catholics had in the RUC was lost. The IRA, whose members had in the beginning acted as stewards to control civil-rights demonstrations, gradually took on what it regarded as its traditional role of protector of the Catholic community. The escalation of hostilities revitalized the IRA and was midwife to the birth of the breakaway Provisional IRA (PIRA) under Sean MacStiofain. Discarding the political interests of the 'Officials' (the IRA proper) under Goulding, the PIRA harked back to an earlier tradition of direct armed violence, romantic nationalism and a self-appointed role as the shock troops of Irish nationalism.

At the same time that extremism was growing in the Catholic community, Unionist opinion also was moving away from the centre. The Stormont government of Terence O'Neill, which had attempted to defuse resentment by offering reform, found itself unable to head off Catholic resentment, but unable, either, to suppress it. Its reformist gestures were too little and too late to appease Catholics, yet too much of a capitulation in the eyes of some Unionists, many of whom eventually gravitated to the more uncompromising brand of Unionism offered by the Rev. Ian Paisley and James Craig.

Violence in Northern Ireland

	1969–73	1974–78	1979–83	1984–88
Incidents:				
Shootings	17,615[1]	8,773	3,483	1,637[2]
Explosions	3,543	2,671	1,585	749[2]
Casualties:				
Deaths: Total	929	953	463	365
Civilians	509	672	228	152
Terrorists	133	74	31	39
Army/RUC	287	207	204	108[2]
Injured: Total	11,338	9,984	4,061	4,362[2]
Civilian	7,708[1]	7,461	2,573	2,534[2]
Army/RUC	3,630	2,523	1,488	1,828[2]
Security:				
Bombs neutralized	1,523[1]	1,437	607	352[2]
Houses searched	128,435[3]	173,131	13,752[4]	3,367[5]

[1] No data available for 1969 [3] No data available for 1969–70 [5] No data available for 1987–88
[2] No data available for 1988 [4] No data available for 1979

The continued descent into chaos inevitably sucked in the British Army, and the small peace-time garrison in the Province was progressively reinforced. Once welcomed by Catholics in Londonderry (much to the disgust of IRA activists) as protectors against Protestant mobs, the Army increasingly assumed police functions, such as house-to-house searches, which brought it into confrontation with the Catholic population. The latter came to see the army as an alien force and its operations as harassment. (At one point, the IRA was chagrined to find that most of its imprisoned members had joined up, not out of nationalist or Republican zeal, but to 'strike back' at the police or the British army.) Bombings and shootings multiplied – both sectarian and aimed at the security forces. In 1971, as tension mounted, the Stormont government resorted to internment, which had worked so well in the Republic of Ireland. But it proved a debacle in the North and was abandoned in 1975; faulty RUC intelligence meant that harmless men were held, while dangerous ones escaped. That no Protestants were detained was presumably because they were not regarded as a threat to the state – an explanation hardly satisfactory to the Catholic population, which felt that a number of them were certainly a threat to life, not to say the peace. Protests inexorably culminated in a NICRA demonstration in Londonderry on 30 January 1972 – Bloody Sunday – when action by British troops resulted in thirteen deaths and accusations of indiscriminate use of firearms against unarmed civilians. Two months later Westminster prorogued the Stormont and imposed direct rule. A few months more and it was the IRA's turn: Bloody Friday, 21 July 1972, when 22 bombs detonated in central Belfast, killing nine.

By mid-1972 most of Londonderry had become a no-go area for the security forces (the so-called 'Free Derry', where the writ of neither

Stormont nor Westminster ran). This situation was only rectified by a massive, and largely bloodless, army operation – 'Operation Motorman' – in July and August. Changes in the law gave soldiers greater powers of arrest; the jury system was suspended and replaced by the verdicts of single judges (a 'Diplock Enquiry' recommendation), thereby reducing the impact of a deliberate terrorist policy of intimidating jurors as well as witnesses. While these measures opened Londonderry, violence did not end; it shifted its focus. In 1972 the Protestant Ulster Defence Association, and more shadowy murder gangs, emerged whose targets were Catholics. In that year there were 122 assassinations; 81 of Catholics. Random murder of Catholics by Protestant terror gangs was matched by similar random killings by the IRA: both sides considered the assassinations as reprisals.

The PIRA now shifted its campaign to Britain, partly to relieve pressure in Ulster and partly in the belief that only by attacking the mainland directly could it force the government to withdraw. The 'mainland campaign' went on for two years – targeting MPs, judges, military personalities, transport facilities, military barracks, London hotels and restaurants – but, despite the number of casualties, it was a failure. The terrorists then shifted to spectacular attacks in the hope of gaining publicity and weakening British resolve. This campaign started in July 1976 with the murder of the British Ambassador to Dublin, the Permanent Under-Secretary of State for Northern Ireland and their driver. Then Earl Mountbatten of Burma and members of his family were killed in August 1979, while on holiday in the Irish Republic. Since Lord Mountbatten had no connection with the Northern Ireland question, his death brought nothing but condemnation, quite overshadowing a major IRA success against the British Army the same day, when a Lieutenant Colonel and seventeen men were killed.

During these years terrorist prisoners probably made more impact on the public than the gunmen. In March 1976 a new prison at Long Kesh, later renamed The Maze, was opened; when previous privileges of civilian clothing and political status were simultaneously removed the prisoners refused to wear prison clothing and began a 'dirty protest', refusing to wash and smearing the cell walls with excrement. In 1980 this campaign was escalated through hunger strikes. Bobby Sands, the PIRA leader in The Maze, and nine other strikers died. The deaths brought no concessions, but they did restore the image of the IRA as 'freedom fighters' and moved *Sinn Fein* into the political arena (Sands had been elected as a *Sinn Fein* MP in the middle of the hunger strike).

Searching for a Political Solution
Having taken responsibility for the province into its own hands in 1972, Westminster tried to chart a political course that would lead first to pacification, and then to a long-term solution. Officials of the Northern Ireland Office may have wondered over the years if Edmund Spenser did not, after all, have the true measure of the Irish problem when,

almost five hundred years ago, he pessimistically speculated whether 'it is the fatal destiny of that land that no purposes, whatsoever are meant for her good, will prosper or take good effect'. Successive British governments have not sought to impose a solution that they might have – had a similar deterioration in public order taken place, for example, in Yorkshire – but have looked instead for some formula to enable those involved to work out their own destiny by compromise and agreement. Given the extremism on both sides, it is not surprising that this has so far yielded little – but 17 years is not a long time in Irish politics.

The first such initiative grew out of a Conference at Sunningdale in 1973, at which Dublin accepted that Ireland could not be unified without the consent of the population in the North, while London accepted that such unification should take place if the majority of the Northern population wanted it. Here, of course, was a formula totally unacceptable to hard-core Unionists on the one side and impatient IRA cadres on the other. An attempt was made to restore local government at Stormont with an executive based on the principles of 'power sharing' between Catholic and Protestant politicians, and an Assembly elected on the basis of proportional representation. Accepted by the SDLP (representing the moderate element of the Catholic community), the proposal split the Unionists. Those opposed to Sunningdale led a general strike, as a result of which a state of emergency was declared, the Assembly was prorogued, and Whitehall resumed the direct rule it had tried to give up. Similar attempts in 1975 and 1980 to coax the Unionist mainstream into co-operating with Catholic leaders to find a political *modus vivendi* came to nothing.

The Hillsborough Agreement, signed by premiers Thatcher and Fitzgerald in November 1985 represents the latest initiative in the search for the beginning of an end to this long and tragic story. It accepts that Dublin has a role to play in the security and political affairs of the North, and looks to greater co-operation from the Republic in British efforts to promote security. As might be expected, the Unionists sniff betrayal in any such discussions with Dublin, while the IRA, of course, read it as an attempt to improve security measures directed against it. It is too early to tell whether even the modest benefits expected from the agreement will be realized, much less whether it is likely to inspire that confidence and co-operation between the Republic and the UK that could serve as an example to the North.

How Might It End?
So far as security considerations are concerned, the problem of Northern Ireland must be put into a proper context. It is certainly true that a very small number of dedicated activists, even without much of a support network, can wreak occasional havoc in any major, advanced state. The October 1984 attempt to assassinate Mrs Thatcher and her cabinet in Brighton did not require major investment in funds or manpower, and, so long as AK-47s can be easily bought on the streets of

Los Angeles or Beirut, urban guerrillas will be able to equip themselves adequately, whether or not they have contacts with Gaddafi or other potential paymasters.

The security threat which the IRA presents to the UK, should not be exaggerated, however. The deployment of British forces in Northern Ireland has exerted only a slight claim on British military capability (peak strength was briefly about 30,000, for 'Operation Motorman' in 1972, but averaged only some 14–15,000 through the 1970s; there are perhaps 9,000 today, compared to a historic peace-time garrison strength of about 3,000), and costs are said to be about £150 m per year.

Meanwhile, the immediate parties to the conflict must begin to recognize that their dependence on force, and their inability to go beyond self-righteous propaganda, are leading them nowhere. The indifference of IRA operatives to casualties among innocent bystanders has earned them the title of terrorists, compromising them in the eyes of those whose support they must win. It is hard, also, to see what their long-term objectives may be for such hit and (more often) miss violence. Any belief that campaigns of this type will 'wear down' British resistance suggests a superficial, even ignorant, reading of Irish history. A movement pursuing mere tactics, rather than strategies, the IRA is already appearing to more and more of its erstwhile supporters as a political dead letter. The Unionist majority, on the other hand, must find some way to conciliate the sizeable Catholic minority and regain its confidence if it hopes ever to deprive the IRA of its vital acceptance in that community. The men of violence on the so-called 'loyalist' side have equally sickened all right-minded people – and alienated moderate opinion – with their mindless sectarian brutality and tit-for-tat murder campaigns. Both extremes therefore face dead ends in their pursuit of armed struggle. The IRA cannot now, or in the foreseeable future, expect to bring about change in Northern Ireland against the will of the majority; nor can that majority ever hope to return to peace and order by police power alone.

Exhaustion is not an attractive formula for resolving civil strife; yet it, too, has a role to play when only the passage of time can moderate the bitterness of age-old conflict. Notwithstanding its ancient lineage, the current problem of Northern Ireland is a domestic political issue, not a threat to the national security of the UK or the Republic of Ireland. As a consequence, the UK, like any legitimate state, must discharge its fundamental obligation to maintain order and protect the innocent in a manner consistent with established procedures of law. It has already made clear that it vests the ultimate national destiny of the province in the hands of its own people – which effectively renders it more a trustee than a sovereign of Northern Ireland. Beyond this, it can contribute little more to a British solution than to assist that other majority in Northern Ireland – of moderates on both sides of the sectarian divide – to assert itself against the warring factions of extremism.

East Asia

CHINA: TWO STEPS BACK, ONE FORWARD

For the decade since Mao Zedong's death, China's history has been characterized by bold domestic initiatives, coupled with a low diplomatic profile intended to maintain a balanced, stable environment in which China can hope to solve its internal problems. It was a formula which transformed the economy and China's place in the world. During 1988, however, economic success in turn created social and economic pressures at home which have required a deliberate slow-down in the economic drive. At the same time, changes in the Soviet Union's foreign policies as part of Gorbachev's 'new thinking' have thrust foreign policy to the forefront. The slow improvement in Sino-Soviet relations which had been gradually gathering force during the previous four or five years suddenly acquired a critical mass, resulting in China's decision to host a summit meeting in May 1989 between Gorbachev and Deng Xiaoping.

The meeting may be one of the last important acts of Deng's long political career. For much of 1988, while his chosen successors struggled with the problems of a run-away economy, he was very much in the background, surfacing only rarely to meet important visitors (like President Bush, on his first visit to China since his election) or to support with his still great authority difficult decisions being made by the new, younger leaders of the party. Deng, now 85 years old, has likened himself to 'the setting sun' – still around, perhaps, but no longer of great use. But none of the men whom he helped bring to the fore by forcing out a reluctant older generation during the 13th Party Congress in November 1987 have yet shown that they have, or can soon acquire, the power and influence that would allow them to replace him for the long term. As the continuing effort to reform Chinese life brings mounting social and economic problems in its wake, the question of whether a more stable leadership will emerge remains unanswered.

Achievements and Problems

A large part of the problem for China in 1988 was that its sustained, rapid growth had been achieved against a background of structural imperfections. The country's GNP grew by 11.2% between 1987 and 1988, and its national income was up 11.4%. With the exception of grain, agricultural production was up, with the total rural output value improving by 10% over 1987. Industrial output increased by 17.7% over 1987, and there were small increases in electrical generating capacity, oil production and coal mining.

China's leaders would have been delighted with this record of growth if it had not brought with it a widening gap between demand and supply, and consequent retail price inflation which has been estimated as high as 30% by Western economists, and which even the official figures put at 18.5% at the year's end. Perhaps more significant was the panic buying in major cities which blew up in August, when rumours swept the country that plans had been finalized to introduce price reforms in September. Like all Communist economies, China had controlled prices of consumer goods closely, but many of the prices were set as long as 25 years ago and are now totally out of synchronization with costs. In addition, the decentralization of economic powers and the introduction of some free markets have created a dual price structure, with inevitable opportunities for corruption. It had become all too easy to buy at the controlled state price for goods produced in the state system and to sell the same goods on the free market for vast profits. London's *Financial Times* reported the case of one factory which had stopped working entirely; it flourished simply by taking its allocation of state-priced steel and selling it on to the highest bidder.

The Politburo, which has been discussing the need for price reform for many years, had apparently decided to bring in a five-year plan for reform which would have allowed prices to rise by up to 90%, while wages would have correspondingly risen by 100%. It was the rumours during August that such a price reform was to be brought in on 1 September that emptied the store shelves. There were corresponding runs on the banks, as depositors, fearing that their money was fast losing its worth, scrambled to make purchases before it was too late.

Faced with a deteriorating situation, the leadership backed away from its plans. At its working summer holiday at Bedaihe (clearly this year more work than holiday) it decided to freeze the price reform for two years and to move back towards the more centralized control it had been dismantling for the preceding four years. Banks had been pumping money into the economy at a very rapid rate during the spring, because they had no way to control borrowing; now loans are to be frozen. New efforts to collect taxes have been centrally instituted, the ability of localities to set prices has been rescinded, and investment funds are to be cut by about 20%.

Without such measures the economy might well have spiralled out of control. Nonetheless, it is doubtful if, by themselves, the measures will be sufficient to create the conditions necessary for continued effective growth. They do nothing for the underlying structural problems which created the difficulties in the first place. Yet to bring about the necessary reforms means moving much further away from the dual-track command-economy and market system that now characterizes Chinese life. There is little sign that the leadership is united or determined enough to bring about this kind of necessary change.

Who is in Charge?
When Deng Xiaoping engineered the removal of the older, more conservative members of the Politburo and Central Committee at the 13th

Party Congress in November 1987, it was in with the expectation that a smooth succession to a new arrangement for running the country would be achieved. Zhao Ziyang, a man closely linked with the Dengist reforms, was made General Secretary of the Party, and two technicians – Li Peng and Yao Yilin – were put in charge of day-to-day operations of the economy as Premier and Vice-Premier. If these three, and the other three members of the Standing Committee of the Politburo, were not always in complete agreement over the speed and scope of the reforms, they were closer in spirit than the previous members of the ruling bodies. But the persistent, even growing, problems in the economy seem to have accentuated their differences. There were strong rumours during the summer that the discussions at Bedaihe were acrimonious, and since then there have been veiled references to the return of factional infighting.

It is in the nature of a hermetic society (and the Chinese leadership's decision-making is still very much a hidden process) that periods of policy reversal open the possibility for political power struggles. Where power to rule is highly dependent on the influence an individual ruler can exercise, as in China, it must be assumed that even a perception of loss of influence will affect a leader's position. Thus, even though there is little firm evidence that the men making the decisions differ over the necessity for a pause (or even a temporary reversal) in the movement for economic reform, there is a presumption that Party General Secretary Zhao Ziyang has suffered a loss of influence, if not yet any considerable loss of power.

Of the three top leaders, Zhao has been the most vocal on the need for price reform, on promoting rural industries, on extending the special economic zone enterprises. All these policies have been set aside, at least temporarily. When Zhao moved from head of the government to head of the Party in late 1987 it was thought that he was leaving his own power base for a post in which he would have to have time to build a new one. His misfortune is that, instead of his policies having continuing success, he has been forced by circumstances to admit that they need adjustment, and the adjustment seems closer to the views of Li Peng and Yao Yilin than to his own.

Yet it is difficult for these two to avoid being tarred by the same brush. It is true that they have generally been thought by Western observers to be less bullish about rapid reform of the economy than either Deng or Zhao. But there is little doubt that they did not agree with the more conservative older Politburo members whom they replaced, who had been totally out of step with the reforms. Li and Yao have been handling the day-to-day operations of the economy for the past year, and, while they are perhaps not guilty of the earlier excesses, it would be difficult for them to behave as though they were free of any blame for what has happened. In fact, in his speech to the National Peoples' Congress in March 1989 Li accepted part of the responsibility for the past problems and the present course, though at the same time subtly suggesting that his predecessor was more culpable.

Perhaps more significant than possible factional scrambling for advantage is the feeling that the leadership as a whole has lost its way. Rather than questioning the effectiveness of individuals to meet the challenge, radical reformists, like the physicist Fang Lizhi, are arguing that the fault lies with the Party itself and its refusal to allow arbitrary personal rule to be replaced by greater intellectual freedom, more democracy, written regulations and law. The present crisis hardly provides an atmosphere in which the leaders can be comfortable with such changes, but without them it is likely that the crisis will be difficult to overcome.

A Happier Foreign Outlook

If China was sailing in very rough water at home, its passage through foreign seas was remarkably smooth. Japan's Prime Minister visited Beijing during the year, apologized for yet another outspoken Ministerial remark about the Japanese role in the Sino-Japanese war of the 1930s, and offered a $US 6-bn package of soft loans to aid the development of China's coastal areas. India's Prime Minister Rajiv Gandhi visited as well, bearing assurances that his country wished to improve its relations with China. In January 1988 Cuban foreign minister Malmierca, the first holder of his office to visit China in 29 years, arrived in Beijing with the clear intention of improving Cuban relations with China as well. Trade with South Korea has boomed, and China brought it out into the open, noting that 'North Korea is certainly concerned . . . but expresses great understanding'. Trade between China and Taiwan, more indirect and still shrouded in ambiguity, exceeded $US 2 bn in 1988, and the partial removal of restrictions on travel brought over 300,000 Taiwanese to China for visits.

Central to all of these moves has been the remarkable improvement in Sino-Soviet relations. There has been a gradual improvement in trade between the two countries, and a slow improvement in political relations for many years. This has been accelerated, however, by Gorbachev's determined effort to woo East Asian countries through diplomacy and trade, rather than through the threat of military might. In September 1988, in a speech in Krasnoyarsk, Gorbachev reiterated the points made in his earlier 1986 speech in Vladivostok, promising that the USSR would work to reduce military activity in the area, help to resolve regional conflicts, improve multilateral co-operation and strive for better bilateral relations throughout the region.

It was clear in both speeches that Gorbachev had China in mind as the prime target of this new regional diplomacy. And in his speech to the UN he went further, promising the withdrawal of a large portion of the forces the USSR has long kept in Mongolia and outlining plans to reduce its troops on the border. This pledge went a long way to removing one of the 'three obstacles' that China has insisted have stood in the way of improvement in relations. A second obstacle fell when the USSR completed the withdrawal of its forces from Afghanistan and made it clear that they would not return, no matter what happened to the Communist government there. The third and toughest obstacle – Vietnam and its presence in Kampuchea – is more stubborn, but it became clear during 1988 that the USSR is now at the least advising Vietnam, and at the most putting considerable pressure on it, to withdraw its troops from Kampuchea. Moscow also agreed to discuss the issue with China and exhibited a willingness to make its own contribution to a solution to this knotty problem.

All this was enough to lead Deng to declare in October 1988 that the Soviet moves were sincere and had opened the way for further improvement. In December Qian Qichen was welcomed in Moscow – the first formal visit of a Chinese foreign minister since 1957 – and the talks he held with Soviet leaders were positive enough for China to agree to Gorbachev's long-expressed desire to visit Beijing. Soviet Foreign Minister Shevardnadze's return visit to Beijing at the beginning of February 1989 completed the preliminaries and firmed up a date (15–18 May 1989) for the summit meeting.

While in China, Shevardnadze reiterated Moscow's plans to cut the number of its troops along the Sino-Soviet border by 260,000 men and to remove three-quarters of the 50,000 troops now stationed in Mongolia. Eventually, he said, border troops would be held at the lowest level commensurate with minimal defence, thus assuring 'absolute trust' along the border, and working groups are to be established to reach an agreement in two years' time on the proper manning levels.

But the major new advance was with regard to Kampuchea. At the conclusion of the visit a nine-point communiqué on Kampuchea was issued which indicated agreement on a number of points: a control mechanism for supervising Vietnamese withdrawal; an end to military aid to both sides; the removal of foreign troops and bases; a role for the UN; free elections; and an international conference 'when conditions are ripe'. To be sure, a number of disagreements remained, with the precise shape of the government that will span the period between the Vietnamese withdrawal and subsequent elections prominent among them. Yet enough common ground had been found to raise hopes that the two powers will be able to influence their respective clients in Southeast Asia to achieve a settlement in the struggle for Kampuchea.

China has been eager to assure the West, and the United States in particular, that a *rapprochement* with the USSR does not mean a return to the form of alliance that existed in the early 1950s. As Beijing sees it, regularizing relations will merely maintain the balance between the great powers that has been at the centre of its foreign policy for the past eight years. Even if the relationship continues for many years to be more tentative than concrete, however, it will provide China with a flexibility and manoeuvrability in its relations with the other great power that it will greatly prize. President Bush has said that he sees no threat in the improvement of Sino-Soviet relations, but he was careful not to make too much of the slight that Chinese leaders dealt him during his visit to Beijing in February 1989, when they refused to allow the dissident Fang Lizhi to attend the banquet to which Bush had invited him. The United States has also muted its complaints about the Chinese repression of the Tibetan resistance, which flared and was put down with considerable force in March and July 1988, and which flared again – requiring an even stronger Chinese response, involving more troops, many Tibetan deaths and a news black-out – in March 1989.

While the Sino-Soviet reconciliation has global implications, its greatest initial impact is on relations in Asia. With the change in the Soviet approach, Vietnam finds itself without the almost automatic anti-Chinese reaction from the Soviet Union that it had relied upon to support its policies in the region. Hanoi is now not only beginning to withdraw from Kampuchea, and appears willing to negotiate some settlement to the long-running dispute, but, if it can no longer play China off against the USSR, can be expected to adjust its policies towards China and the US. With a change in Vietnamese policy, Thailand finds itself freer to move closer to China, and it has been improving its political, and even military, relationships with the Asian giant. Indonesia has at last agreed to open diplomatic relations with China. The Indian government, too, has recognized that a change in Sino-Soviet relations necessitates an adjustment to its antagonism towards China and the US. Even North Korea is reluctantly accepting that the change, which brings with it a new positive relationship between South Korea and China and the Soviet Union, will compel it to rethink its policies towards South Korea and China. In Asia, as in the rest of the world, Gorbachev's willingness to overturn previous Soviet policy has created an unaccustomed reappraisal of the stagnant pattern of links and affiliations that had dominated Asian international politics for many years. When the swirl of activity set in motion by the Soviet moves settles, a new set of relationships will have been established and a new balance achieved.

INDOCHINA – THE STALEMATE BROKEN

From shortly after the Vietnamese invasion of Kampuchea in late 1978 until the end of 1987 the military and diplomatic positions of those involved in the conflict seemed to be deadlocked. In 1988 things changed dramatically. In the preceding years, the Vietnamese-installed People's Republic of Kampuchea (PRK) regime had remained in power with the military support of a Vietnamese occupation force of some 140,000 troops and the assistance of Soviet finance and material aid. Military resistance to the Vietnamese occupation came mostly from the forces of the ousted *Khmer Rouge*, whose finance and supplies came principally from China, channelled through Thailand to its camps on the Thai-Kampuchean border. The notorious *Khmer Rouge* won widespread diplomatic support only after it agreed in 1982 to form the Coalition Government of Democratic Kampuchea (CGDK) with two non-Communist resistance factions, the Kampuchean People's National Liberation Front (KPNLF), led by Son Sann, and FUNCINPEC, led by Prince Sihanouk. None of the parties to the Kampuchean conflict, it appeared, could impose a decisive military solution, nor were they prepared to make the compromises necessary to achieve a political settlement.

Vietnam was subjected to an economic aid embargo by supporters of the CGDK, particularly the US, China and the countries of the Association of South East Asian Nations (ASEAN). The governments of a number of potential major trading partners also quietly discouraged companies based in their countries from trading with Vietnam, while the United States already had legislation explicitly barring such commerce. Hanoi thus came increasingly to rely on trade with the Soviet bloc and on Soviet economic assistance to prop up its catastrophic economy, a reliance that Moscow increasingly came to see as unduly onerous.

Since Gorbachev became Soviet leader, he has overseen a reformation in the USSR's Far East foreign policies sparked by intensified efforts to further improve Sino-Soviet relations. This has required Moscow to play a more active role in solving the Kampuchean conflict. In 1987 the Soviet Union signalled through diplomatic channels that it was encouraging Vietnam to pull out of Kampuchea, but it warned that results would take time. It could put pressure on Vietnam by cutting financial and military support for the Vietnamese occupation, or by broader sanctions curtailing Soviet economic assistance to Vietnam itself. But such action would put at risk Soviet-Vietnamese relations, which provide Moscow with both a strategic and a political presence in South-east Asia. The value of that presence can hardly have diminished since, under Gorbachev, Moscow has further emphasized the USSR's status as a Far Eastern power. Nevertheless, the Soviet Union has put pressure on Vietnam, though it has not appeared willing actually to force Vietnam into changing its Kampuchea policy. Only when it appeared that Hanoi, for its own reasons, was willing to begin considering a withdrawal from Kampuchea was Moscow willing to risk continued pressure for this result.

Vietnam's Indochina Policy
During the 1984–5 dry-season offensive, Vietnamese and PRK forces were able to destroy the CGDK camps on the Kampuchean side of the border with Thailand. This encouraged the resistance forces to become more mobile, which in turn forced Hanoi and Phnom Penh to spread their forces more thinly. The offensive thus seemed to be a qualified victory. Yet, in retrospect, it appears to have caused Hanoi to reassess the need for a continued Vietnamese military presence. In August 1985 it was announced that all Vietnamese troops would be withdrawn from

Kampuchea by 1990. At the time this was widely seen as a diplomatic ploy by Hanoi. But the announcement in 1987 that 20,000 troops were being withdrawn, and one in May 1988 that a further 50,000 troops together with the Vietnamese high command in Kampuchea were to be withdrawn by December, strongly suggested that Hanoi was in earnest. While it is impossible to verify Vietnam's mid-December claim that it had completed its 1988 withdrawal, it appears that Vietnamese troops in western Kampuchea have been thinned out. This has left the PRK's armed forces to bear far more of the fighting.

Following the withdrawal announcements both Phnom Penh and Hanoi expressed confidence in the growing strength of the PRK's armed forces and their ability to resist the *Khmer Rouge*, once Vietnamese troops leave. Without a political settlement, however, this may be a recipe for a civil war in which the *Khmer Rouge* enjoys control of large regions in western Kampuchea. In such a situation, Vietnam's national security would be unaffected, but Thailand's unstable border region would remain a problem for Bangkok.

The PRK's doubts about its armed forces' ability to withstand the *Khmer Rouge* is implicit in its calls to accelerate a build-up of the armed forces, so that they can fulfil their duties in 1990. It seems equally unlikely that Hanoi can be fully confident that the PRK armed forces are a match for the *Khmer Rouge*. The *Khmer Rouge* had been comparatively inactive on the battlefield for the two years before the start of the 1988 Vietnamese withdrawal and is thought to have been concentrating on political proselytization. Yet it was still receiving arms shipments and other supplies from China, which presumably it has stockpiled. This military inactivity may have encouraged Hanoi in its belief that the conflict had taken a decisive turn for the better back in 1985, but Vietnamese military intelligence is unlikely to be so naive as to entirely discount the threat of *Khmer Rouge* military power, even without continued Chinese supplies.

Changes in Vietnam's Foreign Policy
Besides Soviet pressure and Hanoi's own analysis of the military situation in Kampuchea, there may be a third, and ultimately more important, factor which now underpins the decision to withdraw Vietnamese troops. In 1988 Vietnam undertook a far-reaching reappraisal of its foreign and defence policies. In May its leadership reportedly decided to improve relations with its two principal adversaries, the United States and China.

The nascent change in attitude to the US was reinforced and encouraged by changes in Washington's policy towards Vietnam. In January it had begun to encourage private US humanitarian aid, and then, as the presidential elections loomed, efforts were made to accelerate the return of the bodies of US servicemen killed during the Second Indochina War. Perhaps most significant is that a growing number of US Congressmen support the normalization of relations with Vietnam.

Progress in improving relations has been slow, however, with signs of disagreement in Hanoi over its new policy.

Vietnam's decision to improve relations with Beijing was partly the result of concern over the constant high level of defence preparedness it has had to maintain because of poor relations with its much larger neighbour. The decision was also a response to the changing strategic landscape in Asia. Vietnam had always considered one of the major benefits of its relations with the USSR to be an implicit Soviet deterrence of Chinese use of military force against Vietnam. But the Soviet Union's efforts to improve its own relations with China were now undercutting that benefit, and indeed Moscow had been urging both Vietnam and China to improve their relationship. The non-committal Soviet response to Sino-Vietnamese clashes in the contested Spratly Islands in the South China Sea in March probably reinforced Hanoi's fear that, if the situation deteriorated further, it would be left to deal with China alone.

In September, the Vietnamese Politburo reportedly passed an as yet unpublicized resolution on 'post-Kampuchea' foreign policy that formalized a number of new policy directions, including attempts to improve relations with China and the United States. If reports of the meeting are correct, a decision has been taken to try to reduce Vietnam's reliance on the Soviet Union and alleviate its international isolation by revising its Indochina policy, improving relations with China, reducing defence expenditure, and broadening its commercial relations. Some indications of these policies already exist.

Hanoi is most probably motivated principally by its failure, despite the advent of a new reformist leadership in 1986, even to begin to extricate itself from economic stagnation. Indeed, the problems seem only to be getting worse, and the thrust of Hanoi's new foreign policy appears to be to try to end Vietnam's economic isolation from a number of potentially major trading partners and financial backers in an attempt to breath new life into the economy.

Obviously, withdrawing Vietnamese troops from Kampuchea will remove an immediate obstacle – indeed there are already signs in many of the countries imposing a ban on aid that government and public resolve has softened in the wake of the recent major troop reductions there. But, with the Kampuchean obstacle removed, other problems will appear. Western governments and international bodies are unlikely to be willing to offer assistance on the scale of that provided by the Soviet Union in recent years – estimated at over $US 1 bn a year. Nor, for that matter, does Moscow seem willing to sustain such levels of assistance any longer. What Hanoi may be seeking to do is diversify its sources of finance.

Similarly, Vietnam is aiming to diversify its economic relations by attracting more private foreign investment. At the start of 1988, it promulgated a new foreign investment code, considered by Western businessmen to be very liberal for a Communist country. However, the government admits that it has been slow to prepare detailed regulations, organize cadres to implement them and create relevant institutions. Furthermore, it acknowledges that the country's infrastructure is inadequate, and that it has been difficult to raise domestic capital for joint ventures. A Finnish company's reported withdrawal in October from negotiations on a joint venture to build a shipyard near Haiphong, citing 'Vietnam's chaotic economy and complicated investment regulations', is an ominous portent for the government's plans to boost Western investment. Vietnam may find the rewards of withdrawing from Kampuchea to be less than it hopes for.

Changes in Vietnam's Defence Strategy
Not only does Vietnam appear to be intent on withdrawing its troops from Kampuchea, Laotian leaders claim that in 1988 it also withdrew all its estimated 50,000 troops based in Laos. More important even than the troop withdrawals are reports that Vietnam has abandoned its 'special relationship' with Laos and Kampuchea, by which it defined the three Indochinese countries' strategic, political and economic relations: this would imply that Vietnam no longer sees its own security in terms of Indochina. The inference is born out by a Vietnamese report, in mid-December 1988, of the implementation of plans for strengthening the border in the Seventh Military Region, where the worst *Khmer Rouge* raids occured in the late 1970s. If Vietnam is now strengthening defences on its border with the PRK, this would suggest a defence strategy that renders the concept of a strategic relationship between the two countries obsolete.

The very concept of national defence as one of Vietnam's 'two strategic tasks' appears to have been downgraded. In November 1988 Senior Lt-Gen. Nguyen Quyet, a Central Committee Secretary, referred to the two strategic tasks and for the first time identified 'the economy and nation-building as the primary one'. This implied a cost-cutting reorganization of the armed forces. Secret talks with the USSR on military restructuring reportedly took place in March 1988, with Moscow urging that Vietnam's armed forces be streamlined, and Hanoi demanding Soviet help in providing them with more and better equipment in return.

The first indications that a big reduction in the size of Vietnam's armed forces was planned came in June. In September Vietnamese government and military sources were quoted as saying that the 1,250,000-strong armed forces would be cut by about 50%, in 1990. In November, Nguyen Quyet, while giving no figures, outlined 'a basic change of direction in strategy' for the army, involving 'a standing force which is numerically small but high in quality' with 'a very massive reserve force'. Many of the troops withdrawn from Kampuchea and Laos will apparently be demobilized as part of the cuts. There is evident opposition to the new defence policy in both the Communist Party and the army, not only because of the demotion of defence in national priorities, but also because of the social strains that demobilization on such a scale will cause in a country already suffering from high unemployment.

Talks on Kampuchea

Talks held in December 1987 between the PRK's premier, Hun Sen, and Prince Sihanouk were followed up in 1988 by further rounds in January, in November (with Son Sann in attendance) and, at working-group level, in December (with KPNLF and *Khmer Rouge* representatives also present). Despite initial optimism, however, the talks failed to make any significant progress.

In late July Indonesia managed to bring Vietnam to the negotiating table. Three days of talks – which became known as the JIM, the Jakarta Informal Meeting – were held at the Indonesian resort of Bogor, under a formula by which the Kampuchean parties to the conflict met first and were then joined by the ASEAN and Indochinese states. Assessments of the talks differed. Indonesia was keen to present them as a success, allowing the Indochinese states to claim that a breakthrough had been made in identifying for the first time a link between the withdrawal of Vietnamese troops from Kampuchea and the prevention of a return to power by the *Khmer Rouge.*

Timetable for a Vietnamese Withdrawal

Since 1985 Vietnam had been saying that it would withdraw its troops from Kampuchea 'by 1990'. In February 1988 it was even more precise: its troops would be out before the end of 1990. In July, General Secretary Linh announced that the troops would be withdrawn by the end of 1989 or early in 1990.

Linh made his statement in Moscow, apparently prompted by Soviet pressure. At the JIM talks, five days later, PRK premier Hun Sen reiterated Linh's statement but added a rider. He stipulated that 'in December 1989, or in the first quarter of 1990 at the latest, all remaining Vietnamese volunteer forces in Kampuchea will be withdrawn at the same time as an end to assistance and sanctuaries provided by foreign countries to the Pol Pot genocidal group and other opposing Kampuchean forces'. On the second day he developed this link into what proved to be the theme of the talks, the 'two key questions' of the withdrawal of troops and the 'elimination of the risk of the Pol Pot regime's return'. However it soon became clear that the 'breakthrough' acceptance of the link between the two issues by the JIM participants was little more than wishful thinking. No side had made significant concessions on the positions held at the start of the talks.

In fact, the apparently real prospect of a Vietnamese withdrawal by the end of 1990 had already raised international concern about a possible *Khmer Rouge* comeback. The linking of a late 1989 or early 1990 troop-withdrawal deadline with action to emasculate the *Khmer Rouge* did little, if anything, to change positions on that. It seems unlikely that Hanoi or Phnom Penh would have expected Beijing, or even Thailand, to radically reduce their support for the *Khmer Rouge* just to get Vietnamese troops out one year earlier.

The late 1989/early 1990 deadline was actually a negotiating tactic designed to put the *Khmer Rouge's* backers under pressure to make concessions in answer to Vietnam's willingness to withdraw its troops. Yet an unconditional withdrawal at the end of 1990 still apparently remained on the cards, if Hanoi's conditions for an earlier withdrawal were not met. Indeed, Vietnamese Foreign Minister Nguyen Co Thach, in reviewing the Jakarta conference, again underlined the unconditional deadline for complete withdrawal: 'I say a political solution should be achieved before the end of 1990, or else Vietnam will still pull out all its troops by the end of 1990'.

Vietnam and the PRK have consistently argued that aid to the Kampuchean resistance should be cut off as Vietnamese troops withdraw. China's position had been that it would continue to supply the resistance so long as Vietnamese troops remained in the country. In late 1988 Beijing made two major changes in its negotiating position which indicated that it had decided that the benefits of the stalemate in Indochina had all but run their course, and that changes in the overall international environment – and in Sino-Soviet relations in particular – demanded a more constructive Indochina policy. In November, Chinese premier Li Peng specified a June 1989 deadline for the total withdrawal of Vietnamese troops from Kampuchea as the 'most desirable' timetable. Nine days later he said that, if Vietnam were to produce a timetable for withdrawal, subject to international supervision, military aid to the Kampuchean factions ought to be gradually reduced and eventually stopped. In mid-December China explicitly stated that the Vietnamese withdrawal and the cessation of aid to the resistance could be done 'in step'.

The gap between the Chinese and Vietnamese positions had narrowed considerably. Both Hanoi and Beijing now recognized that the difference over the withdrawal schedule – as little as six months – was undeniably negotiable. This may have caught the Indochinese states, and Phnom Penh in particular, unprepared. The PRK's premier Hun Sen, in a December news conference on the 1988 Vietnamese withdrawal, referred to 'the two years we have to build up our forces to assume the tasks once the Vietnamese army is withdrawn'. That would indicate an anticipation that the withdrawal would be completed by the later deadline of the end of 1990. In early January 1989 Vietnam reduced the gap between its own and China's positions even further, saying it would withdraw by September 1989 if support for the Kampuchean resistance were also to cease. However, Hanoi has yet to accept Beijing's other condition: systematic international supervision of the withdrawals. Vietnam has invited foreign observers and journalists to view the most recent partial withdrawals, but the opportunities for cheating on such haphazard verification have been widely recognized.

JAPAN: END OF AN ERA

On 24 February 1989 representatives of 164 countries and 28 international organizations attended the solemn state and religious funeral of Emperor Hirohito. The 87-year-old Emperor's death on 7 January, after a long illness, resurrected dormant controversies over his role in World War II and awoke bitter memories among prisoners of war who had been mistreated by Japanese forces. Pressure developed in some countries, particularly the UK, Australia and New Zealand, to reduce the level of their representation; the prompt decision of President Bush (who, as a young US Navy pilot, had been shot down over the Sea of Japan) to attend helped to tip the scales in favour of attendance and ensured that the Emperor's funeral would be by far the largest gathering of world leaders ever.

Within Japan itself the immediate difficulty centred around how to separate state functions from Shintoist ceremony in the preparations for the funeral and the succession of Prince Akihito as Emperor. The Constitution separates religion from the State, and this has been a constant point of debate in the post-war period. The final decision was a compromise which sanctioned optional attendance of the religious and traditionalist aspects of the occasion, while focusing more on the state aspects. This allowed members of the Socialist Party, for example, to pay their respects but to absent themselves from the parts of the ceremonies they could not support.

Japanese feelings ranged from those of some who maintained their reverence for a pre-war Imperial role to those of the majority which felt the late Emperor had ably carried out his role as a 'symbol of the state and unity of the people' as called for in the constitution established in 1947. Although a distant figure, he retained the affection of most Japanese, who felt that his efforts since the war to smooth the way towards a more democratic Japan transcended concern over his exact role during the war. Even the younger generation, less concerned about either the old or the new Emperor, feels that the constitutional arrangements serve well as a symbol of peace and prosperity. As a result there is little call for constitutional revision, whether to strengthen the status of the Emperor or to abolish the Emperor system.

US–Japanese Relations

President Bush's decision to attend the Emperor's funeral underscored the emergence of Japan on the world scene as an economic super-power, as well as the immediacy of the problems which have affected US–Japanese co-operation. Foremost among these, of course, is the continuing unbalanced trade relationship, one that stubbornly resists the efforts of both sides to correct it. Although Japan's trade surplus with the United States fell by almost $8 bn in a year, it still amounted to $52 bn at the end of 1988. The small decrease was partly due to Japan's decision to abide by a February 1988 GATT ruling that restrictions on a series of agricultural imports should be liberalized. Restrictions were duly reduced on a number of processed foods and peanuts. In June a compromise was reached on the more important beef and citrus food imports; they are to be liberalized in stages – beef and oranges by April 1991, and orange juice by April 1992.

Japan had hoped that these decisions would affect the passage of the controversial Omnibus Trade and Competitiveness Bill being debated in the US Congress. Although President Reagan had vetoed the first version of the bill in May 1988, this was mostly because of amendments which had little to do with the central question of requiring retaliation within three years of a determination that an individual country was unfairly restricting US imports. Somewhat less protectionist in its second version, the bill was signed by the President on 23 August. The new law will give the Congress and critics of Japanese trading practices a powerful new weapon with which to pressure the Bush Administration into taking tougher measures against Japan.

Another area of controversy was eased in May 1988, when a compromise over US bidding for construction contracts was reached. For many years Washington had been upset over the imbalance created by Japanese construction firms winning contracts for projects in the US, while US firms were prevented from bidding for Japanese projects. In November 1987 Japan agreed to allow competitive US bidding on a construction contract at the new Kansei airport, but the US argued that restrictions should also be lifted on public works. When Japan demurred, the Congress refused to allow Japanese construction companies to bid on extensions to the Washington subway. This was enough to bring senior Japanese negotiators to Washington, and the compromise agreement was achieved, allowing US companies to bid on a few more selected contracts.

In these conditions, occasional discussion of the concept of a Japan–US free trade agreement will remain theoretical, notwithstanding both countries' apprehension about the '1992' process in Europe. Even so, strong interdependence already exists: Japan buys half of all US government bonds, for example, while some 200 US companies in Japan produce $50-bn-worth of goods. Most Japanese automobile companies now have factories in the United States, and in early 1988 Honda was importing automobiles from its US plant into Japan. Yet the economic relationship remains a lopsided one, between the world's largest creditor and debtor nations, and until that imbalance is adjusted there will continue to be considerable difficulties.

Other International Relations
Prime Minister Noboru Takeshita's diplomatic performance – demonstrated in negotiations with the US over these crucial and politically heated economic issues, as well as in a number of timely proposals he made at the Toronto economic summit – surprised many critics who had argued that, while a master of domestic politics, he lacked inter-

national experience. Until the last few months of 1988, when he became bogged down with the Recruit Cosmos insider stock trading scandal and the Emperor's last illness (which began on 19 September), Takeshita managed the diplomatic agenda well, conducting a surprisingly activist and generally successful foreign policy.

Metaphorically flying a banner emblazoned with the slogan 'Japan as a Contributor to the World', he visited a large number of countries in Asia, North America and Western Europe. He made a positive gesture at the Toronto economic summit, proposing cancellation of some of the external debts from which some third-world countries were suffering. In a complicated formula, Japan offered to replace aid debts built up by the poorest countries from 1978 to 1987 (and the interest on them) with grants equivalent to $US 5.5 bn. Takeshita also pledged to double the Japanese ODA (Official Development Assistance) to $50 bn over the period 1988–92. The $10 bn per year that he has promised will surpass US aid, although at only 0.31% of GNP, it still lags behind the average 0.34% granted by the members of the Development Assistance Committee of the Organization for Economic Development and Co-operation (OECD).

The sharp increase in Japanese aid, which is denominated in dollars, was aided by the sharp appreciation of the yen. From 240 to the dollar in 1985, the yen rose steadily to a high point of 120 to the dollar in the middle of 1988; it has since fluctuated in the 120–130 range, having effectively doubled in a little over three years. In addition to thrusting Japan more into the centre of the world economic arena, this rise has proved an effective tool for enhancing Japan's diplomatic role.

The domestic attitude to Japan's global role has also been slowly evolving. Although Japan continues to be reluctant to send members of its Self-Defense Forces (SDF) overseas in any capacity, the government is searching for a new international role commensurate with its economic might. As part of this new look, the Takeshita cabinet decided to send a civilian to the UN peace-keeping team monitoring the truce in Afghanistan and two more to join the UN team observing the cease-fire between Iran and Iraq. Early in 1989 the government announced a plan to send about 30 civilian specialists to participate in UN supervision of the election that is to precede national independence for Namibia. Though still modest, these moves represent the beginning of a more visible Japanese presence on the international stage.

Yet another new development came in the wake of political unrest in Rangoon in the summer of 1988, when Tokyo stopped ODA to Burma on the grounds that the military government was not making adequate efforts at political and economic democratization. Using its ODA in this way to make political points is another departure for Japanese diplomacy. Japan may also try to play a slightly more visible political role in Indochina. In July, at the ASEAN meeting, Foreign Minister Uno proposed the establishment of a UN observation team in Kampuchea. Other signs of an extension of Japan's diplomatic reach came with

Uno's visit to Israel, the first to that country by a Japanese minister. And the head of the Defense Agency, Tsutomu Kawara, became the first minister in charge of defence to visit South-east Asia.

There are, however, continuing obstacles to an active Japanese diplomacy towards Asia, and some of them are as much at home as abroad. Political leaders of ministerial rank have in the past offended Asian neighbours by revising the history of Japan's role in the Pacific war. In April and May Minister Seisuke Okuno again created difficulties with China and South Korea when he more than once stated in the Diet that Japan had had no intention of invading China during the War, and that its actions could not be considered as aggression. As a result, Okuno was ousted, and Takeshita visited Beijing in August to help mend relations. But in early 1989 he himself invited similar criticisms with similar remarks. Nevertheless, Japanese political relations with South Korea and China were basically good, though potential difficulties remained which would need delicate handling. The Seoul Olympics, for which Japan and South Korea co-operated over anti-terrorist measures, helped to strengthen relations, and Takeshita's visit to China with a large aid commitment helped forge better relations there.

In the meantime, Gorbachev's efforts to normalize relations with China and establish non-political contacts with South Korea have changed the diplomatic framework in north-east Asia. Japan's interest continues to be to maintain stability on the Korean Peninsula. As a means to ensure that North Korea does not begin to feel isolated, a few days before the start of the Olympics in September Japan lifted the sanctions it had imposed on Pyongyang for its role in the November 1987 destruction of a Korean Airlines flight. There are not many in Tokyo who express concern about Soviet courting of South Korean capital and technology for the development of the Soviet Far East, or about Seoul's use of its new contacts with Moscow as a card against Washington. But a considerable number are somewhat apprehensive about the *rapprochement* between the two Communist giants; the unknown changes that this might bring – and particularly for South-east Asian countries, Japan's important political and economic partners – awakens disquiet.

Tokyo's greater interest, of course, is in what Gorbachev's policy priorities are for Japanese–Soviet relations. During 1988 the USSR sent various conflicting signals about the key territorial issue: the four Northern islands (Habomai, Shikotan, Etorofu and Kunashiri) which the USSR occupied after World War II. When Nakasone visited Moscow in July 1988 Soviet leaders indirectly hinted that they would at least be willing to discuss territorial disputes with Japan, although there was no indication that the outcome would be what Japan wanted. Even with no firm response, on 19 December 1988 Shevardnadze made the first visit to Japan by a Soviet foreign minister since January 1986, and the two governments agreed to establish a working committee to discuss 'the matters related to the conclusion of the Peace Treaty'. Whether the working committee will produce some fruitful outcome, leading to a visit by Gorbachev to Tokyo in 1989, or whether it will be used as an excuse to put off any solution to the territorial issues yet again remains to be seen. There are signs, however, that as part of Gorbachev's 'new thinking' some advances in this outstanding problem may well be on the way. If the Soviet leader cannot make progress on this core issue, which would set a precedent in terms of Soviet attitudes towards the territorial *status quo* resulting from World War II, then Japanese–Soviet relations would probably be such that Japan would remain the one industrialized nation impervious to the 'Gorbachev effect'. In particular, the Japanese investment, technology and know-how that the USSR is seeking would not be forthcoming on any significant scale.

Bearing the Defence Burden
There is at the moment no 'Gorbymania' to be sensed in Japan, as there is in Europe, and consequently there is no pressure to reduce defence spending in response to a perceived change in the international security climate. In 1988 Japan maintained its slow but steady incremental increases in defence spending. The government had appropriated ¥ 3,700.3 bn (about $US 29.5 bn at ¥125 to the dollar) for defence in FY 1988, and on 24 January 1989 it submitted to the Diet a FY 1989 defence budget of ¥3,919.8 bn (about $31.4 bn). The latter represented a 5.9% nominal increase over the previous year's budget, or 1.006% of estimated GNP. Expressed in dollar terms this looks quite formidable, leaving only the US and the USSR with larger absolute defence budgets. But it should be remembered that a large part of the tripling of Japanese defence costs in dollar terms from 1981 to 1989 results from the increasing strength of the yen; in yen terms it has risen 'only' 1.6 times, which is still considerably more than the US defence build-up during the two Reagan administrations (a rise of 1.4 times).

Part of the increase has been spent on acquiring modern, sophisticated weapons, such as F-15 and P-3C aircraft, *Patriot* missiles, and locally-produced SSM-1 missiles. In 1988 the northernmost division in Hokkaido was equipped with anti-CW equipment. The budgetary appropriation for equipment was 28.1% of the defence budget, the highest percentage in recent history (during the 1970s it had been below 20%).

There was an increase in military exercising as well. In August 1988 the SDF, practising the defence of Hokkaido in an emergency, for the first time moved reinforcements through the Seikan Tunnel (the world's longest, passing under the Tsugaru strait to connect Hokkaido and Honshu), which had been opened just a few months earlier. But the SDF's capability for sustained combat still leaves much to be desired, with many air bases and radar sites, for instance, left unprotected.

Burden-sharing
In financial terms, host-nation support for US bases and troops in Japan was higher than ever; the government, which includes the estimated

value of the land provided for US troops in its figures, claimed that the support was equivalent to $US 2–2.5 bn a year, or $45,000 per soldier. While this is a somewhat self-serving presentation, the Pentagon expressed general satisfaction with the current effort, and even supported Japanese arguments that non-military contributions, like aid to Turkey and the Philippines and the cancellation of debts owed by third-world countries, should be considered as an integral part of Japan's 'responsibility-sharing' in maintaining international stability. Some US Congressmen who were not impressed with this argument pressed for a larger direct contribution by Japan, as was typically shown in the August 1988 report of the Defense Burdensharing Panel of the House Committee on Armed Services. Friction with the US Congress, if not with the US Administration, will remain so long as Japan spends only some 1% of GNP on defence and a huge bilateral trade surplus of the order of $50 bn continues.

US frustration had also been stoked by illegal sales of sensitive technology to the Soviet Union by the Toshiba Machinery Co. in March 1987. This frustration and distrust were present in the US debate over Japan's use of US military technologies. On 24 June 1988 the two governments signed a contract to allow Japan to produce *Aegis* anti-aircraft cruisers under license, but, even after the contract was signed, some members of Congress attempted to block its implementation. Similar problems, albeit with potentially much more damaging political implications, arose over the agreement on the co-development of Japan's next-generation fighter, dubbed FSX. The US had argued that Japan could buy the F-16 (often considered the best aircraft of its type) more cheaply than it could develop a design of its own, at the same time helping to reduce the huge trade deficit. Japan, however, wanted to build its own fighter. In October 1987 a compromise agreement for joint development of an advanced aircraft based on the F-16 was reached, but it took another 13 months before the sharing scheme was finally worked out and signed. Japan was to cover all the expenses involved, with the US providing 40% of technologies required to build the new model. Certain advanced Japanese technologies would go into construction of the aircraft, and the US could use these under license. Prototype fighters with CCV (control-configured vehicle) technology are to be produced in 1993, with 130 units eventually being manufactured. The estimated cost for one unit is ¥5,100 m ($40.8 m).

In early 1989, under the new Bush Administration, the US Congress and the Department of Commerce began to criticize the FSX deal, arguing that sensitive military technologies might be used by Japan to produce competitive commercial aircraft. In early March 1989 President Bush said that the US intended to honour the November 1988 agreement, but that he would want to review it and probably alter certain aspects. Thus, even if the deal does not collapse, American unwillingness to implement an apparently firm agreement and the increasing Congressional criticism can only encourage Japanese techno-nationalism, which will make future negotiations on co-development extremely difficult.

Domestic Political Developments

The highest priority on Takeshita's political agenda for 1988 was to carry out a long-awaited tax reform. Both his predecessors, Masayoshi Ohira and Yasuhiro Nakasone, had tried to reform the tax system, and both had been defeated on the issue. Takeshita was aided by his adroit political style, which put a premium on developing a consensus before acting, and by a growing realization in the Liberal Democratic Party (LDP) that the inequities of the old tax system bore disproportionately on the salaried workers of urban areas, the very voters the Party must attract if it is to diversify its base of support away from the countryside. After careful preparation, Takeshita summoned a special Diet session on 19 July to introduce a package of six tax reform bills, aimed at tapping new sources of revenue by introducing a 3% consumption tax and correcting the inequity of the taxpayers' burden. These bills, the first major tax reform since the 1950s, were passed after long and arduous debate at dawn on 24 December. The new tax, which has adopted the controversial principle of a consumption tax, is intended to meet the future welfare needs of the rapidly aging population.

In the midst of the unprecedentedly long (163-day) Diet session, the Recruit Cosmos scandal loomed ever larger, involving at least 13 members of the Diet, including top figures in the ruling LDP. That Takeshita was able to secure the passage of the bill despite the impact of the scandal was a testimony to his political adroitness. Unlike Nakasone, he worked untiringly to divide the opposition; against his personal desires he even jettisoned Finance Minister Kiichi Miyazawa, a key actor in the tax reform, who was caught in the scandal.

The scandal had broken in the Japanese press in July 1988; it involved the offer of shares in Recruit Cosmos Co. (the real-estate subsidiary of Recruit, an employment and information-processing conglomerate) to the secretaries of a number of political personalities before the shares were listed on the stock exchange. After the listing their worth had risen exponentially, and the favoured figures made profits in the hundreds of millions of yen. Prime Minister Takeshita attempted to blunt the impact of the scandal by changing three-quarters of his cabinet after the tax bill was passed, but this merely backfired. Less than a week later the new Justice Minister was forced to resign because of his implication in the scandal; at the end of January, even more embarrassingly, the Director General of the Economic Planning Organization, whom Takeshita had put in charge of a parliamentary committee to investigate the affair, was also forced to resign; his replacement, though still in office at the end of February 1989, also proved to have been involved in the scandal.

By February 1989 the affair was in the hands of the Public Prosecutor's office, and arrests for bribery were being made. Seven senior figures – including Recruit's flamboyant founder, the chairman of Nippon Telephone and Telegraph, and a senior Ministry of Labour bureaucrat – were taken into custody. Nobody doubted that there were many more revelations still to come. Former premier Nakasone's role was being questioned. Nor was the scandal confined to the LDP; the chairman of the Democratic Socialist Party had resigned in early February over his acceptance of Recruit shares.

The unravelling scandal had exposed the surprising extent of the role of money, and consequent opportunities for political corruption, in the Japanese political world. It reminded people of the deficiencies of the political system, in which a multi-seat constituency election system means that a party must win many seats in each constituency and that members of the same party find themselves opposing each other. The process requires extraordinary outlays of cash. One finding revealed that, even in a normal non-election year, an average politician needs some ¥30–100 m ($240,000–800,000) to retain his constituents' favour.

Taken in conjunction with the unpopularity of the tax bill (the consumption tax will raise prices, disproportionately affect the lower paid, and tax previously exempt sectors, like agriculture), the exposé greatly affected the popularity of the LDP and the Prime Minister himself. His popularity plunged to 19% in February 1989 public opinion polls, and a by-election that month resulted in the loss of a hitherto safe LDP seat. The government faces the prospect of an election for the Upper House in the summer of 1989, and Takeshita, who must avoid electoral defeat if he is to remain at the head of the party, has hinted that he is considering reforms in the system.

Beginning a New Era
With the burial of Emperor Hirohito, there was very much the sense that a new period was truly beginning in Japan. This was, of course, literally true, for the *Showa* era ended with Hirohito's life, and the *Heisei* ('achieving peace') era was ushered in with Akihito's ascent to the imperial throne. The new Emperor indicated in the early days of his reign that it would be more open and visible than his father's had been.

Beyond this, reactions to the Recruit scandal have put the question of reforming the political system, and political ethics, at the top of the agenda. That there is even debate on this subject is a measure of the change in Japanese public opinion, which hitherto had always accepted considerable corruption as the price of politics. Prime Minister Takeshita is said to be considering replacing the multi-seat electoral system with a single-seat system, and to be re-examining the possibility of public financing of election campaigns. But this might change the party system and factional politics so drastically that no party, least of all the LDP, would carelessly leap at such reform at the moment. In addition, the ordinary voter, who now gains from the lavish gifts that politicians hand out in their search for votes, may not yet be willing to forsake this advantage for an unknown new system. The odds must remain that, although greater controls on political corruption will ensue, the politics of the new *Heisei* era will retain a large measure of the old.

THE KOREAN PENINSULA

In 1987 democratization was launched in South Korea; in 1988 the government and the people struggled to make it seaworthy. Student demonstrations and labour unrest continued during the year, but not on the scale of 1987. Instead, the focus of opposition activity shifted to the National Assembly, after the April 1988 elections had for the first time deprived a President of an overall majority for his own parliamentary party. The spirit of grudging accommodation which typified the immediate post-election period ended after the Olympic Games, as the opposition began to pursue investigations into the murkier aspects of the previous Administration. During the course of the year, the continuing element of volatility in Korean politics was demonstrated by the fate of Chun Doo Hwan, who exchanged residence in the *Chong Wa Dae*, the luxurious presidential palace, for a humble Buddhist temple.

In his inaugural speech in February 1988 President Roh Tae Woo expressed the hope that Korea, 'once a peripheral country in East Asia', would take 'a central position in the international community'. The September 1988 Olympic Games, attended by a record number of countries, were symbolic of that aspiration, and they were a sporting, diplomatic and economic success for South Korea. North Korea was not only left almost totally isolated in its Olympic boycott but was forced to watch East European states and even its closest allies, China and the Soviet Union, develop significant economic and semi-official links with South Korea. While South Korea's economy recorded another year of high growth, North Korea's continued to stagnate, and Pyongyang seemed increasingly out of touch with trends in the region, not least the movement for political reform and economic restructuring in other East Asian socialist countries.

South Korean Politics: Coping with Democracy
President Chun managed to hand over the presidency peacefully to his long-time friend, Roh, at the end of February 1988, but after that little went right for him. Almost as soon as he left office revelations of corruption under his Administration began to appear. Roh, who had been widely criticized for retaining in his first cabinet one-third of the ministers from the outgoing Chun cabinet, slowly tried to distance himself from Chun. The arrest of Chun's younger brother for embezzlement of funds from the *Saemaul Undong* (rural development agency) forced Chun in April to resign from his remaining party and government advisory posts. This left Roh freer to promote the interests of his own supporters, within the Democratic Justice Party (DJP).

However, Roh's calculations and Chun's fortunes were hit by the unexpected results of the April National Assembly elections. The campaign was in many ways a replay of the December 1987 presidential election campaign: it was more about personalities than policies, regional loyalties than class divisions, and the past than the future. A combination of DJP complacency, opposition enthusiasm, a revised electoral constituency system and strong regional voting biases gave the DJP a poor total of 125 seats, and it failed to achieve an overall majority. As in December 1987, Kim Young Sam and the Reunification Democratic Party (RDP) took a higher percentage of the vote than Kim Dae Jung and the Party for Peace and Democracy (PPD), but the quirks of the electoral system gave the RDP only 59 seats compared with the PPD's 71. The New Democratic Republican Party (NDRP), led by Kim Jong Pil, gained 35 seats and thus emerged as the key balancing element to be courted by both the DJP and the other opposition parties.

The elections confirmed both the political longevity and the personal rivalry of the three Kims. The new constitution, which came into force in February 1988, has diluted some of the executive's powers *vis-à-vis* the legislature, and during the summer there was much cautious testing of strength between Roh and the three Kims. Although the opposition claimed some early successes in forcing Roh to rescind the appointment of a controversial Chief Justice and vetoing two motions for National Assembly investigative panels on the Chun administration, it seemed as concerned as Roh to limit the confrontation until after the Olympics.

Post-Olympic euphoria was short-lived for Roh, as opposition demands for investigations into the irregularities of the Chun administration and the responsibility for the 1980 Kwangju incident (when South Korean troops bloodily suppressed a civil uprising) mounted. Roh appeared to favour clearing up the legacies of Chun's maladministration, but wanted to avoid being too directly implicated himself. Senior figures from his predecessor's regime were called before National Assembly public hearings, but Chun himself refused to testify. A number of Chun's relatives and associates were arrested on corruption charges, and eventually Roh persuaded Chun to make a humiliating nationwide television apology for his past misdeeds, which he did on 23 November before leaving Seoul for internal exile. Roh then appealed for leniency and a new start, promising further democratic reforms, and in early December he reshuffled both the cabinet and the DJP leadership to remove those associated with the Chun era.

With an eye on their future electoral prospects, all three Kims have tried to cultivate an image of responsibility and moderation. At the beginning of 1989, Kim Dae Jung, at least, had appeared to think that he had Roh on the defensive and began to demand more forcefully that the President honour his election promise of offering a post-Olympic referendum on his record in office. By March, however, no longer certain that the voters would pronounce in his favour, Kim agreed with

Roh's decision that such a referendum could be postponed to a later, undetermined date.

Surprisingly, extra-parliamentary forces looked less threatening in 1988 than at any time in the previous three years. The students remained both vocal and visible, but their summer campaign for immediate contacts with North Korea failed to evoke the wide popular support aroused by their 1987 struggles for democracy. Although the students' criticisms of Chun accorded with the popular mood, the methods they employed did not. Labour militancy was also at a lower level, with economic concerns dominating political ones. The military remained ever-present in the background, and its sensitivity to its slowly declining influence on politics was clear on occasions – for example, in September, when a journalist who had written critically of the military's political role was knifed by soldiers in disguise. Nevertheless, the military seem prepared to live with Roh's assurances that stability could be maintained.

The process of democratization, itself in part a product of socio-economic change, also in turn affected economic policy-making. Roh found it necessary to take into account the voices not only of opposition parties but also of various economic interest groups. For the third year in succession economic growth reached 12%, and total trade for the first time exceeded $US 100 bn. Roh's economic advisers, however, appreciated the need to alter the imbalance in development between regions and industrial sectors, and a high-level non-governmental advisory committee reported in the autumn on the need for adjustment. Moreover, sustained growth heightened tensions with major trading partners, while increased economic self-confidence combined with the assertiveness of political parties and economic interest groups to evoke a more 'nationalistic' response from the Roh government to external economic pressure.

South Korean Diplomatic Progress
Before becoming President, Roh had stressed that continuity would be the keynote of his foreign policy. There has indeed been no dramatic change, but Roh nevertheless has subtly altered the atmosphere and context of foreign policy, not least through added emphasis on the 'northern diplomacy' introduced by Chun in 1983. Democratization has meant a greater say for the opposition in foreign policy, just as much as in domestic policies. This has complicated relations with traditional friends, but has helped in developing new contacts with the socialist world.

While the United States remained South Korea's key partner, the relationship became slightly more troubled during the year. With exports to the US exceeding imports from it by as much as $US 10 bn, the main source of tension continued to revolve around economic issues. The Reagan administration resisted some of the more extreme protectionist demands of Congress, but itself pushed hard for Korean concessions in several trade- and investment-related areas. Economic interest groups hit by US pressure therefore found themselves at one with those younger Koreans who accused the United States of political support for authoritarian government.

The anti-American feelings that were growing during the year were accentuated by incidents during the Olympic Games period and by the National Assembly hearings on the Kwangju uprising. The previously taboo subject of US–South Korean security arrangements was now openly debated, and in the autumn, as a way of trying to diffuse the anti-American sentiment, Washington and Seoul began talks on revising the complex joint command-and-control arrangements, relocating a US army base away from Seoul, and South Korean financial support programmes for US forces. These discussions may well be the prelude to the phased withdrawal of US ground troops from South Korea.

The South Korean 'northern diplomacy' was not an issue between the two countries, for, as President Reagan made clear to Roh when they met in October, the US supports the concept. During 1988 US officials, reflecting improved relations with the USSR, were much more prepared than in earlier years to discuss the Korean situation with Soviet as well as Chinese officials. In November, after the peaceful conclusion of the Olympics, the US announced that it would remove restrictions on diplomatic contacts with North Korea. Roh's government has encouraged such modest moves; indeed, in July it announced that it would not oppose trading in non-military materials and would even be willing to co-operate in promoting cultural and sports contacts between the US, Japan and North Korea. Nevertheless, South Korea is, as ever, concerned about Japan and other Western powers taking the spirit of reconciliation too far without some real North Korean change of attitude.

Whereas US–South Korean relations have become somewhat more difficult, Japanese–South Korean relations improved in 1988. A number of factors helped; the trade imbalance at last decreased, Japanese attitudes showed signs of some convergence with South Korea's own policies, Japan was prepared to join the US in assisting South Korea with counter-terrorist operations before and during the Olympics, and Roh seemed more relaxed than Chun about cultural contacts with Japan. Prime Minister Takeshita attended Roh's inauguration and the Olympic opening ceremony and, although Roh's November visit to Japan was postponed because of the Emperor's illness, a business-like, if not necessarily warm, relationship has emerged between the two leaders. Nevertheless, the legacies of the past still resurface on occasions; Japanese ministerial comments in April 1988, appearing to condone Japan's wartime role, and the death of Emperor Hirohito in January 1989 provoked widespread comment in the Korean media on Japan's colonial and wartime record.

Roh's government has had its greatest success in changing attitudes and relationships with the socialist allies of North Korea. China, the Soviet Union and the East European countries all sent delegations to the Olympics, and other sporting and cultural links developed. Commercial relations expanded rapidly – trade with China alone reached an estimated $US 3 bn in 1988 – but it was the East Europeans who were able to be more open than the USSR and China in 'officially' endorsing these contacts. During 1988 trade offices were exchanged between South Korea and Hungary and Yugoslavia, and negotiations with Bulgaria and Poland were set in motion. On the eve of the Olympics, the Hungarian government announced that it would establish a permanent mission in Seoul, and it extended this to full diplomatic recognition in February 1989.

Both China and the Soviet Union concentrated on building up trade and even encouraging South Korean investment. The USSR and South Korea began negotiating about trade representatives and established their first joint venture, but Beijing allowed only Chinese provincial governments to establish trade offices. Soviet President Gorbachev publicly mentioned the development of economic relations with South Korea for the first time in his September 1988 Krasnoyarsk speech. However, on his December visit to North Korea, Foreign Minister Shevardnadze reiterated that diplomatic relations with the South were not yet conceivable. For all that the Roh government has made it clear that Communism within South Korea would still be severely dealt with, external contacts have been liberalized.

If the Olympics acted as a diplomatic key to relations with socialist countries, they also provided a celebration of South Korean prestige and accomplishment. Roh has tried to capitalize on this by taking a higher international profile. In October he became the first South Korean head of state to address the UN General Assembly, and in early November he set off on a two-week tour of South-east Asia and Australasian countries. Commercial ties with South-east Asia are increasing, and Roh also succeeded in obtaining for South Korea the status of an ASEAN dialogue partner. Ironically, while the country's profile in the region was rising, relations with one of its closest allies, Taiwan, deteriorated, primarily because of Seoul's very successes in developing contacts with Beijing.

North Korea in Isolation

The rationale for South Korea's northern policy is that friendly links with socialist countries will eventually have a positive effect on reunification with North Korea. With democratization moving ahead, reunification rose higher on South Korea's political agenda. Nevertheless, relations between North and South retained their long-standing element of shadow-boxing during 1988, although the initiative did seem to have passed to the South.

Certainly Roh felt under greater internal pressure to make some attempt to reopen dialogue with Pyongyang. Demands for action came not just from the opposition political parties but also from the students, who twice (in June and August) attempted to march to the border at Panmunjom to meet with North Korean counterparts. While most

131

South Koreans saw the students' actions as naive, they did prompt Roh to try to take the initiative, first through a major policy declaration on 7 July and then in a speech to the UN General Assembly on 18 October. Roh said that he would do away with the 'hasty and confrontational policy' of the past. In the July declaration he announced a number of measures to liberalize inter-Korean economic exchanges and in October he proposed a north-east Asian consultation conference for peace.

Although by the end of the year reports of the first trade contacts for importing Northern products were beginning to appear, there was no revival of the joint economic talks that took place in 1984–5. The only form of dialogue that did begin was preparatory talks for a full-scale joint parliamentarians' meeting. Proposed in mid-July by South Korea's National Assembly speaker as a last-ditch attempt to induce the North to participate in the Olympics, the agenda broadened to include the promotion of inter-Korean exchanges, the signature of a non-aggression pact and the holding of a North–South summit. Seven meetings were held between August and December 1988, but the two sides failed to iron out differences about the size and scope of the proposed conference.

During the second half of the year both sides made a number of other proposals. The North continued to push for tripartite political and military talks (to include the US), and in his January 1989 New Year speech Kim Il Sung proposed a political consultative meeting to which South Korean party, religious and dissident leaders would be invited. The South, in turn, urged Red Cross talks, education talks and, finally, discussions at deputy-prime minister level. The last proposal was accepted by Pyongyang in mid-January 1989, but with the premise that the annual US–South Korean combined forces' *Team Spirit* exercise be cancelled. While North Korea's renewed references to *Team Spirit* cast some doubt on its commitment to serious progress in the dialogue, it did seem that the North was becoming slightly less rigid in its attitude to the South.

The North Korean economy continued to be a major problem, and almost all the senior government personnel changes during the year involved economy-related ministers. Partial cabinet reshuffles occurred four times before Li Gun Mo retired on health grounds, to be replaced as Premier by Yon Hyong Muk in December 1988. Like his predecessor, Yon is an economic technocrat. The policy emphasis within the current Seven Year Plan was shifted to agriculture and light industry from heavy industry, but there were few signs of economic restructuring on the Chinese, or even Soviet, model. A new Ministry of Joint Ventures was established in December, however, and the North Korean media began to admit the utility of 'material incentives', as an adjunct to the constant ideological campaigns, as a means of improving productivity.

The Soviet Union continued to provide economic and military aid (including the transfer of MiG-29 aircraft), but Soviet leaders, just as much as Chinese ones, encouraged North Korea to be more open to the

West. However, even though Kim Il Sung told a visiting Chinese delegation in July that China's open-door policy was a 'great encouragement', by the end of the year North Korea had in fact become more isolated both economically and politically. As Sino-Soviet relations
improved, Moscow and Beijing became less concerned about competing for influence in Pyongyang than with developing economic inter-
course with South Korea. Although the celebrations of the fortieth
anniversary of the founding of the People's Republic in September,
were marked with congratulatory visits and messages, North Korea's
relations with the USSR and China did little more than mark time. Its
relations with East European countries, however, deteriorated.
Hungary's *rapprochement* with South Korea was particularly galling to
Kim Il Sung, as one of his sons, Kim Pyong Il, had arrived to take up the
ambassadorship in Budapest only a few weeks before (he was recalled in
protest).

Economic restructuring was tentative at best; political restructuring
was non-existent. Despite the replacement as Chief of the General Staff
of the long-serving Oh Guk Ryol by Choe Gwang, a veteran comrade-
in-arms of Kim Il Sung, and the sudden emergence of Kim Pyong Il as
an ambassador (he was appointed to Sofia after the Budapest fiasco),
there was no change in the pre-eminence of Kim Il Sung and his chosen
successor, his son Kim Jong Il. Economic stagnation and diplomatic
isolation have not loosened their control over every aspect of North
Korean life.

BURMA: NEAR CIVIL WAR

During 1988 Burma was recalled to the attention of the world community for the first time since the 1960s. From the military coup of 2
March 1962 until the resignation on 23 July 1988 of U Ne Win, the man
who dominated Burma's politics during the intervening 26 years,
Burma had withdrawn almost completely from involvement in Asian
politics. While there had been major conflicts between its neighbours
and the super-powers during this period, including the Sino-Indian border clashes and the American war in Indochina, Burma remained
largely untouched by these events. The end of the Ne Win era, however,
has raised questions as to whether Burma might now be drawn into
regional conflicts. Not since the 1950s – when there were cold-war conflicts between China, on the one hand, and the United States and
Thailand, on the other – has there been so serious a risk that Burma's
neutralist position in Asian politics might be undermined.

Background
The Ne Win era began with a nearly bloodless coup in 1962, when the
army, in the form of a Revolutionary Council, replaced the government

of Prime Minister U Nu. Fearful that Nu's attempts to negotiate greater autonomy for minority-designated states on the country's borders with India, China, Laos and Thailand might lead to a deterioration of the strength of the Union, as well as concerned that the civilian government was deviating from the socialist intentions of the 1947 constitution, the army quickly moved against the existing political order and replaced it with the beginnings of a one-party socialist system modelled on similar systems in Eastern Europe.

The heart of the military's strategy was composed of three elements: a cadre party, the Burma Socialist Programme Party (BSPP); an autarkic economic development programme; and an attempt to redefine ethnicity in an effort to undermine the appeal of separatist minority groups. The restructuring programme of the Revolutionary Council reached its culmination with the introduction of a new constitution in 1974 and the nominal return of state power to an elected *Pyithu Hluttaw* (People's Assembly). Despite these formal changes, the newly renamed Socialist Republic of the Union of Burma still remained largely governed by the same group of men who had carried out the 1962 military coup. Gen. Ne Win, who became the first chairman of the BSPP, remained in power as President, and the bulk of government ministers and other top officials were retired or serving military officers. One of the weaknesses of the regime, as the events of 1988 demonstrated, was its inability to draw non-military personnel into positions of trust and authority, leading the government to become increasingly remote, isolated and ossified.

The attempt to develop an autarkic economic development strategy proved in the end to be a failure. The reason is not difficult to perceive, once the political constraints under which the regime operated are recognized. The strategy was based upon three elements: the strong belief of the Revolutionary Council's older civilian advisers in the moral superiority of socialism over capitalism and its alleged twin, imperialism; the fear of peasant revolt and possible support for the continuing insurgency of the increasingly isolated Burma Communist Party (BCP); and the fear that active collaboration with Western industrial nations would inevitably undermine the country's neutralist foreign policy, creating the possibility of eventual conflict with Communist China. Behind all these elements there lay a strong belief in Burmese nationalism and state sovereignty – which, in the army's view, could only be safeguarded by the military itself.

The government's autarkic development strategy finally collapsed because of an inability to raise sufficient capital for investment. For political reasons the regime was unwilling either to impose heavy taxes on the peasantry, which is the backbone of the economy (rice and other commodities are the country's major export items), or to accept foreign investment. With little foreign aid or borrowings until the mid-1970s, the economy lacked any force for growth. The low purchase prices that the state set for rice and other agricultural crops lowered incentives,

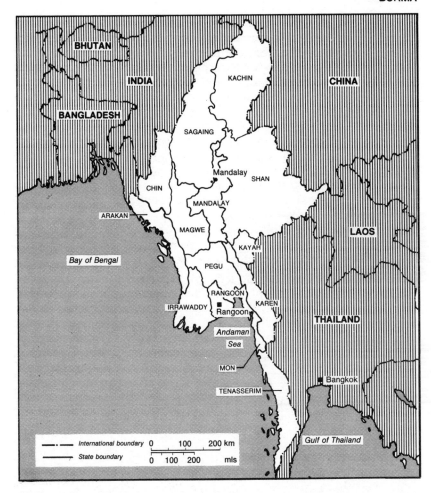

and, as the population grew, Burma's food surpluses declined, thus undermining foreign-exchange earnings. After a re-evaluation of the economy in the early 1970s, aid and borrowings (mainly soft loans) were again sought, and this boosted economic performance in the late 1970s and first two years of the 1980s. However, the early 1980s slump in world commodity prices, coinciding with the start of major debt repayments, saddled Burma with a growing debt service ratio, probably rising as high as 80% of exports by the beginning of 1988.

The collapse of both the domestic and international economic position of the government undermined the official economy. The growing black market, which had flourished in the face of great shortages of consumer goods from the mid-1960s onwards, provided a financing mechanism for the country's major insurgencies. While the BCP in the north and some of the various warlord bands in the Kachin and Shan

135

states thrived on the smuggling of opium into Thailand, the Karen National Union (KNU) and its armed forces, the Karen National Liberation Army (KNLA), financed itself entirely through this illegal border trade. Despite the military's stronger attempts in the 1980s to isolate and defeat the numerous insurgent groups which persist in the border regions, success has proved elusive.

By the middle of 1987 the economic crisis of the government was obvious. The debt service burden was becoming unmanageable, and even the limited amount of normal trade that Burma had officially conducted since the 1960s was becoming impossible. According to IMF figures, Burma's official foreign exports fell by 58% in the seven years between 1981 and 1987. In each year but one exports fell compared to the previous year – by as much as 65.9% in 1987. The collapse of export earnings then hit imports of increasingly scarce consumer goods as well as of industrial spares and raw materials, bringing domestic industrial production and transport almost to a halt. Total official imports fell by a massive 70.2% between 1981 and 1987. All this not only increased the incentives to black-market and smuggling activities, it also intensified inflationary pressures. At the same time, the government was starved for revenue and unable to improve salaries, as all available funds were being used to fund the military and to service the foreign debt. By the third quarter of 1987 Burma's reserves were barely sufficient to cover two weeks' trading, and servicing its debt, now over $US 4.0 bn, was proving impossible. The government was forced to appeal to the UN to be declared a 'least developed country', so as to qualify for softer financial arrangements with foreign donors. The autarkic goals of 1962 had turned Burma into a pauper nation.

Attempts to Stem the Tide
Faced with this massive financial crisis, BSPP Chairman Ne Win called an extraordinary meeting of government and Party officials in August 1987, when he tacitly admitted that the 25-year reconstruction that he and the army had undertaken was a complete failure. Officials were told that they had to reconsider all the government's and Party's policies and strategies, and the possibility of changes not only in economic policy but also in constitutional structure was mooted.

In September there followed the first of a series of economic changes which were probably intended to revive the economy, but which can be seen retrospectively as the beginning of the end of the Ne Win era. First, the government declared that the state monopoly of the official trade in rice, pulses and other primary crops was ended, and that private traders were to resume control of domestic trade. The possibility of private traders being involved in foreign trade was also suggested, but many obstacles were placed in the way, not least bureaucracy and a highly artificial official exchange rate – at least three times less than the black-market price for the national currency, the *kyat*.

Trade liberalization was initially hailed as a step towards a return to market forces in the economy and was expected to increase production, but the result – rampant inflation – was predictable. Prices rose steeply, and by July 1988 the price of rice in Rangoon had increased by 400% over the previous year. The final straw for the credibility of the government's economic policy came in September 1987, when higher-denomination bank notes were withdrawn from circulation. Although the government had done this twice before, presumably in unsuccessful attempts to squeeze the profits of black marketeers, on this occasion no compensation was provided. At the time a few students attempted to organize public demonstrations against the demonetization, but there was little other open public response. Nevertheless, it is safe to assume that public morale fell even further, and officials were able to devote less and less of their time to public duties as they sought to find a means to feed their families.

The Government Stumbles
As the economic crisis deepened the government appeared to do little more than tamper with the taxation system on the margins. In March, as an indication of growing public discontent, clashes between university students and townspeople broke out, and public protests increased in May and June, with conflicts between traders and consumers in a variety of towns throughout the country.

On 23 July a special meeting of the Central Committee of the BSPP was held, at which Chairman Ne Win announced his resignation and called for the Party to consider holding a referendum on whether the one-party system should continue. The Party, though accepting his resignation, rejected the call for a referendum, and for the next three days the political situation in the capital was very confused. On the 26th former General Sein Lwin, one of the Party's two joint Secretaries General, was declared Party Chairman. Dubbed 'the butcher of Rangoon', Sein Lwin's brief period in office saw widespread demonstrations and military and police repression, with reports of 1,000 or more killed throughout the country.

Sein Lwin was forced to resign on 12 August and was succeeded on 19 August by the only civilian figure in the upper reaches of the Party, Dr Maung Maung. Maung Maung attempted to calm the situation by making concessions to the demonstrators, including the ending of the one-party state, and promising eventual multi-party elections. But the demonstrators, now becoming better organized under the leadership of various political figures, mainly from the 1950s and 1960s, refused to believe the military's promises and demanded the establishment of an interim government. Though the bloodshed of the Sein Lwin period was over, political tensions remained high, and civil servants went on strike. On 18 September, unwilling to see the stalemate continue, the army – led by Minister of Defence Gen. Saw Maung – conducted a coup and, under the name of the Council for the Restoration of Law and Order in the State, abolished the 1974 constitution and took complete power. There followed several days of conflict and some additional shootings in the cities, as several thousands (perhaps as many as 10,000) students fled to the border areas in the hope of organizing an armed resistance against the military government.

During the three months of protests and repression in Rangoon and other major towns, the various insurgent organizations, despite their claims to the contrary, were unable to capitalize significantly on the military's political preoccupations. Though the insurgencies were briefly boosted by the addition of students to their ranks, insurgents and students became disillusioned with each other, and by November many of the latter were returning to the cities. The Thai government was very co-operative in helping the Burmese government organize a system for the reception and return of Burmese students who had fled over the border, and by the end of 1988 nearly 2,000 were back in the cities.

Relative Quiet, But . . .

Since the coup the military government has continued to promise to hold elections. By January 1989 at least 170 different political parties had registered with the government's election commission. New electoral rolls were being prepared but the prospect of serious early elections remained dim, since most of the parties – including the major grouping, the National League for Democracy (NLD), led by former general Tin U and Aung San Suu Kyi, daughter of Burma's national hero, Gen. Aung San – refused to accept elections held under the auspices of the current government. The inability of the civilian groups to organize effectively for elections was underscored in December 1988, when NLD President Aung Gyi, a former General and one of the 1962 coup makers, was voted out of the Party and then formed the United National Development Party (UNDP).

The BSPP itself had been renamed the National Unity Party and is preparing to compete in elections when they are held. A major change from past political practices is that military and civilian government officials are formally forbidden to participate in Party life. Though it seems likely that elections will be held in 1989, the result will be less important than the fact that, for the foreseeable future, the army will continue to determine the general direction of foreign and domestic policies. The campaigns against insurgents have continued in the border areas with increasing co-operation from neighbouring governments, but the most significant changes in domestic policies have come in the economic sphere, with the introduction of investment legislation giving foreign companies extremely good conditions for operations in Burma. Some major multinational firms have already expressed interest, though doubts remain about the bureaucratic and political obstacles that may lie ahead.

As a result of the harsh repression of student and other urban protests in 1988, major aid donors, led by Japan and West Germany, froze all their aid programmes in mid-1988 and have vowed not to resume assistance until elections are held and the government improves its human-rights record. The latter stipulation concerns not only an end to repression of the urban protests but also insistence that the army government come to some form of negotiated settlement with the ethnic insurgent bands on the border. Much of the criticism of Burma in the foreign press actually emerged before the mid-1988 disturbances, as a result of increasing political agitation by separatist groups and anti-government organizations (in the US and West Germany in particular) which had gained some hearing from foreign governments. Several highly critical reports on the army's human-rights record *vis-à-vis* the Karen, Shan and other rebels were published by Amnesty International during the year.

The effective semi-boycott of the government of Burma organized by Western governments during the latter part of 1988 was not endorsed by neighbouring governments. China, Thailand, Bangladesh, India, Singapore and South Korea, in particular, continued to encourage trade and other forms of co-operation with Rangoon. They are concerned that any further destabilization of Burmese domestic politics could result in an expansion of international disorder, which in turn could feed back into Burma to create a condition of civil war, such as occurred between 1948 and 1952. Civil war would then raise the prospect of the government becoming dependent upon one or more outside powers for support, thus upsetting the balance of power and interests in the region.

It must be remembered that, although Burma has not been at the centre of the world's attention for many years, it sits at the hub of several zones of conflict where South, South-east and East Asia meet. Being metaphorically the still centre around which Asian international politics rotate, Burma, and the continuation of its neutralist foreign policy, are essential for ensuring that a new zone of conflict does not emerge which could adversely affect the continent.

South and South-west Asia

AFGHANISTAN: TOWARDS AN ISLAMIC REPUBLIC

1988 was a decisive year in the Afghan war. Early in 1989 the Soviet
Union completed the withdrawal of its troops from Afghanistan without achieving its long-standing aim of securing a non-hostile regime in
charge in the country. This failure to assure its own basic interests was
due more to the overall diplomatic and political constraints which the
USSR had placed upon itself during 1988 than to the domestic situation
in Afghanistan. The military situation did not by itself require Soviet
troops to leave, but Mikhail Gorbachev, in his speech of 8 February
1988, had claimed that the resolution of the Afghan problem would provide a model for solving most of the world's regional problems, and he
had committed himself to a rigid timetable. This pedagogic approach
created a straitjacket for the Soviet Union; it found that it could no
longer react flexibly to events in the field and yet maintain the schedule
it had set. After this decision, time was on the *Mujaheddin*'s side, not
the Soviet Union's. When it transpired that the situation inside Afghanistan was worse than the USSR had assumed when signing the Geneva
Agreement on 14 April 1988, there was little it could do to rectify
matters.

The Agreement and the Withdrawal
The Soviet withdrawal adhered to the pattern established by Gorbachev
in his February 1988 speech and confirmed by the Geneva Agreement
in April: it was 'front-loaded' and rapid. The withdrawal began on 15
May; by 15 August half the Soviet troops in the country had returned to
the USSR. After a pause in the autumn of 1988, the withdrawal
resumed at the end of January 1989 and was completed on schedule by
15 February. But in fact, things did not go as smoothly as this chron-
ology makes it seem.

Gorbachev's 8 February speech was the public acknowledgment of a
decision that had been taken earlier, after preliminary informal discussions held with the US in the autumn of 1987; US Under-Secretary
of State Armacost and Soviet Foreign Minister Shevardnadze informed
their respective allies of the new developments in January 1988. But
when the negotiators met more formally, in March in Geneva, new
obstacles appeared: Washington refused to stop supplying weapons to
the *Mujaheddin* from the beginning of the withdrawal, as the Soviet
Union insisted, and Islamabad wanted a new regime in Kabul before
the withdrawal was completed.

It appears that in 1985, in informal discussions with UN negotiator
Diego Cordovez, the State Department had in fact agreed to stop sup-

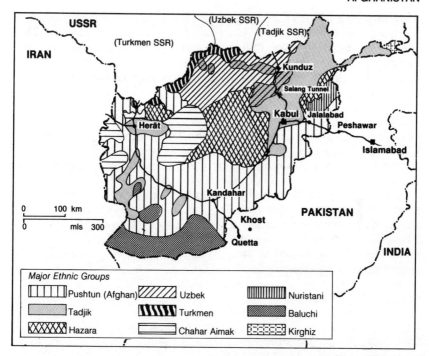

Major Ethnic Groups

Pushtun (Afghan)   Uzbek   Nuristani
Tadjik   Turkmen   Baluchi
Hazara   Chahar Aimak   Kirghiz

plying the *Mujaheddin* as soon as the Soviet Union began to withdraw, but this position was never officially endorsed. And the US Congress pre-empted any informal agreement on 1 March 1988, when it unanimously passed a resolution urging the Administration not to halt the supplies so long as Moscow did not stop supporting Kabul, even if the USSR were to withdraw its troops. After a month of negotiations in Geneva both sides dropped their demands for a commitment from the other to cease supplying its allies. Instead, Washington made a unilateral declaration pledging 'positive symmetry' – that is, it would halt supplies only when the Soviet Union did.

The Pakistani government justified its demand for a real political settlement before a complete withdrawal on the basis that a sudden Soviet pull-out would leave a dangerous political vacuum in Afghanistan. Neither Moscow, which argued that the Najibullah regime should maintain its supremacy, nor Washington, which was eager not to become too deeply involved in Afghan domestic politics, would agree to such a commitment. Except for some general and mutual pledges from Pakistan and Afghanistan not to interfere in each other's affairs (ineffective pledges, so long as both Moscow and Washington retain a right to support their allies directly), the only real accomplishment in the Geneva Agreement was a firm schedule for the Soviet withdrawal.

Under these circumstances, the Agreement could in no way be considered a Peace Treaty. Having established the conditions for a Soviet

141

withdrawal it left open the key question: who will run Afghanistan after the troops leave? Apparently both sides were willing to gamble. The USSR continued to hope that, with some continued assistance, the Kabul regime could survive; the US thought it would crumble very soon. The military balance between the regime and the *Mujaheddin* remained the ultimate arbiter.

The Course of the War
Soviet policy was two-fold: while committed to leave Afghanistan, the USSR attempted to strengthen the Kabul regime militarily and at the same time to create conditions for the emergence of a broad-based regime. The complete victory of the *Mujaheddin* would be a devastating defeat. Although Moscow had given up the idea that the 'April Revolution' was irreversible, it nonetheless thought the best way to ensure its strategic interest was to ensure that the People's Democratic Party of Afghanistan (PDPA) participated in a broad-based coalition government. It therefore moved to an unusual 'deconstruction of socialism'. Everything which characterized Afghanistan as a 'revolutionary' and 'progressive' state was eradicated, to such an extent that the USSR's so-called 'internationalist' duty to support a fledgling revolution no longer held any meaning. Relations between the Soviet Union and Afghanistan were redefined on a state-to-state (rather than Party-to-Party) basis to accord with the patterns of the last hundred years, with no reference to the 'April Revolution'.

This policy was a failure. No significant part of the population was attracted into the 'national reconciliation'. Instead the *Mujaheddin* went cautiously over to the offensive. In October 1988, confronted with the growing efficiency of the *Mujaheddin*, Moscow began to introduce new weapons into Afghanistan: MiG-27 fighter-bombers and *Scud* surface-to-surface missiles. But these deliveries were so obviously designed to convey a political message and were of such limited military value that they failed to produce any tangible effect.

When Soviet troops began to withdraw from the countryside, the government troops left with them, either because they were unable to resist *Mujaheddin* attacks without direct Soviet fire support or because they were needed to replace the departing Soviet troops in the more sensitive areas – that is in the large cities. Dozens of outposts and small bases were abandoned, most of them in the south and in border areas. In August the situation deteriorated badly for government forces, when the first provincial capitals fell into *Mujaheddin* hands: Bamyan, Taloqan (Takhar) and Kunduz, followed in November by Chaghasaray (or Assadabad, in Kunar). The Soviet Union decided to sacrifice the small towns (some provincial capitals are in fact merely bazaars) but to prevent at all costs the loss of the big cities. It used heavy retaliatory bombardments and artillery shellings to deter the *Mujaheddin* from attack. Kunduz was retaken with heavy civilian losses one week after its fall, and the *Mujaheddin* were kept out of Kandahar and Herat by these tactics. The defence of Khost and Jalalabad was easier for the government, for it had many more supporters in those areas. By the end of 1988, a new military balance was thus established, but the regime's lines of defence had shrunk considerably.

The *Mujaheddin* continued to bring in arms from Pakistan. New weapons were introduced, like the Franco-German *Milan* anti-tank missile, but the *Stinger* anti-aircraft missiles no longer played the decisive role they had when they were first introduced. Soviet pilots had learned new tactics and used new decoys: the more vulnerable Mi-24 helicopters were no longer used over the battlefield, while fighter-bombers would cruise at high altitude before diving suddenly. The consequent lack of precision was partially offset by the use of laser-guided bombs. Nevertheless, Soviet troops kept mostly to a purely defensive stance.

In fact, except in the north-eastern areas controlled by Ahmad Shah Massoud, most of the cities which fell into *Mujaheddin* hands were not taken by assault but were occupied after being abandoned. The *Mujaheddin* still lack both heavy weapons and the tactical skill necessary to take well-defended objectives. These military limitations have been reinforced by the political divisions within the resistance. Every offensive has to be discussed and agreed by all the political parties involved in the local battlefield. Without this precaution, ignored groups could easily jeopardize actions taken by the others. Another consideration, more purely political, is that most of the *Mujaheddin* commanders are reluctant to take a decisive military step which will bring to the forefront the very difficult question of political power.

Most of the *Mujaheddin* commanders were, and still are, obsessed by the shadow of civil war, even if there had been no evidence of an increase of internecine feuding during 1988. In order to avoid the possibility of an outbreak of civil war, most commanders seem more eager to maintain the delicate balance of power which exists than to rush forwards. Their strategy has not been to race to Kabul but, before every military move, to ensure that they could assume the political responsibilities which a military victory would entail. They have preferred to avoid pitched battles by slowly strangling the cities and disrupting lines of communication, thus increasing insecurity within the cities and destabilizing the government. During the summer of 1988 both the number of car-bomb explosions and surface-to-surface missile attacks increased, and the economic situation in Kabul seriously worsened, forcing the Soviet Union to establish an airlift to bring in supplies. Even without pitched battles, the cost to the USSR mounted.

Political Developments
The Kabul government's response to the Soviet withdrawal was to try to establish an orthodox hard-core while opening the regime to other groups, without ideological or even political requirements. Under the policy of 'national reconciliation' the PDPA had tried to enlarge its sup-

port while maintaining a grip on all facets of the government. Now it was simply trying to buy time and avoid an immediate *Mujaheddin* victory. The strategy was two-fold: to prevent the fall of Kabul for as long as possible and to drop all that made the regime unacceptable (one-party rule, secularism, references to socialism and Communism, as well as the presence of Soviet troops). The Party hoped that the permanence of a military stalemate would soon seem unbearable to many of the *Mujaheddin* and to Pakistan, since the motivation of fighting a Communist regime and a foreign invasion would have disappeared.

This 'deconstruction of socialism' had in fact begun in 1987. It was characterized by the proclamation of Islam as the state religion, the authorization of other political parties, the appointment of a non-party figure, Hassan Sharq, as Prime Minister in June 1988, the demotion of hard-liners and the promotion of non-PDPA members. To achieve these aims, however, President Najibullah was forced to dump the orthodox hard-core of the PDPA's *Khalq* faction, which opposed any concession, believed that the *Mujaheddin* could be resisted after a Soviet withdrawal and considered the avowed renunciation of revolutionary rhetoric as unnecessary treason. Thus he sent the *Khalqi* leader, Minister of Interior Gulabzoy, to Moscow as ambassador, and at the Party's October Plenum engineered the demotion of a large number of *Khalqi* radicals. However, this turn against the hard-liners was not accompanied by the creation of new well-trained troops. Rumours that a *coup d'état* would be mounted against Najibullah after the Soviet troops departed spread through Kabul during the winter.

The new open policy of the regime was based on the incorrect assumption that it would be acceptable to the population, because of its weariness with war, and to the *Mujaheddin* commanders, because it gave them much without the necessity of fighting on. But no more than 100,000 refugees returned to Afghanistan in 1988, no *Mujaheddin* commander agreed to a settlement with the government, even on a local basis (Massoud, who was said to have agreed a cease-fire with the Soviet Union, took a provincial capital, Taloqan, during the so-called cease-fire), and the Peshawar Alliance remained adamant in its refusal to agree to any coalition government which included the PDPA.

Soviet–Mujaheddin Relations

Although it tried, the Soviet Union was unable to play upon the real divisions which exist among the *Mujaheddin* (between local commanders and the Peshawar parties, between Shi'ites and Sunnis, between ethnic groups, between moderates and fundamentalists). The local commanders, after fighting for ten years, were not interested in giving up their hard-won expectations for a token share in a PDPA-led government, and anyone prepared to make a deal with Kabul would be sacrificing any hope of a political future. Even the Shi'ites were advised by Tehran in December 1988 to work out a deal with the Sunni majority. The death of Pakistan's leader, Gen. Zia, in August reinforced cohesion among the *Mujaheddin* by reducing the status of his favourite among them, the most radical leader, Gulbuddin Hekmetyar. The moderates in the resistance, who had been considering making a deal with the Soviet Union in order to prevent Hekmetyar from coming to power, now lost that fear. Although the convergence among the *Mujaheddin* was a negative one, built on an agreement that there should be no sharing of power with the PDPA, it was strong enough to limit the effectiveness of Soviet manoeuvring.

Failure to attract a part of the *Mujaheddin* forces obliged Moscow to accept direct negotiations with them. In October, Deputy Minister for Foreign Affairs Vorontsov was appointed ambassador to Kabul. After trying unsuccessfully to meet secretly with Rabbani, leader of the Sunni *Jamiat-i-Islami*, he agreed to meet him in Taif, Saudi Arabia, as head of a delegation of the Peshawar-based alliance of seven *Mujaheddin* factions; the *Mujaheddin* looked upon this meeting as a political victory. The Soviet aim now was to create a political settlement in Kabul, and one which would include both the PDPA and the *Mujaheddin*. This was in sharp contrast with Moscow's attitude at the Geneva conference, where it had been Pakistan that was urging the establishment of a coalition government in Kabul. It is not clear whether Moscow was just trying to save face or whether it really believed it could maintain a place for the PDPA in a future government. Even with Pérez de Cuéllar, the UN negotiator at the conference, favouring a coalition government in Kabul under the leadership of the former King Zaher, it is obvious that in the long run the *Mujaheddin* will not share power with the PDPA.

The US Role
Washington remained strongly committed to supporting the *Mujaheddin* even after the Geneva Agreement (belying the doubts raised in Congress by many conservatives, who expressed their concern in a Congressional Resolution urging the Administration to remain steadfast). Not only did the US not stop the supply of weapons (with the exception of *Stinger* missiles for a short period in the spring of 1988), but it continued to insist on the necessity for the Soviet Union to respect the withdrawal schedule, and it refused to pressure the *Mujaheddin* into accepting any face-saving agreement for the Soviet Union.

The only noticeable change in US policy concerned its attitude towards Gulbuddin Hekmetyar, head of the *Hezb-i Islami* party, who had been the main beneficiary of US supplies. The official explanation for supporting him had been that he was the best commander (or at least the worst for the Soviet Union) and that he was Pakistan's choice – and Washington was very eager to grant Pakistan a primary role in the daily management of the resistance. The first assumption was obviously wrong, and it soon proved that Hekmetyar could be more dangerous than helpful: he was responsible for most of the clashes between *Mujaheddin* groups, and there is also strong evidence that his group sold *Stinger* to Iran. In July 1988 the US embassy in Islamabad began to put some pressure on the Pakistani government to reduce the share of arms going to Hekmetyar.

Pakistani and Iranian Perspectives

Gen. Zia's sudden death was not necessarily linked with the Afghan conflict. The USSR did not reduce its pressure on the Pakistan border area, as if it knew that there would be no new Afghan policy in Islamabad. In fact, the continuity of that policy was stressed by Benazir Bhutto: the two men who had been in charge of it (Gen. Hamid Gul of the Inter-services Intelligence and Yaqub Khan, Minister of Foreign Affairs) remained in charge. This continuity could easily be explained in terms of the strategic constraints on Pakistan.

Yet Pakistan seemed also to have reduced its ambitions. At the time of Zia's death the Pakistani army seemed to have been betting on a quick military victory by the *Mujaheddin*. Zia's great design was to see a fundamentalist regime in power in Kabul and to create a 'Muslim belt' south of the Soviet Union and west of India, thus revitalizing the old CENTO pact, but with a purely Muslim colour. But Benazir Bhutto's government seemed more concerned with ensuring that there would be stability in Afghanistan, which would allow the refugees in Pakistan to go home, than with creating a grand design.

Paradoxically, it was now Iran that was supporting Gen. Zia's grand design of a 'Muslim belt', but its aim was to prevent a return of the US influence into the area after the Soviet withdrawal. Since the beginning of the war, Iran's policy had been to adopt a low profile as far as the USSR was concerned, while strengthening its influence among the Shi'ites, using them as leverage to retain some influence in Afghanistan. But in 1988 Tehran realized that its effort to export its Islamic revolution had been a failure. Minister of Foreign Affairs Velayati, in particular, drew significant conclusions from this failure and from the end of the Gulf War. He decided not to link Iranian influence solely to the local Shi'ite minorities, but to join the diplomatic process in collaboration with Pakistan. In the autumn of 1988 Tehran stopped its severe criticism of the Geneva Agreement and also dropped its appeal to the *Mujaheddin* to fight for the establishment of a true Islamic Republic by shifting their base from Pakistan to Iran. Velayati pushed the Shi'ite alliance of eight parties, based in Tehran, to join with the Peshawar-based 'Seven Alliance'. Rabbani, head of the Sunni *Jamiat-i-Islami* was warmly welcomed in Tehran, and on 15/16 January 1989 a conference of both Alliances, held in Tehran under the auspices of Velayati, made this new policy official.

There was opposition within Iran to the new policy. The radicals, spearheaded by Minister of Interior Mohtashemi, still considered Afghanistan as Iran's backyard and had not given up the idea of using the Shi'ites as the main tool for extending Iranian influence. But most of the Afghan Shi'ites themselves favoured Velayati's policy, and they were not backing an 'Islamic Revolution'. Iran's re-entry into the negotiating process deprived the USSR of the possibility of playing Iran off against Pakistan, and the Shi'ites against the Sunnis, as Soviet negotiator Vorontsov tried to do when he visited Tehran early in 1989.

The Mujaheddin and the Prospects for Power

Time is now working very much for the Afghan resistance, which is not eager to make a political deal with either the Soviet Union or the Kabul regime, but is more concerned with finding a way to deal with both the traditional segmentation of Afghan society and the new political segmentation which resulted from the creation of the seven Sunni and eight Shi'ite parties. There is an absolute incompatibility between the *Mujaheddin*'s Islamic beliefs and any secular government, even if that government gives up all references to Marxism. The Communist regime is doomed to disappear, even if it takes some months after the Soviet forces pull out completely. Talk of a settlement based on a coalition government including some Communists is linked to external pressure from Pakistan and the UN, but, even if such a government could be put together, it would not last.

The strategic dimension has shifted from an East–West context back to a regional one. With a nominal Islamic *Mujaheddin* government in Kabul, Afghanistan could be considered stable, even if the countryside is disrupted by local conflicts. Only if these local conflicts take either an ideological form (fundamentalists versus moderates) or an ethnic form (Pushtuns supported by Pakistan and Shi'ites by Iran, for example) would Afghanistan develop a potential for destroying regional stability. But at the moment that looks unlikely to happen.

Among the *Mujaheddin* the conflict is not so much between 'fundamentalists' and 'moderates' as between ethnic groups. The Pushtun tribesmen who are supposed to adhere to the 'moderate' parties are in fact as 'fundamentalist' as the northern people, at least as far as everyday life is concerned. The next regime will probably be a conservative and puritan Islamic Republic, even if it might be headed by the former King. Part of the problem now is how to assure the legitimacy of any new government, and this is put more in ethnic terms than in constitutional ones. The 'moderates' advocate a *jirga*, the 'fundamentalists' want a *shura*: both define this entity as an elected assembly, but *jirga*, a Pushtun word, refers to a traditional tribal assembly of notables, while the term *shura* implies that its members have a religious legitimacy. Will the next regime remain tribal and Pushtun? Will it embody the power of the notables or that of the local commanders, most of them new men, without traditional legitimacy? Thus, beyond the ideological opposition of 'moderate' and 'fundamentalist', there is an ethnic conflict and a generation gap.

The war has brought about a new balance in Afghanistan, and the Pushtuns have ceased to be the obvious legitimate power. But this shift can in itself be the source of new tensions. The weight of the Pushtuns may have diminished, due partly to emigration and changes in the leadership, but their pretensions have not. Yet these pretensions do not have a political outlet; in fact, there is no party within the resistance whose *raison d'être* is the single issue of ethnicity, even if ethnic identity does play a role in political affiliation. Paradoxically, the establishment of modern political party structures in Afghanistan could result in either of two outcomes: it could bypass the traditional segmentation (as has happened in the north-east), or (as in the centre north) it could give a new boost to intra-political, intra-ethnic and even intra-tribal segmentation.

A civil war in Afghanistan soon, based on ethnic affiliations appears unlikely, because ethnic conflict can be expected only at the local or regional level. The most probable outcome is a coalition *Mujaheddin* government in Kabul, but one that is weak and ineffective because it will have to reach a consensus on every issue. In the countryside there will be a mosaic of power, made up in part of large political units (under Massoud, for example, or Ismail Khan), in part of loose tribal confederations (in Kandahar), in part of areas plunged into anarchy due to local feuds (as in the centre north). Patchy as this sounds, it could still provide an equilibrium stable enough to maintain a regional stability which would not provoke foreign intervention and would allow Afghanistan to regain its historical status as a buffer state.

PAKISTAN AFTER ZIA

The death of General Zia ul-Haq in a mysterious air crash on 17 August 1988, and the phoenix-like ascension of former Prime Minister Zulfiqar Ali Bhutto's Pakistan People's Party (PPP), under his daughter Benazir, transformed many of the accepted notions governing Pakistan's domestic and regional environment. The General's demise opened up dramatic possibilities for political liberalization; power was transferred to a civilian regime peacefully and in accordance with the constitution for the first time since 1971; and 35-year-old Benazir Bhutto became the first woman leader in the modern history of any Muslim nation. Contrary to what Zia had always claimed, Pakistan's electorate demonstrated its readiness for democracy, for free and fair elections. The new, however, co-existed with the old. The tumultuous events of 1988 brought home once again the pivotal role played by personalities and by civil–military relations in shaping Pakistan's politics.

Zia's Legacy
General Zia, like his military predecessors in power, had little respect for civilian politicians. Their inability to negotiate peacefully with one another, he felt, endangered Pakistan and Islam. Although he paid lip service to democracy, he argued that it was Islam that should form the source of laws and govern the rules of public discourse, not Western,

secular ideas of parliamentary democracy. Islamic courts should test the conformity of the legal rules of the land to sacred texts and mete out Islamic punishments. During his eleven-and-a-half years in power – the longest tenure of any Pakistani leader – Zia, who retained his title of Army Chief of Staff, symbolized the unification of army and state.

He sought to bring about conservative-oriented social and political change, first under martial law and, after 1984, through a joint military/civilian enterprise, the result of a referendum on Islamization which also awarded him the Presidency and of non-party elections in 1985. His experiment in joint rule failed. When his hand-picked Prime Minister, Mohammed Khan Junejo, became too independent, particularly about foreign and military policy matters (such as the signing of the Geneva Agreement on Afghanistan and the investigation of the accident at the Ojhri ammunition depot near Islamabad, in which thousands died), Zia accused the politicians of corruption and mismanagement, fired Junejo and dissolved the Parliament on 29 May 1988. A caretaker cabinet was installed, and 16 November was announced as the date for new, presumably non-party, elections.

By 1988 Pakistan was a country at war with itself. Zia's successes were few. Despite years of good harvests, unprecedented infusions of US economic and military aid and remittances from migrant workers in the Middle East, Pakistan's economy was weakening. The country was tormented by ethnic fratricide and by the spin-offs of the Afghan war next door: air raids and acts of sabotage, the spread of heroin and arms, and friction between Afghan refugees and the local population.

A Triumph for Democracy

The military man's promise of elections was never tested. His death freed Pakistan's other institutions – the judiciary and the political parties – to act. A senior civil servant and Senate leader, Ghulam Ishaq Khan, took over as Acting President and successfully guided Pakistan through free elections and a constitutional transfer of power. The once-moribund judiciary quickly handed down a series of judgments vital for the restoration of democracy. As a result of its verdicts, party-based elections – the first since 1977 – could proceed.

In the November elections, platforms and promises seemed hardly the issue. Benazir Bhutto opposed nationalization, advocated good relations with the US, continuation of Zia's policies on Afghanistan, and a strong defence. Her principal opponent, Nawaz Sharif of the *Islamic Jamhoori Ittehad* (IJI), the representative of 'Ziaism', advocated much the same. Strictly speaking, even parties were not at issue as, in a 'bandwagon' effect, hundreds of old-style politicos flocked to join the PPP, the party most likely to win. The PPP which ran in 1988 was a motley band of old stalwarts, young radicals, feudal leaders and traditional power-brokers. In this election it was cults of personality and interpretations of history which mattered. When the results were in, they revealed a divided electorate, but with the larger proportion favouring the political resonance of the Bhutto name.

Pakistanis made eager and discriminating choices in the 1988 elections. They voted out politicians with bad records, military men of any party, and numerous feudal chieftains, religious right-wingers and extreme left-wingers. Although it did not win either a national majority or a majority in every province, the PPP did emerge as the strongest single party, winning 94 of the 205 national seats, as well as showing a presence in all four provinces. On 2 December, after consultations with political and military leaders, Ghulam Ishaq Khan invited Benazir Bhutto and the PPP to form a government.

Outstanding Problems

Key messages of the 1988 elections relate to centre/province and inter-ethnic relations, Pakistan's deepest and most deadly problems. Each regime since Independence has had to face the dissent of a particular province. Generals Ayub Khan and Yahya Khan dealt with the dissatisfaction, and ultimately the secession, of East Pakistan. Bhutto's bête noire was Baluchistan, where he deployed nearly 80,000 troops against an insurgency during 1973–7. Under Zia, Sind was the most fractious province, plagued by a sense of political and economic inequity, by bloody ethnic wars (in which thousands have died) between muhajirs (immigrants from India, whose newly-formed group, the Muhajir Qaumi Mahaz or MQM, now controls the powerful city of Karachi), militant Sindi 'sons of the soil', and others, including migrant Pathans and Punjabis. It also suffered from an increasing death toll resulting from the spread of guns and drugs, dacoits (rural bandits) and the continuing presence of army garrisons. The PPP, along with the MQM, swept the seats of Sind. All IJI candidates were defeated. In 1988 Sind's message was that only under a Bhutto, herself a charismatic Sindi, was it prepared to give all-Pakistan mainstream politics another chance.

The new provincial government of Sind is a coalition between the PPP and the MQM. Even here, however, difficult problems await Bhutto. The woes of the province are complex, the central government's coffers are empty, and the carefully negotiated PPP-MQM power-sharing agreement is tenuous. Only days after her assumption of office, ethnic violence returned to Karachi. The new Prime Minister believes that Sind's crises are the 'scars' of unrepresentative, military rule and that the solutions lie with democratic government. But whether the new political partnership will be able to bring peace and prosperity to this southern province is still in grave doubt.

Bhutto's initial relations with the opposition have been confrontational. Within two weeks of her nomination a mini-constitutional crisis broke out in Baluchistan, where the PPP is weakest. In a controversial move the assembly was dissolved by the Governor, who then called for new provincial elections. The opposition charged that Bhutto had prior knowledge of the event and had played foul. The Prime Minister denied the charge.

And in Punjab, Pakistan's most powerful, populous and prosperous province (and home to much of the army), the PPP was defeated by the army's choice, the IJI, and the two parties' leaders have already locked horns. The new Chief Minister of the Punjab is the young Punjabi industrialist Nawaz Sharif, Bhutto's principal opponent in the electoral battle and the bearer of Zia's message and mantle. To counter the IJI 'Bhutto named a PPP loyalist and retired general, Tikka Khan, as governor. A hostile opposition government in the Punjab weakens the centre and makes for an unsteady apportionment of powers. Bhutto's unhappiness with this state of affairs has been palpable. Yet Pakistan's political stability will depend in large part upon the ability of the centre to negotiate new forms of accommodation with the Punjab government and a genuine devolution of powers to the smaller provinces, as well as upon the restraint of the IJI over stirring up anti-centre, anti-Bhutto sentiment.

Despite the opposition of Islamizers in the IJI and the religious establishment (who publicly protested that the appointment of a woman as head of government was repugnant to Islam), Benazir Bhutto took the oath of office in a moving ceremony on 2 December 1988 as Pakistan's, and the Muslim world's, first constitutionally-elected female leader and one of the world's youngest Prime Ministers. While the euphoria of Pakistanis about the beginning of a new era gives her some freedom for manoeuvre, the expectations of Bhutto's supporters are high – as is the scepticism of her opponents. Her government has few funds, and she is constrained by the enduring reality of the army's influence and interests in the political arena. She has pledged herself to promote costly programmes of employment, education and health, to reduce drugs and guns, to free the press and political prisoners, to cancel all laws prejudicial to women, and to restore labour and student unions. Yet she has inherited a straitened economy, meagre foreign-exchange reserves, an agriculture damaged by floods, and an agreement with the IMF to impose austerity measures across Pakistan in return for a three-year, $US 1-bn loan.

Bhutto's Enduring Opposition
Benazir Bhutto faces both a weaker civilian mandate and a stronger army than did her father. He swept the vote at a time when Pakistan's army was humiliated by the debacle in Bangladesh, and he was able to trifle with, and then ban, opposition parties in the North West Frontier Province (NWFP) and Baluchistan, secure passage of the 1973 Constitution and partially reorganize the army's top brass. Despite this, Zulfiqar Ali Bhutto was toppled by General Zia in the summer of 1977, after opposition allegations about rigged elections led to mass civilian unrest. Following a controversial court verdict he was hanged in April 1979 for conspiring to kill a political opponent. Benazir Bhutto's disadvantages of power, especially in relation to the army, are evident. She is

151

also circumscribed by Ghulam Ishaq Khan, now President of Pakistan, with whom the army is comfortable and who possesses broad powers to override the Prime Minister under the terms of the Eighth Amendment to the Constitution, passed under Zia. One of her ambitions is to rid herself of this rankling amendment.

The results of the 1988 elections were finally sufficient to convince the army to return to the barracks, but they do not necessarily signify a conclusive return to civilian political control. Bhutto gained the premiership only after Gen. Aslam Beg, the new Chief of Army Staff, assented (and his fundamentalist views on defence and foreign policy – on Afghanistan, India and the United States – are unlikely to be easily overridden). She will need masterly political acumen, restraint over policies dear to the army, and the ability to negotiate with opponents in the civilian arena if she is to keep the army in its barracks.

Given her domestic societal and political vulnerabilities, Bhutto must clearly function within an Islamic framework. This could also help to soothe the anxieties of Pakistan's conservative and revolutionary Islamic neighbours and friends, particularly Iran and Saudi Arabia. The Saudi authorities, champions of Zia and Islamization, do not accept a woman as the head of a Muslim government. Yet Bhutto's politics and her mandate are undoubtedly secular. 'Top-down Islamization', which was Zia's principal vehicle of legitimacy and of social change, is not likely to make great advances in her time. Yet Bhutto is constrained in rescinding all that the mullahs have wrought; she has said she will repeal Islamic laws prejudicial to women, while simultaneously avowing that she will function within Islamic law.

A Changing Foreign Scene

Pakistan's present situation is remarkable because the sudden, dramatic liberalization of the domestic political environment is paralleled by a notable fluidity in the regional sphere. The Soviet presence in Afghanistan – the central determinant of Pakistan's foreign relations during the 1980s, defining its ties with the US and the Soviet Union and making its relations with India more contentious – has been withdrawn. As a result, all these relationships can be expected to change. Pakistan has already indicated its desire to improve diplomatic, political and economic ties with the USSR; as US–Soviet relations continue to improve, as other neighbours – Iran and China (Pakistan's firmest ally) – enhance their links with the Soviet Union, and as India continues to have close ties with Moscow, Pakistan feels that it cannot stand isolated from global and regional detente.

So far, however, Bhutto has promised simply a 'continuity' of policy towards Afghanistan. Until a more friendly government is established there, the interests of the army and traditional Pakistani concerns remain paramount. Standard promises to observe the April 1988 Geneva Agreement – as well as to maintain Pakistan's role as a conduit for weapons supplied to the Afghan *Mujaheddin* and to see a representative government installed in Kabul – have been repeated by the PPP government. And direct talks with the Communist regime of Najibullah in Kabul have been ruled out. Unlike Zia, Bhutto and the PPP are not admirers of the Afghan *Mujaheddin* and have publicly voiced their especially low regard for Zia's favourite freedom fighter, the fundamentalist *Hezb-i-Islami* leader, Gulbuddin Hekmetyar, who previously received more than half of the foreign funds and supplies allocated to the *Mujaheddin*. Nevertheless, on 23 February, Pakistan aided the creation of an Afghan interim government in which Hekmetyar acquired the powerful ministries of Defence and Agriculture.

If the conflict in Afghanistan continues Bhutto's main concern will be with the safe (and, most important, speedy) repatriation of the approximately 3.4 million Afghan refugees in Pakistan. Housed mainly in tented villages and refugee camps in the NWFP and Baluchistan, these refugees are an economic burden on the government and a source of controversy and discontent across Pakistan. Their presence has been blamed for the air-raids from Afghanistan, for daily cross-border violence and acts of sabotage which Pakistanis must endure, for the spread of weapons and narcotics, for competition with locals for pastureland, firewood, rights of passage and jobs, for the high pitch of ethnic conflicts and for interference in local politics. Popular sentiment increasingly advocates their repatriation. In the 1988 elections the PPP argued that Zia's supporters would use the refugees to cast illegal votes, and for the first time they were confined to their camps and barred from entering the cities and towns of Pakistan. The uncertain and painful process of repatriation, however, involves considerations beyond Pakistan's control: inter-Afghan relations and the restoration of physical security and agricultural and irrigation infrastructure inside Afghanistan will be the factors which determine the method and financing of the Afghan return.

The Soviet withdrawal from Afghanistan will modify US interests in the area, leaving Pakistan to contend more independently with the consequences of a continuing inter-Afghan conflict. The shift in American policy, combined with US budget constraints, could lead to cuts in US military and economic aid to Pakistan. It will be hard to justify further $US 4.2-bn aid packages to the Congress. The issues of nuclear non-proliferation and the narcotics trade are also likely to re-emerge to complicate the US–Pakistani agenda.

Bhutto, however, has certain assets in the US Congress which Zia could never muster. She symbolizes the struggle for a successful return to democracy in Pakistan, and, like US President George Bush, she has declared a war on drugs. With her present pro-Western stance, and with Pakistan's economy deteriorating, Bhutto is clearly interested in maintaining strong ties to the US. However, she will probably prefer to shift the emphasis of the aid relationship away from military assistance towards economic and other transactions. Pakistan's location also retains strategic meaning for the US Central Command. All these factors suggest that a much-desired honeymoon between Benazir and Congress could result.

This is not to suggest that the deeper and more difficult issues in US–Pakistani relations will disappear. Under the protective umbrella of the Afghan conflict Zia successfully gained from the US more than $US 7 bn in aid, as well as the turning of a blind eye towards Pakistan's enrichment of uranium. Addressing her first press conference, Bhutto indicated that she would like to slow down the country's nuclear programme. She reportedly said that her government's nuclear policy would be 'weapons-free': 'We do not want any doubt to cloud the issue and isolate Pakistan'. Elsewhere she has suggested that she would permit 'inspection' of facilities. Regardless of her own views, Bhutto will face pressures to continue the programme as in the past, for pro-nuclear forces include members of the opposition and the army, influential policy-makers and experts, and national public opinion, which supports an overt nuclear capability. She will have to be sitting much more firmly in her seat to effect radical changes in this and other sensitive policy areas.

As ties to the international powers are subject to modification, so too is Pakistan's central relationship with the South Asian regional power, India. Although Zia carefully averted a major conflagration with India (a mini-war continues along the northern Siachen Glacier), his relations with India were unsteady. Within weeks of taking office, however, Bhutto repeated her desire for a new, less 'tense' involvement with India. She suggested that, since she and Rajiv Gandhi are both members of the post-partition generation, the possibilities for a personal and political South Asian dialogue are measurably better than under Zia. All Zia's public protestations of goodwill towards India had fallen on deaf ears; they were suspect. But Bhutto's is a democratic voice, and Indians, too, have been swept up in her victory.

In the face of a disheartening history of hostile Indo-Pakistani relations, Bhutto is trying to navigate a smoother course with India. Zia's death, the Soviet departure from Afghanistan and Bhutto's own expressions on subjects of pressing concern to India – Pakistan's nuclear programme, its alleged involvement in supplying and training of Sikh terrorists in the Indian Punjab (she has said firmly that Pakistan will not interfere in India's internal affairs), and the 'no-war' pact which Zia had touted (she, like Rajiv, prefers the 1972 Simla Accord signed by their parents as the proper framework for bilateral relations) – have created a thaw in a relationship marked most often by suspicion and war. Bhutto made use of the opportunity presented by the fourth summit of the South Asian Association for Regional Co-operation, held in Islamabad in January 1989, to welcome Rajiv Gandhi and to finalize and sign formal accords (arranged earlier) for the first time in sixteen years. These included agreements not to attack each others' nuclear facilities, to increase cultural co-operation and to avoid double taxation on the income from air transportation. These are all good beginnings. Whether they truly mark a new phase in this structurally volatile relationship remains to be seen; the anti-Indian stance of IJI leaders has already forced her regime to reiterate that Kashmir and Siachen remain outstanding problems in relations with India.

Prospects

Although Benazir Bhutto's popular mandate is for change, the old political, bureaucratic and military infrastructure demands continuity. But, chastened by the demonstration of democracy and reassured by Bhutto's lavish praise of the army, the military seems for the moment willing to give civilian politics a chance. It is Pakistan's deteriorating economy that will be the new government's biggest challenge and Bhutto's greatest handicap. She has promised much, but she has no funds in hand and faces a hostile opposition, an army waiting in the wings and, perhaps most importantly, the highest expectations of the people. In the coming year she will have the hazardous task of stewarding an embattled country in a rapidly changing external environment. It has still to be seen whether she can emerge from her father's and the army's shadows and place her own unique stamp upon the political history of Pakistan.

The Middle East

There was a marked reversal of trends in the Middle East during 1988. The previous years' preoccupation with the Iran–Iraq War ended (as did the war), though not before it had bequeathed a new preoccupation with non-conventional weaponry. The Palestinian issue, once again dominant, moved the PLO and the super-powers to centre stage, and King Hussein of Jordan, who by late 1987 had become the pre-eminent inter-Arab player by orchestrating Arab support for Iraq, now beat a strategic retreat into relative passivity. Egypt regained its position as a member of the Arab world. And, for the first time in years of confronting Palestinian nationalism, Israel lost the initiative.

In Lebanon, which had been disintegrating slowly for over ten years, the situation took a rapid turn for the worse in the autumn of 1988. In September a sharply divided and depleted Lebanese parliament failed to elect a new President to replace the outgoing Amin Gemayel, leaving the country without a chief executive, but with two competing governments. The government left over from the Gemayel regime was led by the veteran Sunni Muslim politician Salim Hoss. A second administration, a military caretaker government appointed by Gemayel before he left office, was headed by the army chief-of-staff, Gen. Michel Aoun, a Maronite Christian. Neither government presided over more than a few square kilometres of Beirut.

The factional strife in Lebanon continued to slip and slide, kaleidoscope fashion. Syria moved to expand its deployment in Beirut and cement alliances with the Shi'ite *Amal*, the anti-Arafat *Fatah* rebels and the Druze. The last, led effectively by Walid Jumblatt, fortified themselves in a semi-independent canton in the Chouf mountains. Another faction was led by the Maronites, whose enclave also increasingly resembled a semi-independent canton (their Lebanese Forces militia reacted to the collapse of the presidency by swallowing up Gemayel's 2,000-strong personal Falange militia and placing him under house arrest). They were supported by a curious coalition of anti-Syrian forces that included Arafat's PLO and Iraq. A third faction consisted of Iran and its Lebanese Shi'ite proxy, *Hizbollah* – its status 'enhanced' by its nebulous control over some 20 US and European hostages.

Iraq's entry into the Lebanese fray – on the side of anyone that opposed Syria – was the major inter-Arab event of 1988 in the Lebanese arena. The most significant development, though, appeared to be the increasing disintegration of the remnants of constitutional control, coupled with the corresponding evolution of a canton-like structure. While this offered little political or economic security for most Lebanese, it did seem to suggest the possibility of a tolerable form of stability amidst the chaos.

If a tolerable form of stability also replaced the chaos of the Gulf War during 1988, there was not much room for hope of a comparable solution to the continuing Palestinian uprising in the West Bank and Gaza. Yet there was a sense that both Israel and the PLO, with support from the moderate Arab states, would need to discover an answer to their continuing conflict if they were not to find themselves losing control of the Palestinians in the occupied territories.

ISRAEL AND THE PLO: YEAR OF THE INTIFADA

The dramatic changes brought about by a year of *intifada* (the Palestinian uprising in the West Bank and Gaza) are perhaps best illustrated by the striking contrast between the totally abortive initiative with which US Secretary of State Shultz began 1988 and the opening of a US–PLO dialogue with which he ended it. What happened in between involved a complex interaction between the dynamic of the *intifada*, and Israeli, Jordanian, PLO and American reactions to it.

By the end of February 1989, after 14 months of the uprising, even official Israeli statistics (which outside observers generally consider undercount events somewhat) described a heavy toll in civil conflict: over 360 Palestinians killed, 7–8,000 wounded, a total of 22,000 arrested, of whom an average of 6,000 – one third of them administrative detainees – were under detention at any given time. The day-to-day scenario of Palestinian–Israeli clashes was made up largely of stone- and petrol-bomb-throwing incidents against Israel Defence Force (IDF) troops and Israeli settlers, and the barricading of roads. The Palestinians successfully restricted their struggle to means that the world would applaud and that the IDF would be hard put to counter by conventional means: by late February 1989 fewer than 20 attacks on Israelis by Palestinians using firearms had been recorded, and only two IDF soldiers and a handful of civilian settlers had been killed.

Intimidation of Arab collaborators by Palestinians was more frequent. The uprising's leadership inside the territories and in the PLO abroad sought to foster self-reliance among the Palestinians of the occupied territories by cutting institutional ties with Israeli authority. Thus leaflets called for Arab policemen and administrators to resign (most did); Arab towns and villages to establish their own security patrols, health services, school systems and informal local government; and Arab workers and businessmen to disengage from the Israeli economy and boycott taxes. PLO funds were infiltrated into the territories through a variety of conduits.

Israel tried to counter the uprising with a reinforced military presence, heavy physical punishment and deterrence, and economic and administrative pressure. Army deployment (police were used in East Jerusalem, which is officially part of Israel) was increased several fold.

This effort to control and deter through physical force short of shooting proved highly controversial both inside and outside Israel. It was especially damaging to Israel's image among US Jews, whose support for Israel is considered vital. Criticism focused on Defence Minister Rabin's specific enunciation of a policy of 'might, power and beatings' and on the inevitable excesses by individual IDF members that ambiguities in the new policy caused. Moreover, as Arab rioting spread throughout the West Bank and began to affect Jewish settlements there, some settlers began to play an independent 'vigilante' role in patrolling Arab areas; the settlers' acts were controversial enough for Rabin to label the settlements a 'security burden'.

In response to Palestinian civil disobedience, Israeli authorities acted on the principle that civil authority could not be transferred to the local population unless negotiated with Israel, and that Israel could relatively easily outlast the Arab population in terms of economic pressure. Thus they instituted curfews, denied fuel to Arab petrol stations, cracked down on Arab money changers, closed schools and outlawed *Shabiba*, *Fatah*'s youth movement. Indeed, Palestinian civil disobedience proved a far less successful tactic than stone-throwing by youths.

Israel also escalated its response to violent Palestinian protest. By April 1988 the IDF had generally abandoned its tactic of attempting to quell disturbances only with riot sticks and tear gas, relying more on automatic weapons firing rubber bullets and, under extreme duress, live ammunition. At the same time it instituted a policy of selectively closing operational zones to the press – widely enough to reduce the catalysing effect of media attention, but selectively enough to avoid blanket castigation of Israel for seeking to hide from press scrutiny. By September the grass-roots people's committees that had created a local Palestinian infrastructure of autonomous services, education and self-help groups were made illegal and their leaders arrested. In October the existence of special IDF units that infiltrate villages and disrupt the uprising's organizational efforts was revealed.

One cost of this struggle, impossible to quantify but of increasing concern to Israelis, was in IDF morale. On the one hand, hundreds of investigations were required against soldiers for violent misbehaviour in suppressing disturbances. On the other, a small movement began among reservists to refuse to serve in the territories.

By early 1989, after over a year of mutual attrition, the *intifada* appeared to be becoming smaller in scope (large-scale rioting had ceased) but 'younger' in terms of the Arab protesters involved, and more violent. This was generally attributed to the IDF's use of plastic bullets – which began in August 1988, but became widespread and systematic only with the onset of winter. The introduction of plastic bullets appeared to give the army a more effective 'stone' (really a lead round with a thin plastic coating, intended to be fired in volleys at a range of about 70 metres) than those of the Palestinian youths who attacked it. When properly used, the plastic bullet inflicts non-lethal wounds at greater than stone-throwing range, so the IDF gained a tactical advantage in countering the uprising 'at its own level'.

The massive use of these munitions against demonstrators – with the deliberate goal, enunciated by Rabin, of 'hurting them . . . leaving scars' – produced a higher daily rate of wounded and even dead, and smaller demonstrations. The plastic bullet appears to have been the most effective single weapon Israel developed in reducing the scope of the uprising. But because it can be lethal when misused at close range, deaths resulted (47, according to IDF figures), and this generated an internal Israeli controversy and heightened criticism abroad. Moreover, relegating IDF regular and reserve troops to repeated riot-control duty at the expense of normal training routine was potentially highly detrimental to the country's military readiness – and hence its deterrent image – in Arab (particularly Syrian) eyes.

In its broadest sense the Palestinian uprising appeared to reflect significant, at times contradictory, trends. For one thing, internal Palestinian divisiveness was manifested in the emergence of *Hamas*, the Islamic Resistance Movement. *Hamas* distributed leaflets containing directives for activists contradictory to those of the PLO. It advocated an Islamic state in all of Palestine (including Israel) and rejected the PLO's growing reliance on political struggle and a compromise solution. Its activity was strongest in the Gaza Strip, where it was led by Palestinians who had had fundamentalist indoctrination from the Muslim Brotherhood while studying in Egypt.

For many Palestinians the PLO remained their leader, even though it had joined the *intifada* after it began. The PLO's link with the *intifada* was most saliently expressed through the people's committees that were made up of representatives of the diverse components of the PLO. Palestinians on the West Bank have now developed an identity and some leadership of their own, and some resent the PLO's insistence on a leadership role.

Generating a New Political Process

The first signs that the *intifada* was creating a new political process among the Palestinians occurred about half a year into the uprising. First, the Palestinian diaspora organizations established greater solidarity, then they entered upon a course of moderation. The uprising itself had developed popular Palestinian pressure for a political initiative. It had also produced a reserve of world sympathy and condemnation of Israel, particularly in the US, which the Palestinians felt they should exploit politically to generate pressure on Israel to concede territory. In early June 1988 a special Arab League summit was convened in Algiers to discuss strategy and muster support for the PLO. Here the Palestinian issue was restored to its predominant status on the Arab agenda, and the PLO was again recognized unanimously as the sole leader of the Palestinians, destined to represent them at an international peace conference. But the only active support that the summit resolutions offered the PLO was money; even then, the sums involved appeared to be grossly inadequate to support civil disobedience in the territories. And, notably, the summit talked essentially of political, rather than military, solutions to the Arab–Israeli conflict. These results tended to reinforce PLO assessments that time was of the essence in exploiting the uprising for political gain.

Behind the scenes, the efforts of both US Secretary of State Shultz and the Soviet leadership appeared to have been instrumental in moderating any Arab tendency to adopt extreme measures at Algiers. Shultz's fourth Middle East shuttle preceded the Algiers summit only by days. And during the meeting Soviet leader Gorbachev sent three messages to PLO leader Arafat, while Soviet Deputy Foreign Minister Yuli Vorontsov was present in Algiers as the summit opened. To the extent that the US and USSR had begun to move towards a common approach to dealing with the Middle East issue, both had an interest in reducing the level of Arab rhetoric at Algiers.

This approach was reflected in the document circulated in early June, by Bassam Abu-Sharif, Arafat's spokesman, calling for reciprocal recognition by Israel and the PLO and direct negotiations. Meanwhile King Hussein's announcement on 31 July that he was cutting Jordan's links and claims to the occupied territories (see below), created a political vacuum that the PLO apparently felt it must fill. This was the backdrop to a flurry of declarations in August from PLO spokesmen and leaders – most prominently Abu-Sharif and Abu Iyad (Arafat's highest-ranking deputy) that detailed a variety of tactics for establishing a new PLO political programme. The statements focused on the goal of declaring a Palestinian state within Israeli-occupied territory. Some also centred upon a return to 1947 UN Partition Resolution 181, which had been rejected by the Arabs in 1947, when it would have left Israel a truncated state considerably smaller than the one that emerged from the 1948 war.

Not all Palestinian leaders endorsed these new and moderate currents. George Habash and Naif Hawatmeh, both leaders of extreme Marxist factions, tended to be neutral or wavering over support. Syrian-backed Abu Musa, Abu Nidal and Ahmed Jibril's PFLP-GC were adamantly opposed. As Abu Iyad stated, 'negativists exist on both sides [i.e., both in Israel and among the Palestinians] . . . [those on the Arab side] brought only evil to the Arabs. . . . [The Palestinian Covenant's articles] are extremist demands'. Abu Iyad also emphasized that the new Palestinian state would recognize the existence of Israel.

The reaction of the key Arab states was considered crucial by the PLO. Egypt heartily supported the new moderate trend and suggested that the PLO should declare the existence of a state and drop the most provocative clauses from its Covenant. And Jordan's King Hussein promised to be the first to recognize a PLO government-in-exile. Syria provided the principal Arab opposition. It viewed the new PLO line as a dangerous pro-American move, a compromise that would ultimately enhance Arab endorsement of Israel's existence, which Damascus continued to reject. Minister of Defence Mustafa Tlass bluntly declared that, 'with 21 Arab countries, we don't need another'. At the heart of the Syrian approach was the ideological assumption that, along with Lebanon and Jordan, Palestine – whatever its size – was part of Greater Syria. To emphasize its point, Syria sought to crack down on the pro-Arafat PLO inside Lebanon, and PLO leaders interpreted the successful June/July campaign by Abu Musa's *Fatah* rebels, with heavy Syrian support, to expel Arafat's supporters from the Palestinian camps in Beirut as a warning against any PLO tendency to abandon 'armed struggle' and endorse political initiatives like those of Abu-Sharif and Abu Iyad.

The PLO's leader, Yasser Arafat, who remained silent throughout the controversy of July and August, was clearly in a quandary: he wished to proceed towards successful exploitation of the impact of the *intifada*, yet without losing vital support within the PLO mainstream, and without incurring Syrian wrath. He launched an initiative to convene the PLO's governing body, the Palestine National Council (PNC), to endorse some version of the new political formulation, but by late August he was forced to postpone the meeting.

American Involvement

The *intifada* inspired the first concrete manifestation of renewed American involvement in the Middle East peace process since the abortive Reagan Plan of September 1981. This was the Shultz Plan, which was highlighted in the round of shuttle trips that the US Secretary of State made during the early months of 1988, themselves a clear reflection of Washington's fear that the Palestinian uprising would escalate into tension between US allies in the Middle East – Israel, Egypt and Jordan. Shultz presented his plan in early March. It called for the convening of an international conference on 15 April, with the Palestinians represented by a Jordanian/Palestinian delegation; bilateral talks among the Middle East participants in May to establish an interim autonomy regime for the Israeli-administered territories which would begin in February 1989 and last three years; and negotiations for a final Palestinian settlement, based on the territories-for-peace principle, to begin on 1 December. All parties were to reply by 15 March.

The responses of the various parties to Shultz's initiative could hardly be considered encouraging, even though – as Shultz never tired of pointing out – no one said no. Israel's Prime Minister Yitzhak Shamir, for example, was fundamentally opposed to an international conference, citing a long list of his oft-expressed objections. In contrast, Alternate Prime Minister and Foreign Minister Shimon Peres pressed for Israeli acceptance of the Shultz initiative. Jordan's King Hussein appeared to withdraw deeper and deeper into an approach which demanded that the international conference have the power to compel the sides to accept its dictates (a position rejected by the US and Israel alike), and he accepted the PLO's demand to attend the conference as a separate, sovereign delegation, rather than as part of a Jordanian delegation. Angry

161

at Shultz's implicit refusal to meet a delegation of its choice, the PLO called for increased unrest in the territories during his visit, and, indeed, was apparently responsible for an abortive attempt to explode a car bomb near his Jerusalem hotel.

By early June – Shultz's fourth and final shuttle – his initiative was a dead letter. With US presidential elections approaching, there seemed little likelihood that Washington would make any new move before well into 1989. But, while abandoning the initiative, Shultz dropped a hint that the US administration might take one more dramatic initiative on the Middle East before completing its term of office.

The Jordanian Retreat

One key reason for King Hussein's rejection of the Shultz Plan was his fear of Syria. A second reason for his ambiguity was the fact that Jordan had only recently voluntarily forfeited one of its trump cards in the peace process: the commitment that Hussein had given Peres at their secret London meeting in April 1987 that Jordan would appear at negotiations together with Palestinian representatives in a single delegation. Hussein had subsequently concluded that Peres was unable to gain Israeli government sanction for the principles of what they had agreed. Moreover, the Iran–Iraq conflict increasingly loomed as a more pressing inter-Arab issue that warranted concessions on Hussein's part in return for a united Arab anti-Iranian stand. Hence, when he convened an Arab League summit meeting in Amman in November 1987 to reinforce Arab solidarity against Iran, Hussein agreed to a resolution recognizing the PLO's right to appear at any peace conference as a separate, sovereign delegation.

Hussein's hand was therefore considerably weakened when he met Shultz in early 1988 to discuss the Palestinian role in an international peace conference. The king's own assessments showed that not only the Amman conference but the Palestinian uprising had strengthened Arafat's hand and weakened his own. In recent years Hussein had attempted – with the concurrence of governments in Israel – to build a basis of political support among Palestinian Arabs by paying the salaries of teachers and officials in the West Bank, offering Jordanian passports to stateless Gaza refugees, and opening a branch of a Jordanian bank in Nablus. But the rejection of this bid for Palestinian leadership was the theme of much of the initial rioting in the *intifada* and signalled the total failure of his efforts. Pro-Jordanian Palestinians in the territories soon found themselves either 'recanting' or surrounded by bodyguards. In March, 'Communique No. 11' of the uprising actually threatened the lives of members of the Jordanian parliament residing in the territories. By that time, too, Jordanian officials were telling Shultz's emissary, Philip Habib, that to hold local elections in the West Bank and Gaza as a preliminary stage in organizing autonomy – as Washington had proposed and Jerusalem had agreed – would be unwise. It was obvious that the Palestinians elected would not be pro-Jordanian.

Indeed, the *intifada* was perceived in Amman as a threat to Jordan itself. In January the authorities were obliged to quell rioting in Jordan's own refugee camps and university campuses, after which supervision of Palestinian activity was tightened. Ever wary of Syria's predilection for exploiting Jordanian weakness for its own purposes, Hussein announced dramatically on 31 July that 'we honour the desire of the PLO, the sole legitimate representative of the Palestinian people, to detach itself from us in an independent Palestinian state. . . . There is a general persuasion that Jordan's judicial and administrative link with the West Bank contradicts this trend. . . . [Therefore] we have no choice but to [sever] the reciprocal relationship'.

Hussein accompanied this declaration with clarifications. Henceforth, Jordan's only role in the peace process would be to negotiate its final borders with Israel; it would cease paying the salaries of administrative and educational employees in the West Bank; it would no longer provide development funds; within two years its passports held by Palestinians from the West Bank and Gaza would be void; import restrictions might be placed on West Bank and Gaza agricultural exports; and the Jordanian Ministry for the Occupied Territories would now become a department of the Foreign Ministry. At the same time, Jordanian officials emphasized that the PLO's newly-recognized explicit jurisdiction over West Bank and Gaza Palestinians would not apply to Jordanian (East Bank) Palestinians, who were in every way Jordanian citizens.

One of Hussein's goals in cutting loose from the West Bank and Gaza was to prove to the Arab world, and specifically to Palestinians, that they could not get along without Jordan: he wanted the PLO to admit that Amman would have to play a special economic and political role in the future of the territories. He quickly learned that he was mistaken. In the ensuing months the PLO felt little need to request special assistance from Jordan; politically, in particular, the PLO's independent performance during November and December did not suffer from the absence of a partnership with Jordan. Yet Hussein continued to feel that Jordan must play a special role in the peace process – if only to ensure that it would not be engulfed by post-settlement Palestinian irredentism. All the more reason why he would need inter-Arab backing for a Jordanian role in any new peace process that developed during 1989.

Israel's Elections
If Hussein's abdication of responsibility for the territories left the field open to PLO and US initiatives, another player, Israel, was neutralized by the *Knesset* elections of 1 November. For a crucial few months they paralysed the country's political machinery and alienated a key strategic ally: American Jewry.

In fact, Israeli political paralysis became a fact of life virtually from the moment, in November 1986, when Labour Prime Minister Peres turned over the mantle of leadership to the *Likud*'s Yitzhak Shamir. Even before this the *Likud* half of Israel's government of national unity

163

had blocked Peres' efforts in favour of an international conference and collaboration with Jordan; now Shamir's essentially *status quo* policy became dominant. By summer 1988 the *Knesset* elections had become a choice between the two major parties' political policies for dealing with the *intifada* and the larger Palestinian problem. As it turned out, enough perplexed voters were effectively 'turned off' by the parties' conflicting and hesitant messages that the elections produced a worse stalemate than four years earlier.

The results gave the *Likud* 40 seats out of a total of 120, while secular parties that had split from the *Likud* and held views to its political right (*Tehiya, Tsomet* and *Moledet*) received 3, 2 and 2 seats respectively. This created a rightist secular political bloc of 47 seats. Its views on the Palestinian issue ranged from the *Likud*'s *status quo* policy – an ideological belief in Greater Israel (i.e., never giving up the territories), yet practical advocacy of Camp David autonomy – via calls by all three splinter parties for immediate annexation of the territories, to the *Moledet* platform of deporting large numbers of Palestinians ('transfer') to ensure a Jewish demographic advantage.

Labour won 39 seats. Its left and centre allies, the Citizens' Rights Movement (CRM), *Mapam* and *Shinui-Mercaz*, received 5, 3 and 2 seats respectively. This produced a Zionist leftist bloc of 49 seats. Its views ranged from Labour's complex and frequently conflicting package of options (an international conference, Jordanian involvement in a solution, territories for peace, and interim measures that included unilateral withdrawal from some territories, Palestinian elections and autonomy) to the more explicit calls of the CRM and *Mapam* to discuss the establishment of a Palestinian state with the PLO, if it recognized Israel and desisted from terrorism.

Another six seats were divided among three extreme-left lists that, while including Jews, depended essentially on the Arab vote. These – the Israel Communist Party, the Progressives, and a list headed by breakaway Labour MP Abd al-Wahab Darawsha – all essentially advocated 'two states for two peoples', immediate recognition of the PLO, and comprehensive withdrawal from all territories conquered in 1967, including East Jerusalem. Finally, 18 seats were divided among four religious lists; the veteran Zionist National Religious Party (NRP) won 5, and 13 went to the non-Zionist ultra-orthodox parties: *Shas*, the Sephardic Guardians of the Torah (6), *Agudat Israel* (5), and *Degel HaTorah* (2).

The most obvious lesson of these elections appeared to be that, in looking for answers, the perplexed voter had to turn to the political fringes. The non-Zionist Left for the first time addressed Jewish voters with a frank, slickly-packaged appeal to talk to the PLO about a Palestinian state; if nothing else, this legitimized that idea for future debate and encouraged leftist Israelis to consider the Zionist Left's slightly more moderate appeal. The far Right also registered a precedent, with the concept of 'transfer' legitimized for open debate.

Most impressive were the gains of the religious parties. By focusing on 'faith' and presenting charismatic, messianic rabbis, the NRP and *Shas* appealed to a bloc of religious Sephardic Jews who had for years been voting for the *Likud* bloc, but were now dispirited over the prospects for peace and frustrated by the 'rational' alternatives being presented. The banning of Rabbi Meir Kahane's *Kach* Party – due to its openly racist platform, which violated legislation passed during the previous four years – caused many of his supporters to vote for *Shas*. Meanwhile two Ashkenazic parties, *Agudat Israel* and *Degel HaTorah*, waged a spirited electoral fight for the votes of Israel's growing (mainly by high natural reproduction) ultra-orthodox community. Eighteen seats for religious parties is not an unusual outcome in Israeli elections, but there had been only 11 in the previous *Knesset*, and this was the only significant electoral change registered by the voters. The particular innovation of 1988 was the heavy ultra-orthodox emphasis, at the expense of Zionist religious and non-religious lists.

The elections left Israel in a political stalemate that lasted six weeks, as *Likud*'s Shamir and Labour's Peres vied with each other to woo the ultra-orthodox into a narrow-based coalition and explored the possibilities for a new broad coalition based on the two main parties. Meanwhile, the US and the PLO engineered a dramatic breakthrough.

PLO–US Dialogue

On 14 December 1988 George Shultz announced that the PLO had 'issued a statement in which it accepted UN Security Council Resolutions 242 and 338, recognized Israel's right to exist in peace and security, and renounced terrorism. As a result, the United States is prepared for a substantive dialogue with PLO representatives'. The dialogue would be conducted by US Ambassador to Tunis Robert Pelletreau, a veteran State Department Middle East expert. Shultz stressed that the opening of talks 'should not be taken as recognition' by the United States 'of an independent Palestinian state', and that the US 'commitment to Israel's security remains unshakeable'. On 16 December Pelletreau met the PLO's Yasser Abd Rabu. The American boycott of the PLO had ended.

The US announcement was made in direct response to a statement by PLO Chairman Yasser Arafat, at a news conference in Geneva, in which he renounced terrorism 'of all kinds: individual, collective and state', repeated earlier assertions that the PLO accepted Resolutions 242 and 338 'as the basis for negotiations within the framework of an international conference on the Middle East' and recognized the right of all parties to the conflict 'to exist in peace and security, including the state of Palestine, Israel and their neighbours'. In so doing the PLO had, according to Shultz, fulfilled the conditions set by Washington for opening a US–PLO dialogue. That dialogue would be 'one more step towards the beginning of direct negotiations between the parties, which alone can lead to . . . peace'.

The Shultz announcement generated praise and anticipation throughout most of the Arab world and in the West Bank and Gaza; split the Israeli body politic between Left and Centre-Right – in effect, straight through the middle of the Labour Party; introduced a crucial issue into the already chaotic process of building a new Israeli government coalition in the wake of the elections; won the general approval of US Jews; and placed the US squarely in the centre of the Middle East peace-making process. The announcement crowned one long and intricate process – and was expected to be the opening of another. The conditions that the US had asked the PLO to fulfil had originated in a September 1975 US–Israeli Memorandum of Understanding drawn up by then Prime Minister Rabin and US Secretary of State Kissinger. That stated that the US would not hold a dialogue with the PLO unless it accepted Resolutions 242 and 338 and recognized Israel; the Reagan administration had added the condition that the PLO must also renounce terrorism.

The factors that brought about this *rapprochement* were as complex as the conflict itself. The *intifada* appeared to have tipped the scales in favour of the moderates within the PLO leadership. It had led directly to King Hussein's decision of 31 July to renounce, in favour of the PLO, any further Jordanian interest in representing the Palestinians in peace talks. This spurred the PLO to develop a new political initiative that would reflect its new-found dominance of the political arena. Soviet pressures on the organization, too, were directed at steering it towards of political negotiations.

Finally, the 'lame duck period' of Ronald Reagan's presidency provided Secretary Shultz with the arena and the atmosphere he needed to encourage the PLO to make the final effort to accept US conditions. The outgoing administration had little to fear from domestic political repercussions, while the incoming Bush/Baker team could either profit from their initiative or, if it became derailed, abandon it without bearing the onus of having recognized the PLO. Shultz was also able to take advantage of Israel's battered public image after a year of suppressing the uprising, and of a particularly critical atmosphere towards Israel among American Jews. American receptivity was particularly important for the PLO moderates, who assessed that it would be easier to establish a dialogue with the US than with Israel, and that US involvement was essential, and could be decisive, in bringing pressure to bear upon Israel to negotiate a settlement.

The momentum towards moderation that began in mid-1988 thus was on the way to fruition in mid-November when, after repeated delays due to intra-Palestinian dissent, the PNC convened in Algiers. The challenge for *Fatah* and the more moderate PNC members was to put together a political programme acceptable to the United States, while nevertheless ensuring the support (or at least the 'loyal opposition') of Habash and Hawatmeh for their initiatives; this would enable them to present a broad enough front to withstand pressure from the pro-Syrian radicals. They almost succeeded. On 15 November the PNC unanimously passed a declaration of Palestinian independence and an accompanying political resolution that were labelled by Washington as 'progress, though insufficient'. The declaration of independence opens with phrases deliberately written to parallel those in Israel's of 1948; it goes on to recognize UN Partition Resolution 181 of 1947; announces Palestine 'to be a peace-loving State . . . and . . . therefore rejects the threat or use of force, violence and terrorism against its territorial integrity . . . as . . . against the territorial integrity of other states'. The political statement (which the PFLP voted against, though without walking out of the PNC) calls for an international conference to be held 'on the basis of . . . 242 and 338 and the assurance of the legitimate national rights of the Palestinian people'. It 'declares its rejection of terror in all its forms'. The US rejection of the PNC statements cited the vague phrasing of the denunciation of terrorism and the recognition of Israel, the fact that the meeting was attended by wanted terrorists like Abu al-Abbas, and the frequent verbal references at the meeting to the Palestinian Charter and to PLO adherence to the principles of armed struggle and the 'right of return' (a euphemism for the ultimate destruction of Israel in accordance with the PLO's strategy of stages, also referred to at Algiers). For these reasons, too, everyone in Israel from the centrist factions of the Labour Party to the far Right, condemned the Algiers proceedings as a public-relations exercise. But the Zionist Left pointed out that the acceptance of Resolution 181 implied, for the first time, PLO recognition of Israel. This, plus the rejection of terrorism, however ambiguous, and the acceptance of 242 and 338 as formulae for a settlement, moved the Peace Now movement to declare its support for direct Israeli negotiations with the PLO.

Meanwhile the pro-Syrian Palestinian factions declared Arafat a traitor. Abu Musa, leader of the *Fatah* rebels, labelled the PNC declarations 'a genuine catastrophe', because they implied the end of armed struggle and the demise of the Palestinian Charter. Yet the wave of popular support for the PNC initiatives that soon swept the Arab world, presumably coupled with Soviet pressure, produced a muted Syrian response. Syria (and Lebanon, which it occupies) were the only Arab states not to recognize the new, nebulous 'Palestinian state'. Outside the Arab world many third-world countries recognized it, and the Soviet Union gave it conditional recognition. In Europe, the EC states voiced approval without recognition.

From Algiers via Stockholm to Geneva, it took one month for a series of indirect US–PLO contacts to generate a refined version of the PNC declarations that Washington could accept. First Shultz used the 'stick' – citing Arafat's terrorist associations and background when refusing him a visa to enter the US to speak at the UN General Assembly (where he intended to 'clarify' the PNC decisions). Then came the 'carrot', in the form of a visit to Stockholm by Arafat, where his contacts with the Swedish government and a leftist US Jewish group were carefully co-ordinated with the State Department. This produced a new document in which Arafat declared that the PNC had accepted UN Resolutions 242 and 338, 'accepted the existence of Israel as a state in the region . . . [and] declared its rejection and condemnation of terrorism in all its forms'. But in this document, too, Arafat mentioned the Palestinian refugees' 'right of return'. And his continuing attempt to 'interpret' the PNC decisions was problematic. Shimon Peres noted that Arafat had carried out a 'cunning exercise in public relations' by framing recognition of Israel as an explanation of PNC resolutions that included the non-acceptance of Israel.

Arafat tried again on 13 December, in his speech to the UN General Assembly at Geneva (whither it had transferred so as to enable him to address it). The elements of the speech had been co-ordinated in advance with the US, but at the last minute Arafat, under pressure from his more doctrinaire colleagues, obfuscated a few key phrases. He did, however, for the first time introduce a direct and emotional appeal to Israelis to join him on the road to peace. The State Department proclaimed that 'the speech contained some interesting and some positive developments. But it continued to be ambiguous on the key issues'. Prime Minister Shamir called it a 'monumental swindle'.

The next day, in a press conference, Arafat noted 'the right of the parties to the conflict to exist in peace and security, including Palestine and Israel'; he renounced terrorism 'in all its forms', and he declared that resolutions 242 and 338 'constitute the basis for negotiations within the framework of an international conference on the Middle East'. A positive US response was delivered a few hours later. Arafat's final statement, it soon became known, had been carefully co-ordinated with the United States through a series of indirect contacts that involved Sweden, Egypt and the Saudi ambassador in Washington.

Israel's official response to the US announcement was one of surprise and indignation. It reiterated its view that no PLO statements could cleanse the organization of its terrorist predilections: its very *raison d'être* was to destroy Israel. Foreign Minister Peres was more moderate in his response, but nevertheless critical. He emphasized that the proof of the PLO's renunciation of terrorism should be sought in an examination of its deeds rather than its statements.

On the Left, however, the news of official US–PLO contacts generated calls for Israel, too, to recognize the PLO and open negotiations. A few prominent Labour figures joined the CRM and *Mapam* in arguing that the government should recognize Arafat's statements as a victory for both Israel and the US: an extremist Arab movement had met the rigid conditions established for it to join the political process, and an important Arab element had recognized Israel. On the far Right, leaders from *Tehiya* and *Tsomet* demanded that Israel respond to the US move by establishing numerous new Jewish settlements on the West Bank, and/ or annexing the territories. The American Jewish response was particularly instructive. In view of Secretary Shultz's consistent record of support for Israel, no major US Jewish organization was prepared to condemn his step.

In the immediate aftermath of the US decision, it was impossible to assess just how this initiative would affect Israel. Certainly in the view of the Israeli political mainstream US–Israeli relations had suffered a major blow. Moreover, Israel now had to recognize the possibility that, within the next year or so, it would face a US proposal that it negotiate with the PLO – the start of a political process that would eventually lead to the creation of a Palestinian state.

The Shultz initiative towards the PLO caught Israel without a government. More precisely, the country was still being administered by its previous government – now a caretaker administration – after more than six weeks of unsuccessful attempts to form a new coalition. That period witnessed a seemingly unending series of byzantine machinations and unexpected turnabouts. It also pitted the American Jewish establishment against both the Labour and the *Likud* leadership over the 'Who is a Jew?' issue. Ultimately, it was the collective assessment of key *Likud* and Labour leaders – that the greatest dangers to Israel now lay in isolation, from the US and US Jewry alike, and in pressure to establish a Palestinian state – that broke the stalemate. The *Likud* cancelled its commitments to the ultra-orthodox and the extreme Right, and both *Likud* and Labour made the concessions necessary to form a new government of national unity.

The 'Who is a Jew?' amendment to Israeli law, accepted by both the *Likud* and Labour as a condition for forming a narrow coalition with the religious parties, delegitimizes conversion to Judaism by Reform and Conservative rabbis. It is thus perceived as delegitimizing the branches of Judaism adhered to by the majority of US Jews, including the most actively pro-Zionist among them. Over the past forty years, it had frequently been proposed by orthodox and ultra-orthodox circles, but had always been defeated; now, for the first time, it seemed as if it might become an official part of a ruling coalition's platform – and so nearly certain to pass into Israeli law. This was one reason for US Jewry to react. A supplementary one was apparently the effect of a year of watching on American television Israel's efforts to deal with the *intifada*. Many American Jews who felt strongly tempted to voice criticism had avoided doing so because they accepted that they had no right to intervene from afar in Israeli security affairs. But 'Who is a Jew?' affected them directly and they made their objections felt with special emphasis. Because both Shamir and Peres had shown a readiness to sanction the amendment in order to form a coalition, the anger of organized US Jewry was directed at both.

The thrust of the American Jewish protest was to remind Israelis that their fellow Jews throughout the world were, first, mostly secular, and, secondly, Israel's most reliable and important strategic ally – a source of vital political and financial support. This, too, appeared to affect coalition calculations. An additional factor was public disgust with the conduct of the politicians, both secular and religious, who conducted their negotiations in the worst tradition of back-room politics. Eventually, President Herzog took the unprecedented step of criticizing the conduct of the entire coalition-forming procedure, urging Shamir and Peres to form a new unity government.

By 19 December the two political leaders succeeded in doing just that. The government that was sworn in on 22 December was very similar in structure to its predecessor. Shamir's electoral advantage was expressed in his remaining Prime Minister for the entire term, without 'rotation'. Peres moved from the Foreign Ministry to the Finance Ministry – reflecting both Shamir's exasperation with his independent foreign-policy initiatives and Labour's acute need to control national finances in order to rescue ailing *Histadrut* (trade-union-run) industries and debt-ridden *kibbutzim*. Rabin remained at Defence and Moshe Arens – a Shamir supporter within the *Likud* – took over the Foreign Ministry.

The new Israeli government of national unity began its term with a more harmonious distribution of labour than its predecessor. Areas of responsibility were better defined, with Prime Minister Shamir, Foreign Minister Arens and Defence Minister Rabin dealing with various aspects of the Palestinian situation, and Deputy Prime Minister and Finance Minister Peres restricting his activities to the economic sphere.

One key development that emerged from this new structure was that Shamir, Rabin and Arens advanced a series of fairly compatible new ideas for movement towards a Palestinian solution. By mid-February these were still essentially informal proposals, in line with the new US administration's preference for postponing substantive discussions on the Palestinian issue until early April, when Prime Minister Shamir was invited for talks in Washington.

All the government's new ideas were notable for two elements. On the one hand, they reflected Israeli concern over the need to end the *intifada* by political means and to improve Israel's image. On the other, they rejected direct dialogue with the PLO and, establishment of a Palestinian state. Thus, in mid-January Prime Minister Shamir accepted the principle that the super-powers would play a role in organizing direct Israeli–Arab negotiations, but he also suggested that the UN Secretary-General could convene direct talks, as in the case of Iran and Iraq. A close aide of his also noted that the ultimate solution for the territories should comprise a confederation of Jordan, Israel and a Palestinian entity, to be preceded by an autonomy that might be established after elections in the territories. And Foreign Minister Arens told the *Knesset* Foreign and Security Affairs Committee in mid-January that Israel 'need not maintain its past positions . . . the situation in which we live requires a political initiative'. He suggested that, alongside direct negotiations and gradual solutions, Israel must also address the desires of the Palestinians in Judea, Samaria and the Gaza District.

In late January, Defence Minister Rabin presented a complex, graduated plan involving several stages: a three- to six-month period of quiet in the territories, followed by free elections; Israel would negotiate with the elected Palestinians – regardless of their affiliation – and offer them comprehensive autonomy; after the autonomy stage Israel would propose a federative structure involving itself and Jordan. Rabin's plan was the most detailed of all those broached, and it emphasized the principle that the 1.5 million Palestinians in the West Bank and Gaza should negotiate their future for themselves. Accordingly, he accompanied his initiative with a broad effort at dialogue with local Palestinian leaders, including even Islamic fundamentalist extremists from Gaza. Faisal al-Husseini, the most prominent of the Palestinian nationalists engaged in this dialogue, was released from a year's administrative detention by Rabin in late January amidst speculation that he was being 'legitimized' as a potential negotiating partner who combined a high standing in PLO and local Palestinian eyes with a relatively pragmatic approach to Israel.

As the US–PLO dialogue proceeded apace into 1989, both Shamir and Rabin appeared united in seeking to persuade the new US administration that it should be abandoned, or, failing that, that Washington should continue to reject the Palestinian state solution espoused by the PLO. They were encouraged by early statements from President Bush and Secretary of State Baker which supported the dialogue but rejected a Palestinian state.

By early February, the State Department's annual report on human-rights violations worldwide had added fuel to Israeli–American tensions. The report sharply criticized the IDF's treatment of the Palestinian uprising, citing instances of cruelty and disregard for human life. Israel protested that the report totally ignored the circumstances of the *intifada*. But new damage to Israel's image in Western public opinion was inevitable.

A Cloudy Future

By early 1989. Israel had suffered two strategic surprises in a year: the *intifada* and the Shultz–Arafat breakthrough. Fewer and fewer Israelis seemed to believe that the uprising could be suppressed by force and the *status quo ante* restored; all recognized that Jordan was no longer a principal player in a settlement; and more and more recognized that Israel would have to negotiate with, at the very least, Palestinians affiliated with and approved by the PLO. But the political leadership still hoped it could preserve an Israeli consensus against a Palestinian state. In this sense the *intifada* had not yet brought the Israeli government to accept the PLO contention that negotiations must be based on Israel's acceptance of the Palestinian state principle as an ultimate outcome. Nor was it entirely clear whether Shamir's haste to form (by *Likud* standards) a relatively moderate and broad-based government in the aftermath of the Shultz–Arafat breakthrough reflected a readiness for eventual compromise, or a need for broad backing for an essentially hold-the-line

171

position. Certainly some time would pass before any serious negotiations could begin.

If the super-powers were to intervene, however, the picture might change. The US–PLO contacts might produce some new initiative, or the growing Soviet-American *rapprochement* generate a move towards a jointly imposed solution. Foreign Minister Shevardnadze's visit to Arab capitals in February presaged greater Soviet activism, an activism that the US did not decry. But by late February 1989 it was still impossible to assess the Bush administration's long-term view of a Middle East peace dynamic and the US role in it.

In this regard it is notable that throughout 1988 and early 1989 the Soviet Union continued to improve relations with Israel, while Egypt maintained correct relations, and the overall Arab–Israeli situation did not deteriorate, despite the *intifada*. Indeed, the fact that the world increasingly saw in Israel a Middle East 'super-power' – now possessing a nuclear capability, its own satellite, and intermediate-range missiles – appeared to guarantee that the powers would not seek to isolate it, and the Arab states would seek to avoid a new conflict with it, however great the deterioration in the territories.

As for the PLO, several key questions were still being tested. First, could the Palestinians' extreme political diversity find a cogent expression without generating new internal fighting among factions? In the early months after the December breakthrough, even though Arafat steadily refused additional concessions on PLO positions ('enough is enough'), he nevertheless faced criticism from the more extremist movements of Habash and Hawatmeh for abandoning 'armed struggle'. Both launched armed incursions into Israel to test Arafat's commitment and embarrass him, while a number of prominent *Fatah* supporters insisted on portraying the PNC and Geneva initiatives as little more than steps in the 'strategy of stages' designed to dismantle Israel piece by piece. Arafat, too, embarrassed Washington by threatening to murder Palestinians who called for a cease-fire in the territories and by refusing to condemn armed PLO incursions from Lebanon. Yet it also seemed certain that conditions were changing, and the ageing PLO leadership was indeed mellowing. One key incentive was the fear that, if the PLO were to dilute its support of their proposals for a two-state solution, West Bank and Gaza leaders might elect to 'go it alone' and negotiate with Israel on their own.

The second test, of course, was whether the new political initiative was moderate enough to generate new progress towards integration of the PLO into the peace process by Israel and/or the United States. Many sceptics added an additional test: Was the PLO moving towards a tactical or a strategic change? Was it prepared to abandon terrorism, recognize Israel and genuinely accept the idea of a mini-state alongside Israel as a long-term solution? Or was it merely adopting a sophisticated version of the 'strategy of stages', intending to accept whatever territory it was given and use it as a springboard for further irredentism?

Alternatively, would genuinely moderate Palestinians be able to prevent the irredentists from taking over a Palestinian political entity, once achieved? And how much longer can Israel refuse to negotiate with the PLO?

THE END OF THE GULF WAR

Active hostilities between Iran and Iraq ended on 20 August 1988, little more than a month before the beginning of their ninth year. Iran's acceptance, on 18 July, of the cease-fire and the negotiating package outlined in Security Council Resolution 598 had taken the world by surprise. Certainly, the war had begun to go badly for Iran, which could no longer hope for a military victory or even significant political concessions from Iraq. But few had foreseen Iran being prepared to abandon the war without any visible gains, so closely had the continued vitality of the Islamic revolution become identified with its struggle against the Iraqi regime. Leading political figures in Iran were quick to point out that the revolution had stood alone against Iraqi aggression and the might of an international conspiracy, and that the world sympathized with Iran and condemned the United States for the brutal destruction of a civilian airliner. The regime did not, as some had expected, collapse without the war as a continuing focus for national support based on Persian nationalism and Islamic fervour. Nevertheless, the end of hostilities was followed by increasing evidence of a struggle over the direction of the revolution. Social and economic problems, whose treatment had been delayed because of the war, would soon have to be addressed. For his part, Iraq's President Saddam Hussein claimed a notable victory; Iraq's forces had achieved a string of military successes to crown the stubborn resistance which had preserved Iraq's own independence as well as the interests of the Arab nation. No doubt both governments' claims rang hollow in the ears of many of their constituents, long weary of the war which had been so costly in both lives and wealth, and which, it had been clear for some time, would bring few, if any, lasting rewards.

Exactly when the Iranian leadership decided to end the war, or how the decision was reached, are matters of conjecture. It is known that Tehran used the good offices of the West German foreign minister as mediator well before 18 July. This fact, as well as criticisms of Iran's war strategy from senior politicians, would suggest that some elements of the leadership might have been ready to halt hostilities earlier, but for the opposition of hard-liners or the lack of a suitable moment, or both. At any rate, a number of factors combined during 1988 to make the war progressively harder to sustain, and unwinnable by any of Iran's publicly proclaimed criteria.

At the end of 1987, there were few signs that Iran might be prepared to abandon the war without any political dividend. The Arab League, responding chiefly to Saudi Arabia's concern about rising tension in the Gulf, had declared its unanimous condemnation of Iran's refusal to accept UN Resolution 598 and reaffirmed its support for Iraq. Another Iranian winter offensive was expected, although Iraq's military commanders were rather more optimistic than they had been in previous years. But it never came, because the flow of volunteers had all but dried up. The casualties of the fruitless Iranian assaults on Basra in the winter of 1986–7 and the costly tedium of military stalemate had eroded the Iranian zeal for martyrdom.

In the spring of 1988 Iran launched a series of small operations on the northern front which made some headway. One of these was in support of Kurdish forces which seized the Kurdish town of Halabja in early March. In their counter-offensive on 16 March, Iraqi forces used chemical weapons, forcing the Kurdish irregulars and their Iranian supporters to retreat, leaving hundreds of dead, including civilians caught by the gas.

From April onwards, the deterioration of Iran's military position could no longer be ignored. Its forces began to lose territory. On 17 April, Iraq announced that it had with surprising ease retaken the Fao peninsula, whose loss in February 1986 had caused regional consternation. At the end of May Iraqi forces captured Shalamcheh, near Basra, and on 25 June they retook the Majnoon oilfields, which had been lost in 1985. It has since been acknowledged by senior Iranian sources – and was evident to analysts – that Iran's forces were poorly led, under-equipped and rotated too frequently to gain sufficient combat experience. This probably made them particularly vulnerable to the psychological as well as the physical effects of Iraqi chemical attacks.

The setbacks at the front occurred against the background of an Iraqi missile and air offensive which began on 29 February and continued with varying degrees of intensity until late April. It caused widespread demoralization and the flight of many of the residents of Iran's major cities; it also provoked bitter criticism of the Soviet Union, as the presumed source of Iraq's missiles. More importantly, Iraq's strategic attacks on tankers, refineries and other vital economic targets were becoming increasingly effective; together with the low price of oil, they further limited Iran's ability to bolster its depleted arsenal or run its economy efficiently. Iran was already suffering from chronic shortages of industrial and consumer goods.

Iran was also coming under increasing international pressure to make peace. The US in particular, was proving a tougher opponent than Iranian propaganda had scornfully predicted. On 18 April, a day after the loss of Fao, its naval units shelled Iranian oil platforms in retaliation for Iran's resumption of minelaying in the Gulf. In the ensuing series of confrontations with the Iranian navy, US warships sank or damaged six Iranian vessels. The US efforts to secure Soviet and Chinese support for an arms embargo had come to nothing, but its naval operation in the Gulf had gained greater credibility than had seemed likely at the time of its inception. And the combined effort by the British, French, Belgian, Dutch and Italian navies to clear mines and escort threatened vessels underlined Iran's isolation.

At the beginning of June, Iran's parliamentary speaker, Hashemi-Rafsanjani, was appointed acting commander-in-chief of the armed forces. Mohsen Rezai, the commander of the Revolutionary Guards, was made publicly to accept responsibility for Iran's recent military defeats. Some Iranians evidently believed – since President Khamenei took the trouble to deny the rumour – that Rafsanjani's appointment was a prelude to the war's termination.

In August 1987 Rafsanjani had told an interviewer that the war would continue 'provided that Iran's administration could function normally'. By mid-1988 it was labouring under considerable difficulties, for, in addition to economic disruption and missile attacks, it had to contend with renewed factional squabbling. Radical elements in the government, committed to state control of the economy and the promotion of 'social justice' had by the end of 1987 become frustrated at the obstructionist tactics of the Council of Guardians. This religiously conservative body, empowered to vet legislation for conformity with Islamic law, had continually blocked measures which apparently infringed private property rights. In February 1988 Ayatollah Khomeini ordered the creation of a special assembly to resolve disputes between parliament and the Council. Though some of the assembly's membership was drawn from the Council's ranks, its overall composition and the fact of its creation appeared to strengthen the hand of the radicals. Moreover, Khomeini went on to declare that the new assembly should uphold the interests of the state against the proponents of the 'American version of Islam'.

Khomeini's apparent partiality probably influenced the course of Iran's parliamentary elections, held over two rounds in April and May. On the eve of the first round of voting he also sanctioned a public rift between the umbrella 'Militant Clergy Association' and a radically-oriented splinter group, the 'Tehran Militant Clergy'. The conduct of radical groups during the elections, including their screening of candidate lists and extensive ballot-rigging, led to serious intra-clerical disturbances in Tabriz, Isfahan and Mashad. After the second round, marches of allegiance to Khomeini by rank-and-file loyalists had to be cancelled lest they prove too inflammatory.

It seems more than likely that by July Iran's leadership had decided to end the war and was looking for a pretext or opportunity to do so. In that case, the shooting down of an Iranian airliner by an American warship on 3 July could, in a perverse sense, have been considered fortunate. In the immediate aftermath of an engagement with Iranian gunboats, the USS *Vincennes* mistook an Iranian airliner over the southern Gulf for a hostile fighter and shot it down with the loss of some

290 lives. The Iranian government seized the high moral ground, but otherwise its reaction was surprisingly restrained. On 18 July, after more 'tactical withdrawals' on the northern front, Iran accepted Resolution 598. Ayatollah Khomeini's pained endorsement of the decision served to quell any immediate dissent.

Despite Iran's acceptance of the cease-fire terms, hostilities continued, at sea and on land, until the official truce came into effect on 20 August. Baghdad was openly sceptical of Iran's motives, and Iraqi forces continued to conduct limited offensive operations in order to take more prisoners and, by occupying more Iranian territory improve Iraq's negotiating position. Iraq's continued belligerence caused a brief resurgence of popular support for the war in Iran. So too did the attempt by the *Mujaheddin-e-Khalq's* 'National Liberation Army' to stage its own invasion of Iran; having advanced almost as far as Kermanshah the column was left without Iraqi air cover and destroyed by Revolutionary Guards.

It is not perhaps surprising that executions of many opponents of the Iranian regime were reported in the months after the cease-fire. More unusual was the extent to which prominent members of Iran's government criticized Iran's shortcomings during the war. Certain themes predominated: Iran had by its diplomatic abrasiveness alienated potential supporters, thereby aiding Iraq; the war had been mismanaged; and, as Rafsanjani noted in early 1989, Iran ought to have made peace in 1982 instead of overreaching itself militarily. Such comments can be seen as part of the general mood of critical introspection symbolized by Ayatollah Montazeri's call, on the tenth anniversary of the revolution, for greater tolerance and a franker evaluation of past mistakes. But, at a deeper level, they also reflect an attempt to discredit the hard-liners who were thought to be responsible for Iran's unsuccessful strategy and, more generally, for the revolution's ills. Much to the chagrin of Prime Minister Musavi and his fellow economic radicals, a more pragmatic approach to the management of the economy and Iran's international relations gained ascendancy after the war. Its chief proponents included Rafsanjani, Khamenei and Velayati, the foreign minister.

Though a pragmatic trend, loosely-termed, had made itself felt, it had by no means triumphed. The reaction in Iran to Khomeini's call for the assassination of the British writer Salman Rushdie for blasphemy, and the Ayatollah's opposition to the speed of Iran's post-war liberalization are indicators of the difficulties ahead. Riding the wave of indignation aroused by the Ayatollah, the radicals seem to have again gained at least a temporary ascendancy. Montazeri and a number of other moderates were forced to resign their positions at the end of March 1989, and Tehran once again resounded with cries of revolutionary zeal. As they pursue a power struggle for control in the post-Khomeini era, Iran's leaders have every incentive to maintain a hard bargaining position in the UN-supervised peace negotiations.

So does Saddam Hussein, despite the victory he has claimed on behalf of Iraq and the Arab world. It is true that Iraq's forces maintained their defensive positions more or less intact for five years and ended the war on a high note; it is true, too, that Iraq's large debt is, to an extent, a reflection of the Arab world's concern that Iraq should succeed in resisting any Iranian expansion. Furthermore, the Iraqi state has remained intact. Iraq's Shi'ites spurned Khomeini's blandishments, whilst the long-suffering Kurds (who have felt Baghdad's wrath since the end of the war) failed to advance the cause of their own independence. Nevertheless, since Saddam Hussein took great pains to identify the war as his own, he must bear the odium for its high cost. There is in Iraq none of the relative openness which characterizes Iranian politics, so it is all the more difficult to gauge the degree of dissatisfaction that exists among the general public and within the ranks of the armed forces. Iraq's government remains rigidly authoritarian and highly personalized. It is hard, therefore, not to be sceptical of Saddam Hussein's assurances that the Iraqi political system will be liberalized to allow for more popular participation. On the other hand, it seems quite likely that the trend towards greater private participation in the economy will continue, both because it promises greater efficiency and because it may defuse one form of discontent.

Military Lessons of the War

All wars provide a number of lessons – mainly for the military forces of the combatant states, but also, where similar conditions are applicable, to the armed forces of the world. In the case of the Iran–Iraq War, there are few operational lessons to be learned, partly because of a lack of information, but mainly because the circumstances, in terms of the troops taking part and the terrain fought over, are unlikely ever to be repeated elsewhere.

Probably the most important, and for the world as a whole the most dangerous, message is that sophisticated weapons in the form of ballistic missiles and chemical-warfare (CW) agents are now well entrenched in the Third World and that there is little compunction about using them. Iraq used chemical weapons on a number of occasions, and Iran on rather fewer. In the case of Iraq, their use was of obvious advantage, both tactically in the narrowly divided defensive battles of 1983–4 and as weapons of terror in the closing months of the war. It was the first well-documented use of CW on a modern battlefield since World War I, and its effectiveness was not lost on other third-world countries. At the conference on chemical warfare held in Paris in January 1989, even as a generalized condemnation of chemical warfare was being adopted in the conference hall, some third-world delegates were using corridor talks with Iraqi colleagues to seek aid for CW production of their own.

The so-called 'War of the Cities' also held a significant message for the world. The two countries exchanged more ballistic missile attacks than have occurred in any war since Germany launched V-2 missiles against England and Belgium during World War II. With the rapid proliferation of missiles in the Third World, and particularly in the volatile Middle

East, this form of terror campaign appears increasingly likely, and future hostilities may well claim many more civilian lives far from the battlefield (see pp. 14–25).

Iranian minelaying and harassment of neutral shipping introduced a new dimension into a war area – the involvement of third parties in the form of super-power and West European navies. The minelaying caught most navies, if not by surprise, certainly unprepared; mine warfare operations are the Cinderella of many fleets (the US Navy, for example, has only a very limited mine-warfare capability). But the experience in the Gulf underlines a potential threat both to naval units, including strategic assets putting to sea in time of crisis, and to the maritime reinforcement of Europe. The protection that US and West European units afforded against attacks on merchant shipping by the small Iranian navy indicated that such protection is still a valid concept, yet the difficulties that the mines caused indicated that they are still capable of causing major disruption at minimal cost. And, while the protection of shipping may still be largely effective, appropriate and proportionate retribution for mine or missile attacks on non-belligerent shipping may be harder to judge if the offender's assets do not present discrete and relatively low-cost targets, whose destruction would cause little collateral damage, as the Iranian off-shore oil facilities did in the Gulf.

Another obvious, but easily forgotten, lesson is the importance of nationalism and religious fervour in sustaining an army's willingness to suffer hardship and yet fight on. Iraq's initial attack on Iran, it is true, was undertaken with limited military objectives, and, when those objectives were easily reached, Iraqi forces failed to follow through to defeat an opposition which seemed on the verge of political collapse. Clearly Iraq (and many people outside Iraq) underestimated the determination of Iranians, despite very real internal and military problems, not to accept Iraq's seizure of what they considered their land. They fought with a fury that the Iraqis could not match. But, when Iran forced Iraq back onto its own territory, the situation changed. Now the Iraqis found a new zeal for defence, and the war settled into a modern version of the trench warfare of World War I, with neither side, until the very end of the war, able to move the front-line very far in either direction.

Impact on the Arab World
A war which lasts eight years can hardly fail to affect the surrounding region. The Iran–Iraq War not only involved those states in the immediate vicinity of the fighting, it also impinged upon the interests of others further afield. Within the Arab world, it exacerbated existing tensions as well as catalysing new forms of inter-Arab co-operation. It is probably too early to judge its lasting effects on inter-Arab politics, not least because of the uncertain implications of recent developments in the Arab–Israeli arena. Nevertheless, an assessment of post-war Arab politics might well begin by considering whether or not the war

advanced Arab interests. The answer will depend on the vantage point of the commentator.

Some have argued that the demotion of the Palestinian issue from the head of the Arab agenda was inevitable, because Iran was capable of destabilizing Arab politics in a way that Israel, for all its military might, was not. Years had been spent, and more might be spent, in futile discussions on a common Arab stance towards 'Palestine'; but the Iranian threat was urgent.

This argument has a certain logic to it. Nevertheless, one is entitled to be sceptical of the rhetoric surrounding Iraq's war effort, and of the motives of those who supported it. Saddam Hussein's repeated claim that Iraq fought the war on behalf of the Arab nation needs to be set against Iraq's stated political war aims, which, from the outset, had included the overthrow of the Khomeini regime. Nor did other Arab states support Iraq out of love for its ruler. Jordan came closest to being an unquestioning ally, but the Gulf states, particularly those furthest from Iraq, were equivocal supporters initially, only shedding the cloak of ambiguity when the military situation became grim. Egypt clearly exploited Iraq's need for military aid (and the Gulf states' anxieties) to accelerate its own rehabilitation into Arab circles.

On the other hand, it remains true that a number of important Arab states, including Egypt, were compelled to acknowledge that Iraq was defending their interests. Apart from keeping the Revolutionary Guards from Kuwait's frontiers, Iraq was weakening a country whose regime was capable not only of undermining the governments of the Arabian peninsula but also, if victorious, of stirring up sectarian or extremist forces throughout the region. This general feeling of vulnerability had a reconciling effect. As the war dragged on, it became clear to the members of the Gulf Co-operation Council (GCC) that they could not defend themselves in a crisis – hence Kuwait's recourse to, and the others' acquiescence in, the tanker leasing and reflagging that, in turn, led to the large Western naval presence in the Gulf; hence also the tendency to emphasize 'Arab national security' and to look for the strategic depth which, it was believed, only Egypt could provide.

It is instructive to consider the results of the extraordinary Arab summit held in Amman in November 1987. The main purpose of this meeting, the first for five years, was to secure a solid Arab front against Iran, and thereby to intensify the mounting international pressure on Tehran. The level of tension in the Gulf was high, and the memory of Iranian missile attacks on Kuwait and Iran's disruption of the *haj* still fresh. Rhetorically, the summit achieved some success, since Syria, Tehran's closest Arab ally, agreed formally to condemn Iran. But the price of unanimity was high; no sanctions on Iran were adopted, only Saudi Arabia broke diplomatic relations, and (although the summit resolved that re-establishing diplomatic relations with Egypt was henceforth a matter for individual Arab states) Syria stood firm against Egypt's readmission to the Arab League. Egypt's subsequent reintegration into the Arab system has confirmed what the summit tacitly admitted: to all intents and purposes, the unanimity required by the Arab League had become something of an irrelevance.

Egypt has been a major beneficiary of the war. Whereas President Sadat was content to spurn other Arab leaders, his successor, Hosny Mubarak, made a sustained effort to bridge the gap between Egypt and the Arab world; Sadat had supplied Iraq with arms for cash, but Mubarak sought a political dividend as well. Following extensive Egyptian–Iraqi contacts, Tareq Aziz, Iraq's foreign minister, became the first Arab minister to break the official boycott of Egypt by visiting Cairo in July 1983. In February 1984 the Islamic Conference once more welcomed Egyptian delegates, and Jordan re-established diplomatic relations in September of the same year. Since the Amman summit, all but two of the Arab states which broke off official contacts in 1979 have reopened their embassies in Cairo, and Egypt once more participates in a range of Arab organizations. But it is worth noting that, despite all the references during the war to Egypt's vital role in defending fellow Arabs in the Gulf, President Mubarak steadfastly denied that he had committed, or would commit, Egyptian forces to the war zone. Apart from military advice and the sale of arms and ammunition, the Egyptian contribution was chiefly psychological. Moreover, Egypt's rehabilitation was in no way connected with its success in mediating between the Arabs and Israel or in advancing the Palestinian cause, for there had been no such success.

Notwithstanding Arab solidarity with Iraq, and Egypt's return to Arab ranks, there were many who claimed that the war harmed Arab interests. Specifically, they deplored the fact that the fears of a handful of states had so thoroughly eclipsed the Palestinian struggle, which was far closer to the hearts of most Arabs than any putative Iranian threat. Certainly, the treatment – or rather non-treatment – of the Palestinian question at the Amman summit was noteworthy. Palestinian rights, the central theme of most previous Arab summits, were relegated to a lowly position on the agenda, and this confirmed the impression that the issue had come to be considered as less important than the Gulf War. There is much satisfaction in the Arab world that the continued violence in the West Bank and the PLO's decision to recognize the existence of Israel have since refocused regional and world attention on the core dispute in the Middle East.

Does the end of the Gulf War mean there will be concerted and effective Arab action on behalf of the Palestinians? Probably not. The Arab states subscribe to the principle of a Palestinian state in general, but in the past their relations with the PLO have been fraught with misunderstandings and marred by competing interests. Such obstacles are unlikely to disappear completely. King Hussein, having divested himself of the financial burden of the West Bank, can afford to take a more detached view; and, although Israel is under pressure to counter the PLO's newly-won international sympathy, it is clearly premature to talk of a Palestinian state. For Iraq, which has for some time aligned itself with the moderate wing of the PLO, assisting the Palestinians will be a less onerous task than confronting Iran. Syria, on the other hand, opposes the conciliatory stance that is now the hallmark of the mainstream PLO and will object to any settlement which ignores its own claim to the Golan Heights. But its economy is weak and in need of continued Arab subventions; its patrons in Moscow are themselves pursuing a more pragmatic line towards Israel; and Saddam Hussein has turned his attention to frustrating Syrian plans in Lebanon. Egypt's position is also changed, in that it may now be able to play the mediating role that has eluded it for the past decade. Hosny Mubarak has a strong incentive to emphasize Egypt's vital role in any lasting Middle East settlement.

Realistically, one should expect no more than loosely co-ordinated Arab diplomatic and financial support for the PLO. Neither the Palestinian cause nor such amorphous notions as 'Arab national security' can create a genuinely pan-Arab effort, despite the Arab leaders' devoted repetition of such formulae. The traditional discourse of Arabism is becoming ever less relevant to the realities of Arab politics. Indeed, behind the fog of rhetoric there is a growing realization that the future of Arab co-operation lies not in the increasingly ineffectual Arab League, but in smaller regional bodies like the GCC. Simply by continuing to function for eight years and providing a forum for regular, high-level discussion, this body has accomplished more than all previous Arab attempts at political and economic co-ordination.

Since the beginning of 1989, two apparently similar bodies have been created at opposite ends of the Arab world. The Arab Maghreb Union, comprising the four Maghreb states and Mauritania, is intended to develop into a common market, in order to meet the challenge of a single European market in 1992. This latest attempt at Maghreb unity, conceived in the wake of the 1988 Algiers summit, has a long but undistinguished pedigree; all previous unions amongst Maghreb states have been stillborn. The potential for co-operation is nevertheless large, so long as the recently re-established amity between Morocco and Algeria lasts (see pp. 192–95). On 15 February 1989, two days before the Maghreb Union came into being, Iraq, Jordan, Egypt and North Yemen created the Arab Co-operation Council. It, too, aims to become an economic bloc, open to other Arab states should they wish to join. The friendship between Iraq and its fellow members is a product of the Gulf War, and it is more than likely that the setting up of this body reflects both Iraqi gratitude for past assistance and a certain post-war euphoria. The Arab Co-operation Council has far greater human resources than the GCC, but it lacks the latter's political homogeneity (and geographical contiguity). Its achievements will probably be relatively modest.

The GCC itself has the advantage that the political structures and interests of its members are relatively complementary, despite the disadvantage of the disparity in size and power between Saudi Arabia and the other members. It represents an attempt to meet local security and development needs with local resources. To date, it must be judged a qualified success, but the period ahead will present a number of challenges. An impressive list of economic agreements has yet to be translated into reality. Moreover, as the Gulf War amply demonstrated, the GCC's defences remain inadequate, and the problems of capability and co-ordination clearly need be addressed. The solution to these problems can only be political. It presupposes common economic priorities and, more importantly, a common approach to internal and external security. Achieving this will not be easy, since the GCC's member states are unanimous neither on the external threat nor even on the direction and pace of internal change. They are, moreover, spectators of regional developments over which they have little influence. To complicate matters, they will find it difficult, singly or collectively, to remain aloof from Arab and Islamic politics. If this prognosis sounds gloomy, it should be remembered that the GCC's purpose is the efficient allocation of resources, not simply the convening of ritual summits.

Arab politics are in a state of flux. The distribution of political influence is still unclear, and fledgling alliances have yet to solidify. However uncertain the outcome of current trends, it is tempting to suggest that they will be judged to have been less significant than another of the war's side-effects – the restoration of Egypt's Arab credentials. But the Egypt which once more finds itself in the bosom of the Arab world is now heavily indebted, overpopulated and dependent on the outside world for vital economic support. These weaknesses compromise its ability to play an active regional role, except insofar as others encourage or finance its efforts. Nevertheless, it is the state which made peace with Israel respectable. Inasmuch as this policy has now been endorsed by almost all other Arab states, as well as by the PLO, there has been a sea change in Middle East politics.

Africa

AFRICA: PROSPECTS FOR PARTIAL PEACE

Most states of the African continent suffered major economic and financial difficulties in 1988; these were compounded by political turmoil or ethnic disputes in a number of others; a few more had to deal with agricultural and environmental crises; and some, like Ethiopia and Sudan, had to contend with all these problems, plus civil wars. Only in two widely separated areas of the continent, the Maghreb in the far north and southern Africa, were there improved prospects for peace.

One of the more tragic events of the year was the ethnic massacre in Burundi involving the Hutu tribe, which are the majority, and the Tutsis, the minority but the holders of power. Reports coming out of Burundi in August 1988 accused the Burundian army, composed almost entirely of Tutsis, of killing vast numbers of Hutus in the north. Government sources argued that in fact many Hutu had also been killed by Tutsis armed with bows and arrows. In any case, over 60,000 refugees, mainly Hutu, fled to Rwanda as a result of the crisis.

In Nigeria, it was religious, rather than ethnic, problems that created headlines in November, when the military government bypassed the normal selection procedure and chose a new Sultan of Sokoto who, according to Muslims rioting in the north at this choice, did not have the votes of local king-makers. The events were significant because of the intense debate in Nigeria about whether the country should accept the *Sharia* law. The Sokoto Sultanate is the spiritual head of Nigeria's 50 million Muslims, and the federal government will need its support to hold the country together. A major challenge remains the establishment of a constitution which would pave the way to elections in 1992 and a return to civilian rule.

Throughout much of the rest of Africa there was little cheerful news. The Ivory Coast, long considered one of the few relative success stories of West Africa, began seriously to feel the pinch of declining world coffee and cocoa markets. While President Houphouet-Boigny's decision to hold up supplies to the international market did not cause the great treasury crisis some feared, international financial institutions concerned by the general situation repeated their call for a devaluation of the CFA franc – which would naturally affect the thirteen other African members of the franc zone. Benin's President Mathieu Kerekou was in trouble throughout the year, not only because of his incapacity to establish a badly-needed structural adjustment programme, but also because of army discontent which produced two coup attempts. Chad's President Hissène Habré felt sufficiently confident in the peace process begun early in the year to announce in October 1988 that he would renew diplomatic relations with Libya, even though the dispute over the Aouzou Strip in the north of the country remains unresolved. In Somalia, fighting intensified in the north of the country after the May 1988 peace agreement between Ethiopia and Somalia. Somalian rebels based in Ethiopia streamed across the border and destroyed the northern towns of Hargeisa and Burao. In January 1989 Somalia's ruling party drew up a rehabilitation programme for the north, but doubts still lingered about the ability of President Siad Barre's regime to survive, given the intensity of northern dissatisfaction.

In Sudan, the civil war continued, with both sides frustrating the efforts of relief agencies to tackle the famine conditions in the south of the country. (While the south was badly affected by drought, the north suffered from catastrophic floods; in both areas the difficulties were aggravated by the continuing war.) The southern Sudanese People's Liberation Army (SPLA), led by John Garang, was able to score some military successes – notably in October 1988, when it cut off Juba, the southern capital. The national unity government of Sadeq el-Mahdi, which now included the National Islamic Front (NIF), remained paralysed by its internal divisions, especially over the application of Islamic law. The establishment of a legal, political and economic system which could both harmonize the disparate views of the various northern groups and satisfy the southerners, suspicious that their own identity will not be respected by the north, remains a distant prospect. Nevertheless, Western aid donors, who have called attention to the war's effects on food distribution, and some regional states, including Egypt and Saudi Arabia, have intensified their demands for negotiations and a settlement between the Sudanese belligerents.

Some hopes were raised after one of the ruling Sudanese parties, the Democratic Unionist Party (DUP), signed a peace accord with the rebels on 16 November. This called, *inter alia*, for a cease-fire, the formation of a preparatory committee to convene a constitutional conference before 31 December, and a freeze on *Hudud*, the Islamic punishments carried out under *Sharia* law. The initiative was encouraged by Egypt (historically close to the DUP and worried by the increasing Islamization of the Khartoum government), grudgingly supported by Prime Minister Sadeq el-Mahdi, and eventually officially accepted by the cabinet. But in late December the parliament refused to endorse the plan (which el-Mahdi had put to it only half-heartedly), and the SPLA then vowed to fight on. Angered by this reversal of the peace process, the DUP left the government coalition and tried to continue some form of negotiation with the rebels in Addis Ababa. While the Prime Minister's *Umma* party and its remaining coalition partner, the NIF, retained a technical majority in parliament, the government was clearly weakened by the DUP's departure.

In February 1989 the US sought to mediate between the rebels and the government, and senior US officials, notably James Baker, began more openly to press for some sort of agreement. By the end of the month the Sudanese military demanded that the civilian government stop the war, thus placing considerable strains on a ruling leadership suffering from diminishing support. Meanwhile, the SPLA continued to mount offensives (it had already, in January, captured the garrison town of Nasr, which lies between Juba and Khartoum). Leaders of both sides in the civil war have thus continued to demonstrate a taste for blood which hardly meets the Sudanese people's need for food.

The Ethiopian government was blessed with good rains and a decent, if still woefully inadequate, harvest, but it continued to pursue a rigid socialist economic programme. This brought disputes with aid donors and pressure from the USSR, which is especially keen to see increases in agricultural production. The government announced several times during the year that it was trying to modify its economic policies and succeeded thereby in renewing World Bank funding. But President Mengistu Haile Mariam remained committed to resettling the population in newly created villages and to the creation of producers' co-operatives, measures which drew wide criticism from outside agricultural experts. On the military front, the government displayed some willingness to open discussions with its opponents, while suffering reverses in battle, but no accord is in sight.

In March 1988 the Eritrean People's Liberation Front (EPLF) overran the garrison town Afabet. In June government forces made some advances against the Tigray People's Liberation Front (TPLF), but by the end of August had failed in their objective of controlling the Shire region in north-western Tigray. At the end of 1988, with Soviet encouragement, the Ethiopian government began to seek direct talks with the EPLF, as military operations began to subside. Leaders of the EPLF remained sceptical – all the more so in January 1989, when the government announced that it was considering splitting Eritrea into two self-governing regions, one for the Muslim lowlands, and the other for the mainly Christian highlands from which the EPLF draws most of its support. By February, fighting was again on the upsurge. Endaselassie, an important government stronghold, fell to the EPLF and the TPLF, who for the first time planned and executed a joint operation against government forces. Outside powers are likely to demand that Addis Ababa make a greater commitment to peace-making, yet the intermittent fighting of the last year demonstrates that such powers will remain unable to force a settlement until the local actors show a greater desire for compromise.

In northern and southern Africa international diplomacy had a more substantial impact on local prospects for peace than it did on the conflicts in Ethiopia and Sudan. Algeria placed more emphasis on renewing its diplomatic ties with Morocco than on continuing a high level of support for the Polisario Front, and this made the attenuation of the Western Sahara dispute more likely. Further south, the untiring efforts of US Assistant Secretary of State for African Affairs, Chester Crocker – pursued as the USSR was putting more pressure on both Angola and

Cuba, and as South Africa decided that war was too costly – made possible a peace agreement which will remove Cuban forces from Angola and bring independence to Namibia. While the outlook in the rest of Africa continues to seem very grim indeed, in these two areas at least, hopes for a more stable future have risen.

THE MAGHREB: A SLOW DANCE TO UNITY

For the four North African states of Libya, Tunisia, Algeria and Morocco, 1988 was dominated by moves towards regional economic and political integration. These moves went hand in hand with a general relaxation of tension in north Africa throughout the year and reflected the realization by Maghreb leaders that the major regional problem for north African states, the Western Sahara dispute, was approaching resolution.

The crucial development came on 10 June, when the five Maghreb leaders and heads of state – Col. Muammar Gaddafi of Libya, President Zine el-Abidine Ben Ali of Tunisia, President Chadli Benjedid of Algeria, King Hassan II of Morocco and President Maouiya Ould Sid Ahmed Taya of Mauritania – met for the first Maghreb summit for twenty-five years in Zeralda, Algeria. It had been stimulated by significant improvements in bilateral relations between the states concerned, such as the restoration of diplomatic relations between Morocco and Algeria on 16 May and the gradual improvement in relations between Libya and Tunisia in the early part of the year.

However, it also reflected major domestic changes. Algeria's long-standing economic and social decline had forced its leaders to search for a path towards regional integration and had profoundly modified their original intransigence over the issue of Western Saharan independence. Tunisia's change of government had introduced significant reductions in domestic political tensions and had persuaded the new leadership that the nation's problems could best be solved within a regional context. Libya, too, had come to see that its serious economic problems and popular disaffection from the Gaddafi regime would best be countered by regional integration. In Morocco, the army's success in establishing control over virtually all the Western Sahara made it possible for King Hassan to show a degree of flexibility over the issue that had been impossible before.

Domestic Affairs
Morocco
One factor that might well ease the transition from confrontation to peaceful integration in the Western Sahara – and thereby clear the way for regional political and economic integration – is the domestic administrative reform now being contemplated in Morocco. In late 1988 King Hassan suggested that Morocco decentralize its internal adminis-

tration so as to provide internal autonomy under a federal government that would handle external affairs and national matters. Eight autonomous regions, including the Western Sahara, have been suggested, together with a ninth for Moroccan migrants in Europe and elsewhere.

Not only would the decentralization reform facilitate a final solution of the Western Sahara issue, it would improve Morocco's central government expenditure position. Morocco has been under considerable pressure from the IMF to reduce the role of central government and the public sector in the economy. Indeed, its attempts to resolve its massive foreign-debt burden – $US 17 bn at the end of 1987 – have largely depended on IMF support. This was manifest most recently in August 1988, when a further standby arrangement was granted, offering SDR 210 m (about $US 271 m) over a 16-month period.

The result has been an energetic attempt to reform the Moroccan economy over the past four years. Subsidies on consumer goods, particularly foodstuffs, have been cut, and the private sector has been able to expand its activities into many areas previously reserved for the public sector. The reform efforts have led to a significant reduction in current-account deficits, with the government claiming a surplus in its balance-of-payments current account in 1988. In large measure, though, these improvements have been due to particularly good weather, which has meant exceptionally abundant harvests. The very real progress made by the Moroccan economy cannot be ignored, but the foreign debt nevertheless continued to rise towards $US 19 bn at the end of 1988.

Tunisia
In Tunisia President Ben Ali has pushed the economic reform and liberalization policies of his predecessor, despite difficulties created by a near drought in 1987 and locust infestation in 1988. Value-added tax was introduced in July 1988, thereby improving government tax collection, and privatization of the state textile sector proceeded slowly. Although the trade deficit did not fall significantly, because of agricultural difficulties, the country had no difficulty in satisfying its external financing requirements for the year, estimated to be around $US 0.9–1.0 bn, while medium- and long-term foreign debt remained steady at around $US 7 bn, with a debt service ratio of 24%.

These economic policies have been accompanied by a series of liberalization measures designed to heal the wounds created by the Bourguiba regime in its latter years and to restore stability to government. All political prisoners have been freed, and the reduced role of the former single party, the PSD, has been symbolized by its change of name to the *Rassemblement Constitutionnel Démocratique* (RCD) in February. The opposition (six political parties have now been legalized) has been persuaded to take an active part in Tunisian politics with the promise of new legislative elections in April 1989, and the role of a multi-party democracy has been written into the constitution. At the same time, limited-term tenure of presidential office has been restored, and Ben Ali will have to seek re-election in two years' time.

One major achievement has been to create a political consensus in Tunisia, symbolized in the National Pact announced by the President on the first anniversary of his accession to power. It has enabled all major political trends in the country to coalesce in support of the government, which was reformed in late July, when all remaining Bourguiba appointees were removed. Although the fundamentalist Islamic Tendency Movement is not yet able to participate in the elections – political parties must not discuss race, language or religion in their party platforms – its leaders have now all been released or have returned from exile. Rachid Ghannouchi, the 'emir' of the movement, has expressed his support for the Ben Ali regime, and the Movement is becoming one of several political options open to Tunisians, rather than a semi-clandestine threat to political stability.

Libya

A superficially similar series of political developments has also taken place in Libya, where the decision in February to open the country's borders and to allow exiles to visit their families freely has been mirrored by other developments. Over 400 political prisoners have been released, political blacklists are supposed to have been destroyed, Col. Gaddafi has called for the abolition of capital punishment, and prisons are supposed to have been demolished. In the aftermath of the General People's Congress meeting at the start of March, the Libyan leader also came out in support of human rights, demanded a greater role for women in Libyan society and agreed to the reintroduction of the private sector into the country's economy.

To a large extent, the leadership adopted these policies to make a virtue out of necessity. The domestic situation had become extremely tense at the end of 1987 as a result both of the calamitous military defeats suffered by Libya's armed forces in Chad and the radical decline of the country's oil revenues in recent years. The government has responded by cutting imports, thus creating inevitable shortages of vital consumer goods. The situation was worsened by the steady destruction of the private retail sector over the past five years.

The private-sector reforms are not an indication that Libya has abandoned its radical policies in the political, social and economic spheres. Indeed, proposals at the start of 1989 to dissolve Libyan state institutions suggested that the ideal of *Jamahiriya* or 'Popular Authority' continues to inspire the regime. None of the repressive organs of the Libyan state – the security services and the Revolutionary Committee movement – has been dissolved, even though the latter has been severely criticized. In fact, Col. Gaddafi has made it clear that he has merely paused on his way towards the total transformation of Libyan society. Nonetheless, the compromises made to date cannot easily be reversed, if the regime wishes to maintain its control. Furthermore, if

Libya's integration into the affairs of North Africa continues, it will become more difficult for Tripoli to plough a political furrow that is radically different from those of its neighbours.

Algeria

The effect of economic change on domestic affairs was particularly evident during 1988 in Algeria. The Algerian government, which calculates that its real purchasing power has dropped by 80% since the 1986 oil price collapse, has attempted to respond by reducing imports ruthlessly. As a result, consumer choice has been sharply reduced. At the same time, the government has continued to pursue economic reforms that are liberalizing the state sector but accentuating the growing inequalities within Algerian society. Popular support for the reforms waned and was replaced by growing discontent. The government nevertheless pressed ahead with its programme and on 23 June set up eight trust companies to hold shares in the 120 state companies which now operate as autonomous entities in growing competition with the burgeoning private sector. The trust companies, which may be allowed to accept private capital participation, are expected to provide a route towards the eventual privatization of the public sector through wider share ownership.

The effect of the current problems of the economy has been varied. On the one hand, discontent with shortages and poor services has reached bursting point; on the other, supporters of the more egalitarian state socialist policies of Chadli's predecessor, Houari Boumedienne, have sought an opportunity to reassert their power. Non-bureaucratic resistance to regime policy has also developed at both ends of the political spectrum; supporters of the secular Left – represented by the outlawed Communist party, and fundamentalists on the religious Right, who are particularly strong in areas of the major cities and in the universities, have made their unhappiness clear.

In October the situation exploded: general popular discontent with shortages and poor services combined with industrial unrest in Rouiba and Algiers to produce widespread rioting. Most major urban centres were affected, and the government, shaken by the intensity of popular anger, had to call in the army to restore order. The riots were put down, but with considerable brutality and a significant loss of life.

There were suggestions that Islamic fundamentalists were basically responsible for the riots. There were also hints that the riots had been fomented by Boumediennist elements in the government party, the *Front de Libération Nationale* (FLN), and the administration to try to discredit the Chadli regime and its policies of economic liberalization. While both may have played a role, in reality the basic cause was popular discontent, particularly amongst the young. Recognizing this, the government tried to allay tensions after the riots by ensuring that the supply of consumer goods was radically improved.

At the same time, President Chadli seized the opportunity to reassert his position against his ideological opponents. Recalcitrant army commanders were sacked in a move designed to curb the independence of the armed forces; reforms designed to reduce the power of the FLN were approved by referendum in early November; the FLN's sixth congress was brought forward from its expected date in December to formalize the President's candidature for the forthcoming presidential elections (he was appointed as sole candidate and re-elected in January 1989); and the government and FLN power structures were reformed to remove old hard-liners from power. A referendum on 24 February 1989 overwhelmingly approved constitutional proposals which will ultimately lead to a degree of political plurality in Algeria. There is no doubt that the Chadli regime has bought itself some time, but it will soon have to deliver concrete results to the population at large if a repetition of the riots is to be avoided.

Regional Unity

In addition to these specific domestic concerns, another factor behind moves towards regional integration is an Algerian initiative, begun in 1982, to resolve regional political tensions caused by the Western Sahara dispute and the competition between Algeria, Libya and Morocco for control of the region. This has been underscored by the recent economic problems faced by the Maghreb and the implicit threat posed by the European Community's proposed Single Market after 1992. The five states involved now recognize their common need for economic, if not political, co-operation and integration.

Early in 1983 Algeria moved to isolate Morocco, and to a lesser extent Libya, by signing the Treaty for Concord and Fraternity with Tunisia on 19 March. Mauritania adhered to the treaty the following December. Morocco and Libya responded in 1984 with a short-lived formal alliance (the Arab-African Union) which was suspended by Libya in late 1986 in the wake of an official visit to Morocco by the then Israeli premier, Shimon Peres. At that time, it seemed that the antagonism between Morocco and Algeria would make further movement towards Maghreb unity impossible.

Two factors have transformed this situation. The first was the crisis that has faced the Algerian economy since the collapse in oil prices in 1986. Algeria has had to seek economic opportunities which minimize dependence on external commerce and the danger of the growth of foreign debt. At the same time, the President Chadli's administration has sought a pragmatic approach to relations with its neighbours.

The second factor has been the transformation of the political environment in North Africa over the past two years. The departure of Habib Bourguiba from power in Tunisia, the apparent political and diplomatic moderation of Libya's Col. Gaddafi and Morocco's evident success in establishing its presence in the Western Sahara have changed past assumptions about political differences in the region. As a result,

Algeria has tried to improve relations with Morocco and Libya, the two states not integrated into its 1983 regional treaty system.

Algeria has also sought a diplomatic resolution of the Western Sahara conflict between Morocco and the indigenous national liberation movement, the Polisario Front, which – with its associated government-in-exile, the Sahrawi Arab Democratic Republic (SADR) – is based in the camps around the Algerian border town of Tindouf, where some 165,000 refugees are living. This approach led to a series of high-level visits between Rabat and Algiers in mid-1987. The visits had sought to iron out the two countries' remaining political differences and to formulate areas of potential economic co-operation. In mid-1988, diplomatic relations were renewed.

The Zeralda meeting on Maghreb unity had established a Maghreb Commission which was to plan the detailed structure for political and economic integration. At its first meeting, in early July, the Commission set up five study groups to prepare for another Maghreb summit, held in mid-February 1989 in Rabat. Tunisia chaired the group handling social and security issues, Mauritania took responsibility for that dealing with cultural issues, Morocco handled finance and customs, Algeria economic issues, and Libya questions of political organization.

There are, however, still fears about the implications of closer political links between North African states. The Western Sahara dispute, although no longer so divisive an issue as it once was, is not yet fully resolved. Considerable differences also remain between the governments involved over what regional unity will really mean. Nonetheless, there is a general feeling in North African capitals that developments in 1988 have produced an irreversible change in regional relations. Algerian politicians have accepted that the original objectives of the 1983 Treaty of Concord and Fraternity have now been surpassed, and that there is likely to be a permanent transformation in regional diplomatic relations. The future of regional economic initiatives – which, apart from the gas pipeline project from Algeria to Libya via Tunisia, only involve bilateral co-operation – may, however, be less dramatic.

Bilateral Relations
Bilateral contacts played a major role in cementing moves towards Maghreb unity throughout 1988. The contacts between Morocco and Algeria, largely the result of Algerian initiatives, paralleled similar moves with the other two North African states. These were particularly striking in the case of Tunisia and Libya after the overthrow of former Tunisian leader Bourguiba.

Despite Algerian anxieties over the pace of the Tunisian–Libyan *rapprochement* during 1988, Tunis and Algiers fundamentally agree over regional integration policy. This was evident during a visit to Libya at the start of January by President Chadli. The Algerian leader was able to further economic co-operation between the two countries, although he resisted Libyan suggestions of full political and economic integration; Algeria would prefer an association along the lines of the European Community as an ultimate goal. Although Tunisia has suggested that North African borders should be opened as well, its regional political vision does not otherwise substantially differ from that of Algeria.

Diplomatic relations between Tunis and Tripoli, cut in August 1985, were restored on 25 December 1987, and the latter offered a grant of $US 10 m to compensate the 30,000 Tunisian workers summarily expelled from Libya when relations were originally broken. Agreements were also reached on the settlement of a $US 10-m Libyan debt to Tunis Air, the Tunisian national airline, and on the restoration of joint economic projects dating from 1984. In early February 1988 Col. Gaddafi visited the Tunisian capital. As a result visa restrictions for cross-border visits were removed, and Tunisia decided to accept a 1982 International Court judgment on the maritime frontier between the two countries. (The actual land frontier was opened in April, and by November a million Libyans had visited Tunisia without needing exit visas.) Later in February, after a brief visit to the Algerian industrial city of Annaba, Col. Gaddafi joined Tunisian President Ben Ali and the Algerian leader at the Tunisian border settlement of Sakiet Sidi Youssef, itself a symbol of Tunisian–Algerian bilateral co-operation.

These diplomatic developments were formalized in a further meeting between Gaddafi and Ben Ali on the island of Djerba on 22 May, when agreements on mutual property rights for Libyan and Tunisian nationals, on removal of visa restrictions and on freedom of movement were signed. At the same time it was agreed that Tunisia and Libya would engage in joint oil exploration of their common continental shelf, and that they would participate in the Algerian tripartite gas pipeline proposed during President Chadli's visit to Tripoli in January. President Ben Ali's formal return visit to Tripoli came eventually on 6 August, after a diplomatic postponement from June because of a dispute between the two governments over the division of revenues from joint oil prospecting in the Gulf of Gabes. Proposals for a pipeline to Zarzis and an expressway to Sfax were discussed. Finally, on 4 September, just after the annual celebrations of the Great September Revolution in Libya, the two leaders jointly attended the inauguration of Libya's massive offshore Bouri field, and a 3,000-km² joint exploration area to the north-west of the field was opened.

The Western Sahara Issue
The most striking development during 1988 was the growth of a consensus within North Africa that a solution to the Western Sahara conflict is now not only possible but may soon occur. In large measure this is due to the radical improvement in relations between Morocco and Algeria. It also reflects, however, the growing role of the UN in mediating a solution between those primarily involved – Morocco and the Polisario Front. The mediation process really began in late 1987, with the visit of a technical commission to Morocco, the Western Sahara and Algeria.

The commission contacted the Moroccan and Algerian governments, as well as the Polisario Front, and then reported back to the UN Secretary-General at the start of 1988.

On the basis of the commission's report the Secretary-General formulated a plan for the fulfilment of UN and OAU resolutions on self-determination for the population of the Western Sahara, and this was submitted to Morocco and the Polisario Front in mid-year. The plan called for a referendum under UN auspices in which those concerned could chose independence or integration into Morocco. No provision was made for a third question – about autonomy under Moroccan sovereignty – to be asked. The UN plan also did not require direct negotiations between the Polisario Front and Morocco beforehand, or the withdrawal of the Moroccan military presence and administration, even though these had figured in the original resolutions. The referendum was to be open only to those who could justify their claim to be Sahrawi on the basis of the 1974 Spanish census of the Western Sahara.

The plan was eventually accepted by both parties on 30 August, although with reservations from the Polisario Front. It was clear that the Front had come under considerable pressure from Algeria – which, by then, was anxious to bring the Western Sahara issue to a speedy conclusion so as not to endanger its *rapprochement* with Morocco and the progress being made towards regional unity. In addition, Polisario had been unexpectedly encouraged by aid from Saudi Arabia. The Saudi government had for several years been quietly attempting to mediate in the conflict and, in July, had persuaded both sides to private meetings in Taif. Polisario officials pointed out that the meetings amounted to the direct negotiations that they had been seeking but also explained that they were convinced that Maghreb unity could only be achieved once the conflict was resolved – a not-too-subtle hint to Algeria that the SADR was not prepared to abandon its claims for the sake of Algerian convenience.

Indeed, the Polisario Front had frequently reminded North African statesmen that it was not simply an extension of Algerian foreign policy. In December 1987 and January 1988 there were repeated attacks on Morocco's defensive wall system, a pattern repeated in August and September 1988. It is clear that, although the wall and the 100,000 men Morocco has stationed in the Western Sahara effectively protect the settled areas of the region (where there has now been over $US 2-bn worth of civilian investment), the Front's forces – variously estimated at between 2,000 and 6,000 men – are still well equipped and active. It is also clear that Algeria is not prepared to hinder the Front's activities too greatly, and may have exploited them on occasion for its own ends.

The September 1988 attacks marked a temporary hardening in the attitudes of Algeria and the SADR. Their first diplomatic expression came at the annual Non-Aligned Movement meeting in Nicosia, where Morocco and Algeria clashed over the Western Sahara issue, and Algeria once again called on Morocco to open direct negotiations with the Polisario Front. Then, in late October, the issue resurfaced at the

UN, where the annual resolution of the Decolonization Committee on the Western Sahara duly condemned Moroccan intransigence – albeit with fewer votes in favour than in the past. International disfavour had been incited by a series of Algerian and SADR demands that appeared to qualify the UN Secretary-General's peace plan; these included a formal cease-fire, direct negotiations, the reinstitution of Spanish law in the Western Sahara, the removal of all migrants from the region, freedom of access for supporters of the Front, access for the Front's military forces and a Moroccan withdrawal as pre-conditions to any UN-sponsored referendum.

This aberration was soon overcome. Its major proponent, Algerian Foreign Minister Taleb Ibrahimi, was removed from power a few weeks later as part of a government reshuffle, and Morocco itself began to reassess its position. One month later, in interviews in France, King Hassan suddenly announced that he was prepared to meet leaders of the Front for 'discussions'. Although he was anxious to emphasize that there could be no formal negotiations before the anticipated referendum, Sahrawi leaders were in no doubt that the long-sought direct negotiations were now really possible, and at the start of 1989 Front leaders visited King Hassan in Marrakesh. A solution to the Western Sahara problem now seemed close, and it looked as though Morocco was likely to gain the sovereignty over the territory that it had always demanded.

Problems persist, nonetheless. In response to the Moroccan gesture, the Front declared a unilateral truce during February 1989 to coincide with Algerian President Chadli's first formal visit to Morocco and the all-important Maghreb heads-of-state summit in Rabat on 14 February. But it still insists on direct negotiations, a UN-administered referendum, the withdrawal of Moroccan forces and administration from the region and the return of its own forces and supporters to the territory while the referendum is in progress. There were even rumours in mid-February that the cease-fire would be broken as a result of these tensions. The rumours may well have led to the Moroccan decision not to hold the second round of discussions with the Front before the Maghreb summit, as had been proposed.

Conclusion

In many respects, 1988 has been an extremely hopeful year for North Africa. Regional unity has at last moved from the ideological sphere into the realm of practical politics. A solution to the Western Sahara dispute now seems possible after thirteen years of conflict. Economic reform appears to be about to bear fruit in at least two countries – Morocco and Tunisia – thereby improving national stability. At the same time, however, serious tensions still persist. It is not clear whether the pace of economic and political reforms in Algeria will satisfy a population increasingly confident about its capacity for self-assertion. The economic reforms and political liberalization proposed by the Gaddafi regime lacked conviction and left many Libyans with a profound sense of anxiety about the future. In short, the problems facing the region could still undermine the very real gains in regional and national stability that were registered during 1988.

Indeed, despite the moves that have been made towards regional integration, the future must be treated with considerable caution. In economic terms, all north African states are far more immediately. concerned with their relations with Europe – as a trading partner and a source of finance – than they are with each other. In political terms, the very different regimes involved are bound to place domestic stability and survival above the uncertain benefits of regional integration. In the short term, therefore, they are likely to advance far more slowly towards regional integration than their public statements might suggest. The same is true of domestic political reform. The moves towards democratization are, in reality, regime responses to popular unrest, and not the consequence of ideological conviction.

SOUTHERN AFRICA: SOLVING PROBLEMS

The change in the super-power relationship which helped to produce the peace epidemic of 1988 did not leave southern Africa untouched. Indeed, there were suggestions that the US–Soviet co-operation which produced the Angolan–Namibian settlement could yet develop into a joint strategy for the whole troubled region. The treaties signed at the United Nations in New York on 22 December 1988 between Angola, South Africa and Cuba brought to an end nine months of negotiation under the chairmanship of the United States. They secured the removal of South African troops from Angola and Namibia and the phased withdrawal of Cuban forces from Angola, and they signalled some hope for an end to South Africa's 73-year rule of Namibia – Africa's last colony.

In the first few days of April 1989 the settlement was jeopardized by large numbers of South West African People's Organization (SWAPO) guerrillas moving across Namibia's northern border. The UN Transition Advisory Group (UNTAG) monitors, deploying under Security Council Resolution 435 (see below), had not reached full strength on the border, and South African forces had already withdrawn to barracks; under a UN dispensation, some South African forces therefore returned to the border area, and the ensuing fighting left over 200 dead. Pretoria threatened to abrogate the treaties unless the UN could bring the situation under control. Nonetheless, the underlying dynamics that had produced the 1988 breakthrough still held out a promise of increased international stability for a region of 60 million people, many of them among the world's poorest and all of them affected directly or indirectly by the conflict which had wracked the region for the past thirteen years.

Negotiation over Namibia

Although regarded as an American diplomatic triumph, the settlement depended critically on Moscow's new willingness to assess the political and economic cost of its regional involvements against its own economic needs. The mounting cost of Soviet support for Angola's MPLA government trapped in an unwinnable civil war (estimated at $US 1 bn in 1988), the associated cost of supporting Cuba and its troops, and a desire to defuse East–West confrontation in the region all appeared to have influenced the change in Soviet strategy. Soviet spokesmen have insisted that Moscow's role in the peace process was the product of a major policy revision which now seeks political, rather than military, solutions to Africa's widening conflicts.

For the United States, the settlement (brokered by Dr Chester Crocker, US Assistant Secretary of State for Africa) appeared to vindicate its much reviled doctrine of 'linkage'. This accepted the South African position that Namibian independence under UN Resolution 435 of 1978, should be linked to the withdrawal of Cuban troops in neighbouring Angola. The settlement was also seen to justify Washington's refusal to recognize the MPLA government in Luanda and its decision, once the repeal of the Clark Amendment permitted it, to supply Dr Jonas Savimbi's rebel UNITA forces with weapons – notably $US 30-m-worth of *Stinger* missiles – despite the fact that South Africa was UNITA's other main source of aid and support.

The campaign promise by Democratic presidential candidate Michael Dukakis to reverse this policy, recognize the MPLA government and cease all aid to UNITA served to delay final agreement by Cuba and Angola until such prospects faded with the presidential election in November. By the same token, however, the prospect of a Dukakis presidency appears to have concentrated South African minds on the need for a settlement while Reagan was still in the White House.

Moscow played no direct role in the quadripartite talks involving South Africa, Cuba, Angola and the United States, which began in London in May and continued in five countries before the two separate treaties were signed in New York in December. Nonetheless, Crocker kept his opposite number, Vladillen Vasev, and Soviet Deputy Foreign Minister Anatoly Adamishin informed every step of the way. The USSR finally played a decisive role in the penultimate round of talks in Geneva, where its influence persuaded a recalcitrant Cuba to accept the US-devised timetable for withdrawing its forces from Angola.

If agreement was secured because of a unique 'convergence of interests' (Crocker's words) between two super-powers united in their desire to bring a costly and stalemated conflict to an end, there was an equal convergence of interest in the benefits of peace between Luanda and Pretoria. Pressures on Luanda from the Organization of African Unity, and particularly the Francophone states, to send the Cuban forces home and seek a reconciliation with UNITA had been mounting for some time. The collapse of the price of oil, which provides Angola with 90% of its export earnings, tightened the screws on a resource-rich country which had seen its economy crippled by war. Access to IMF and World Bank funds, needed for economic reform and reconstruction, had been blocked by the United States for as long as Luanda played host to Cuban forces. Cuban troops, which had increased from a few hundred in 1975 to more than 50,000 in 1988, backed up by new Soviet-supplied MiG aircraft and sophisticated air-defence systems which put South Africa's ageing jets at increasing risk in Angolan skies, had begun to hold UNITA and its South African ally in check. Nevertheless, there was growing recognition in Luanda that, although it might not lose, neither could it win this increasingly costly and devastating war.

Similar considerations appear to have been at work in Pretoria after the 1987 offensive, in which South African forces, fearing unacceptable losses of men and aircraft (the latter particularly difficult to replace in view of the UN's arms embargo of 1977), failed to take the strategic Angolan base of Cuito Canavale. In the previous eighteen months there had been the highest number of white South African casualties (50 killed) since the conflict began, and support for a war fought without any clear political objective had begun to wane in South Africa. But Pretoria's reluctance to sacrifice its air force and troops in an unwinnable war, fought for no clear political goal, did more than shift the military balance in southern Angola. It also undermined the long-dominant role of South African Defence Force 'securocrats' in determining Pretoria's regional policy.

The Department of Foreign Affairs, under its new Director General, Neil van Heerden, seized the initiative and began to argue the benefits of a negotiated settlement. Chief among these were the cost to South Africa's dwindling exchequer of both the war (an estimated $US 39 m a year) and Pretoria's annual subventions to Namibia ($US 120 m in 1988). Since the agreement, Pretoria has announced that it intends to reduce the latter to $US 32.5 m for 1989.

Other benefits were more intangible but no less real to a South African government needing to persuade its white electorate that it was not 'selling out' Namibia to a 'Marxist regime' dominated by SWAPO. These included an agreement, enshrined in the eventual treaty, which effectively closed both Angola and an independent Namibia to the guerrilla bases of the African National Congress (ANC). Pretoria could thus claim partial responsibility not merely for the removal of Cuban forces from Angola but also for creating a defensible *cordon sanitaire* around South Africa, with no ANC guerrilla base closer than 1,500 miles from its borders. Namibia's continuing economic dependence on, and military vulnerability to, its southern neighbour, and the fact that it is thus likely to remain a client state of South Africa for the foreseeable future, were equally important in persuading Pretoria of the advantages of a settlement which, it hoped, would also defuse further sanctions legislation in the US and improve its relations with both the rest of

197

Africa and the West. In early August, Angola, Cuba and South Africa signed a joint cease-fire, and South African troops left Angola.

During the round of negotiations in New York which followed, the US scored a major breakthrough when, for the first time, Cuba tacitly accepted linkage between the removal of its troops in Angola and a Namibian settlement. Prolonged negotiations on the timing of the Cuban withdrawal were finally resolved in the Geneva round in October and November, when, under pressure from the Soviet Union, Cuba agreed to a compromise proposal for a phased pull-out over 27 months. Under this agreement Cuba will reduce its troop strength to 25,000 by 1 November 1989 – the target date for Namibian elections. By 1 April 1990, 33,000 troops will have left; and the full complement of 50,000 will have departed by 1 July 1991. After the treaties were finally signed on 22 December 1988 the first batch of 1,500 Cuban troops left Luanda for Havana in January 1989, their departure monitored by a 70-strong corps of international observers (United Nations Angolan Verification Mission, or UNAVEM) under the auspices of the Security Council.

Equally important to South Africa was Cuba's undertaking to redeploy its forces north of the 13th parallel before 1 August 1989, and behind the 15th parallel before 31 October, thus removing both the possibility of Cuban military backing for SWAPO during the run-up to the Namibian elections and the threat of Cuban attacks against UNITA strongholds in southern Angola. South Africa in turn pledged to end all aid to UNITA. US President Bush stressed that the US would continue to support UNITA until the Soviet Union ceased its supplies to the MPLA regime in Luanda. Moscow responded by announcing that it would not support an MPLA summer offensive against UNITA.

Though UNITA was not involved directly in the negotiations, there is hope both in Washington and in those African states which have been pressing for an end to the Angolan civil war that, left to themselves, the MPLA and UNITA will be compelled to seek a reconciliation. A cease-fire offer from Savimbi in October 1988 had been brushed aside by Luanda. By January 1989, however, President Dos Santos was calling for a cease-fire, and on 4 February a promised amnesty for UNITA guerrillas came into force. Despite Luanda's enduring suspicion of Savimbi, there were indications that its need for access to IMF and World Bank funds, coupled with prodding from Moscow and other countries threatening a possible reduction of aid, could bring it to the conference table.

Still No Easy Path

Although the seven-month countdown to the independence elections called for in Resolution 435 began on 1 April 1989, the level of mutual suspicion between all the parties to the agreement, and the opportunities for widespread intimidation by both SWAPO and South African elements in the run-up to the elections do not herald an easy path to Namibian independence. Nevertheless, a momentum has been created which will make it increasingly difficult for any of the parties unilaterally to abandon the agreement without the risk of universal condemnation.

The Resolution, which had been negotiated in 1978 by the so-called Contact Group of five members of the Security Council (the US, Britain, France, Germany and Canada) called for:

- A cease-fire between SWAPO and South African forces and their confinement to base;
- The phased withdrawal of all South African troops from Namibia before the independence elections: within three months from 1 April South African troop levels will be reduced from an estimated 30,000 to 1,600 men, confined to two bases in the north of the territory.
- The creation of a demilitarized zone along the Angolan–Namibian border monitored by the military component of the 7,500-strong UNTAG, which would also include electoral monitors, military observers and police monitors.
- The repeal of all discriminatory laws, the release of political prisoners and the return of refugees.
- The holding on the basis of proportional representation of free and fair elections to a constituent assembly which would formulate a new constitution.
- The appointment of a UN Special Representative to oversee the electoral process and govern the country in conjunction with the South African-appointed Administrator General during the transition.

The first hiccup occurred when, to secure saving of $US 234 m in the cost of UNTAG, the Security Council proposed reducing it to 4,600 men, a proposal vigorously opposed by SWAPO and the 'Front-line States' (Angola, Botswana, Mozambique, Tanzania, Zambia and Zimbabwe).

Despite a South African government undertaking, required under Resolution 435, to disband the South West African Territory Force (SWATF), which in recent years has done the bulk of the fighting in the 'operational area', it issued call-up papers to 2,000 young Namibians in January 1989. Pretoria has disbanded *Koevoet*, the much-feared police counter-insurgency unit, and promised to reduce from 8,300 to 6,000 the South West African Police (SWAPOL), which will be responsible for maintaining law and order during the run-up to elections. There are, however, fears that large-scale demobilization could destabilize the territory.

Questions have also been raised about the alleged fate of 100 dissidents, imprisoned by SWAPO in jails in Angola and other African states, and the effect on Namibia's economy of the return of thousands of SWAPO refugees. Estimates of their number, which could prove critical in the election, range from the UN figure of 30,000 to SWAPO's claim of 70,000. The territory, which is two-thirds the size of South Africa, supports a population of only 1.3 million people, but the economy is largely underdeveloped, depending exclusively on mining and agriculture, and estimated unemployment is 25%. Decades of political uncertainty have produced a highly politicized society, and, despite the sparse population, the country has 42 political parties which reflect both ethnic divisions and political differences.

Although it draws some support from all groups, SWAPO's historic base is the majority Ovambo tribe of 600,000 people, concentrated in the northern part of Namibia. Whites (including 20,000 Namibians of German nationality or descent) are the second largest group at some 70,000, many of them supporting the far-right National Party. Other groups include the Hereros, Rehoboth Basters, Damaras and Bushmen. Under South African rule the territory also had ten legislative assemblies for the ethnically-based second-tier government. The first-tier government (the 'Transitional Government of National Coalition', TNGU), established by Pretoria in 1985, was disbanded on 28 February 1989. It was an uneasy coalition of six parties dominated by the multi-racial Democratic Turnhalle Alliance, which is expected to provide the main opposition to SWAPO.

There is little doubt that SWAPO. will win the elections, but it could fail to secure the two-thirds majority required to impose its own constitution. This could lead to a coalition with some of the smaller internal parties and to prolonged constitutional bargaining within the constituent assembly, thus delaying independence until 1990. The need for coalitions has already compelled SWAPO to abandon its avowedly Marxist plans for the country. Its President, Sam Nujoma, has moderated the party line in discussions with Namibian businessmen and politicians, pulling back from pledges to nationalize the mines (which includes the world's largest uranium mine at Rossing), assuring farmers that their land rights will be respected and urging the white business community to remain. A SWAPO government will also be constrained by the fact that South Africa will retain the former British territory of Walvis Bay (now a South African enclave), which is the only developed harbour on the Namibian coast. All other road and rail links with the outside world are through South Africa.

South Africa: Changing Partners?

The political paralysis inside South Africa, with Pretoria apparently hypnotized by the rise of the parties of the extreme right, stood in sharp contrast to its flurry of activity on the diplomatic front. Although by the year's end there were hints that Pretoria might be ready to place greater emphasis on reform than on repression, President Botha's refusal to retire after recovering from a stroke suffered in January 1989 has complicated the political picture.

Three by-elections in May 1988, at which the Conservative Party broke out of its rural stronghold and into blue-collar urban seats, appeared to confirm the government's worst fears that it was losing its appeal to Afrikaners. In February, in an attempt to reassure right-wing voters that he remained the guardian of national security, President Botha had banned 17 anti-apartheid organizations affiliated to the United Democratic Front (UDF) and detained most of their leaders. He had also curbed the political activities of the black trade unions. By the end of the year the number of banned organizations had grown to 28, including, for the first time, a small fanatical far-right group. This action followed a massacre in the centre of Pretoria when an ex-policemen shot and killed seven blacks and wounded 17 others. However, the largest far-right para-military organization, the neo-Nazi *Afrikaner Weerstandsbewiging*, which reportedly draws much of its support from off-duty police, continued to enjoy immunity.

The Government's action against the UDF spurred world-wide condemnation. It fuelled the passage of further sanctions legislation through the US House of Representatives, although the legislation was abandoned when a matching bill failed to come to a vote in the Senate. Pressure on South Africa from West Germany and the UK, in particular, was more successful, achieving substantial amendments to Pretoria's Foreign Funding Bill, which would have cut off all foreign aid to anti-apartheid organizations.

There were also strong international representations against proposed new provisions of the Group Areas Act, which enforces residential segregation and is one of the foundation-stones of apartheid. The amendments, allowing for some mixed suburbs (or 'grey' areas) but strengthening the Act's punitive provisions to prevent further integration, were introduced to pacify right-wing opinion alarmed at the rapid integration of many inner-city areas. President Botha's determination to push through this legislation nearly precipitated a constitutional crisis when the majority Labour Party in the (Coloured) House of Representatives responded by vowing to provoke the collapse of the tricameral Parliament. The Labour Party also threatened to block all legislation (including the proposed appointment of black cabinet ministers and the postponement of the 1988 general election) unless the Group Areas Act was scrapped in its entirety.

At the beginning of the 1989 Parliamentary session the Government withdrew the bill, and Acting President Chris Heunis, who is also Minister of Constitutional Affairs, admitted publicly that the three remaining pillars of *apartheid* – the Group Areas Act, the Population Registration Act (which codes all South African according to race) and the Separate Amenities Act – were 'obstacles' in the path of negotiating constitutional change with black South Africans.

This fanned hope that the Government had finally overcome its fear of right-wing reaction and was prepared to abandon group identity as the corner-stone of any 'power-sharing' with black South Africans. It suggested a new beginning after the immobility of recent years. For much of 1988, however, the ruling National Party appeared to be mesmerized by the rise of the Conservative Party (CP), and unwilling to institute any major reforms which could stimulate further Afrikaner defections to the right. In the nation-wide local elections in October, however, while the CP scored expected gains in the rural and blue-collar areas of its Transvaal stronghold, it failed to register any significant showing in the other provinces or take control of the cities. Since the elections, attempts by some councils newly captured by the CP to reinstate and enforce social segregation in public amenities have led to commercial boycotts and widespread condemnation – and polls show that support for the CP has shrunk.

Pretoria's initial response to this electoral reprieve was to address some of the more immediate issues of international concern. These included the moves opening the way for the widely expected release of imprisoned ANC leader Nelson Mandela, the release on compassionate grounds of the elderly and frail Zeph Mothopeng of the Pan-African Congress and Harry Gwala of the ANC, and the reprieve of the so-called Sharpeville Six, whose death sentences were commuted to lengthy terms of imprisonment.

The elections for black councils – held at the same time as the white elections – also carried a message for Pretoria: the black electorate intended to continue, if not intensify, its opposition to the Government's mixture of co-option and coercion as the only recipe for power-sharing. Despite a Government clampdown on extra-parliamentary protest and a ban on promoting an election boycott, more than 70% of the black electorate stayed away from the polls, and in the black urban heartland of Soweto the turn-out was less than 10%. Even moderate black leaders such as Chief Mangosuthu Buthelezi, leader of the Zulu-based opposition group *Inkatha* and Chief Minister of the black homeland of KwaZulu, remained steadfastly indifferent to the Government's group-based theories of constitutional change. Here too, however, there appeared to be a tremor of movement at the year's end, when Mr Heunis and Chief Buthelezi agreed to establish a joint committee to explore obstacles to negotiation.

Chief Buthelezi himself was preoccupied for most of the year by a bloody local power struggle in Natal and KwaZulu between *Inkatha* and supporters of the (non-Zulu) UDF. By the end of 1988, despite futile attempts at peace-making by several black leaders, the war had claimed 1,800 lives. In South Africa's black townships, however, the long-running State of Emergency and the mass banning of extra-parliamentary organizations had re-established Government control and quelled the unrest.

Economic Pains

Paralysis on the political front was paralleled by an acute decline in South Africa's economic health, caused mainly by the need to maintain a balance-of-payments surplus to service its $US 22-bn international debt under the standstill agreement of 1986. The effect on a developing country of this persistent haemorrhage of capital was graphically demonstrated when the Government was compelled to strangle a budding boom at birth.

Emerging from a four-year recession during which it recorded an average growth rate of only 0.5%, the economy began to expand again rapidly during the first two quarters of 1988. But increased growth caused the balance of payments to plummet from a R6,000-m surplus to a deficit of R410 m. South Africa needs to record growth rates of 5% a year or more to accommodate an annual population increase of 2.3% a year (some economists estimate that 40% of the economically active black population is now unemployed or under-employed), but Pretoria was constrained to act to keep its balance of payments in surplus. As the rand threatened to go into free fall against the dollar, the Deputy Governor of the Reserve Bank warned that South Africa might not be able to meet its 1990 obligations under the debt rescheduling agreement. Pretoria moved to curb demand through higher interest rates and import tariff increases of up to 60%. By the end of 1988 the trade surplus had been restored, but the 6% growth rate of the first two quarters had slumped to an annual 3% and is expected to drift down to 2% in 1989.

South Africa's economic problems, although exacerbated by a falling gold price and by the need to export capital to pay debts as the balance of payments moved into deficit, are not a direct result of international sanctions. Despite trade boycotts, the plunging rand has assisted an overall trade performance which has actually improved since the US imposed sanctions in 1986. South Africa's trade with the UK, Germany and Japan has improved substantially, while exports to Canada soared by 66% in 1988. The pace of disinvestment has also slowed, with only 25 US companies and 11 non-US companies pulling out in 1988, leaving 138 American and 440 non-American companies with direct investments in South Africa.

Nevertheless, high inflation, low business confidence, the Government's mounting deficit and its inability to raise substantial foreign loans have all contributed to a shrinking formal economy. This has been partly offset by the explosive growth of the informal sector, which, stimulated by Government deregulation, has helped to soak up substantial black unemployment. The black-owned taxi industry, which in the past few years has become an essential part of the South African transport sector, has a turnover of R3 bn a year and a R3-bn asset base and employs twice as many workers as such industrial giants as ISCOR and ESCOM. Some 500,000 street traders now generate a yearly turnover of R1 bn. According to some estimates, the informal sector now contributes 40% of GDP.

The Black Opposition
These developments fuelled new thinking among some black political commentators. Alarmed by the self-defeating factionalism of black politics and disillusioned with the promises of instant liberation, they are beginning to preach economic self-empowerment as the path to political power. Divisions have also appeared between the political and the military wings of the exiled ANC.

These emerged during the 1988 bombing campaign, when the ANC initially seemed to reverse an earlier strategy of concentrating on 'hard' targets (government installations, police stations), rather than 'soft' (civilian) targets. According to the South African Police, there were 281 ANC bombing, grenade and other attacks during the year, which claimed 49 lives. Many of them had taken place in supermarkets and shopping arcades, at bus stops and sports stadia. Both whites and blacks were among the casualties. The police also claimed that 1,000 ANC weapons had been seized and more than 300 guerrillas killed or captured in 1988.

Because of the difficulty of infiltrating guerrillas into South Africa from beyond its borders, it is believed that many of these attacks were initiated by hastily-trained local cadres beyond the control of the ANC's Lusaka headquarters. Nevertheless, when Chris Hani – chief of staff of *Umkhonto we Sizwe*, the ANC's military wing – insisted that the organization would henceforth concentrate on 'soft' targets, this was hastily repudiated by the ANC's President, Oliver Tambo, and its National Executive Committee, fearful that an ANC terror campaign would undermine the organization's diplomatic offensive in Western capitals. A reappraisal of the military element in the ANC's overall strategy would, in any case, appear inevitable after the closure of ANC bases in Angola under the Angolan–Namibian accords and their removal to a base 200 km north of Dar es Salaam in Tanzania.

The ANC and its close ally, the (formerly Stalinist) South African Communist Party (SACP), have also been under pressure from Moscow to moderate their views on the inevitability of a successful revolution. Spokesmen in the Southern African Department of Moscow's Foreign Ministry have admitted that they are engaged in a major review of Soviet policy towards South Africa, on the basis that the way to black majority rule now lies through a political settlement rather than the revolutionary overthrow of the white regime. Spokesmen have stressed that they do not want to see the destruction of Africa's largest and most successful economy.

As part of its policy review, Moscow has begun to reach beyond the ANC and the SACP in an effort to broaden its information base about South Africa. Although South African–Soviet relations have been severed since 1948, a number of Afrikaner academics and journalists were admitted to the Soviet Union last year, a Soviet journalist visited South Africa for the first time, and Boris Asoyan – deputy head of the Foreign Ministry's Southern African Department and a key figure in the policy review – has had extensive contacts with leading figures in the Afrikaner community. Deputy Foreign Minister Anatoly Adamishin and South African Foreign Minister Pik Botha had private talks during the Brazzaville round of the Angolan–Namibian peace talks, and there have been hints in both Moscow and Pretoria that diplomatic relations might be resumed.

President Gorbachev is understood to have spelled out the Soviet Union's new attitude in a meeting with ANC President Oliver Tambo last year, since when both the ANC and the SACP, which previously insisted that they were only prepared to negotiate a transfer of power with a defeated Pretoria regime, now appear more willing to talk. To this end, the ANC has been assiduously seeking contacts with Afrikaners so as to increase pressure on Pretoria to lift the ban on the organization and to open negotiations.

Relations with Other Neighbours

Although South Africa's military strength remains largely unchallenged in the region, the failure of the military solution in Angola gave the negotiators in its Department of Foreign Affairs the chance to persuade President Botha of the benefits of a different strategy. This seeks to stabilize relations with Pretoria's neighbours and intensify contact with other African states in an effort to defuse Western pressure on Pretoria and secure wider international acceptance.

The Department's ascendancy was illustrated by President Botha's meetings during 1988 with the Presidents of the Ivory Coast, Zaire, Malawi and Mozambique. Other states, including Mali, Gabon, the Congo, Togo, Equatorial Guinea and the Central African Republic are now said to be prepared to meet the South African leader, once Nelson Mandela is released. Some also seek more visible ties with Pretoria, which currently trades with 50 of the other 51 African countries (its trade with the rest of Africa has increased to 10% of total exports since 1984). Pretoria's wooing of the Francophones, however, has been harshly criticized by the Front-line States, and President Botha's suggestion of a southern African summit conference seems at best premature.

For the Front-line States particularly, Mozambique remains the test of Pretoria's intentions. These appeared to have been transformed in September when, after lengthy negotiations brokered by the UK (which sees Mozambique as pivotal in the region), President Botha met President Chissano at the border town of Songa to reaffirm Pretoria's commitment to the Nkomati Accord. This non-aggression pact, signed in 1984, had led to the eviction of ANC guerrillas from Mozambique but had failed to end Pretoria's support for the rebel RENAMO movement.

As a gesture of good faith after the Songa summit, South Africa supplied Mozambique with R10-m-worth of defence equipment. Since then, however, RENAMO has increased its attacks in all but three Mozambican provinces and is stepping up its cross-border raids on Zimbabwe's eastern frontier. Hopes that the giant Cabora Bassa hydroelectric project, completed more than a decade ago, could at last begin to deliver power to southern Africa have been dashed by increased RENAMO attacks on the pylons. Zimbabwe, the most inflexible towards Pretoria of all the Front-line States, bears the brunt of the fighting in Mozambique, where 27,000 Zimbabwean troops guard the rail links from Zimbabwe to Maputo and Beira. (A 9,000-strong Tanzanian force sent to aid the Maputo government forces was withdrawn in 1988.) Increased RENAMO activity has created suspicion among the Front-line States that maverick elements within South Africa are continuing to supply RENAMO, though possibly without government consent.

New Hopes

Despite enduring suspicions of South Africa, the Angolan–Namibian accords have stirred tentative hopes of peace throughout the region after more than two decades of war. Support for the agreement also appeared to reflect an emerging consensus among the states of southern Africa in favour of accepting formal peaceful coexistence with Pretoria, and bringing diplomatic, rather than military, pressure to bear on it.

As an example of super-power co-operation in the region, the Angolan–Namibian agreement also raises the possibility of a joint East–West approach on South Africa. In January South African Foreign Minister Pik Botha showed he was sensitive to the possibilities of continuing super-power activity by calling for a US/Soviet role in a Mozambican peace initiative. Soviet strategists, however, insist that they are anxious to devise a bilateral policy with the United States towards South Africa itself. The ANC might be forced to abandon violence and bargain realistically with the Pretoria government – a move which would have the wholehearted support of Western governments. British Prime Minister Margaret Thatcher, for example, is anxious to play a mediating role and could use her influence to extract a positive response from South Africa.

President Botha would be unlikely to entertain any negotiations with the ANC. His successor – either the conservative F.W. de Klerk, who was narrowly elected to the National Party leadership in February 1989 while Botha was in hospital, or de Klerk's rival, Finance Minister Barend du Plessis from the Party's more liberal wing – could adopt a more flexible approach. The 'convergence of interests' between the super-powers which produced the Angolan–Namibian agreement may have established a precedent that can be applied to the search for a solution to southern Africa's other problems. However, Botha's insistence on resuming his duties after his return from hospital in March was not conducive to new initiatives by the National Party.

Latin America

One of the more hopeful, and certainly one of the most highly touted, political developments in Latin America during the 1980s has been the emergence of democratic forms of governance throughout much of the region. The exuberant blossoming of popularly-elected governments, however, has merely been the most colourful stage of what is necessarily a long-term process. If democracy is truly to take root and flourish in the region, conditions in the external environment will, at a minimum, need to avoid subjecting these governments to extreme duress. A review of the record over the past year produces the distressing conclusion that events have not been especially nourishing to the region's emerging democracies.

The most critical problem confronting these democracies is economic stagnation. Growth on a regional basis has been sluggish, and, given demographic trends, income per capita has generally deteriorated. Efforts to regenerate growth have been vitiated in almost all cases by the crushing burden of debt. For economies striving to modernize and retool their productive plant to meet the challenge of competition in the international market place, the net transfer of nearly $US 30 billion to the region's creditors in 1988 constituted a crippling handicap. The argument has been repeatedly made that externally-imposed austerity measures have put the region's fragile political institutions under severe pressure. In early 1989 this message was delivered with shocking clarity, however, by austerity-induced street riots in Venezuela. Some 300 lives were lost, and the stability of one of the region's more securely-grounded democracies was cast into doubt.

Another threat to democracy in Latin America is the pernicious influence of the drug underworld. This malignancy has manifested itself in several forms. One of them has come to be known as 'Colombianization', a reference to that country's tragic experience with the corrupting and subversive influence of drug 'cartels', which illustrates the damage that can be inflicted upon even a relatively prosperous and institutionalized democracy. At the other end of the spectrum, military regimes have sometimes been enlisted as outposts of the expanding drug empire. A previous government in Bolivia and the current regime in Panama provide examples, with signs that the new leadership in Paraguay may be similarly inspired. In between these two extremes is Peru, where a fledgling democracy is struggling with a spreading and subversive threat made all the more ominous by its expanding links with the drug underworld.

If the circumstances of 1988 were not especially propitious for the region's democracies, neither did they smile on the two Communist strongholds. Cuba, maintaining its rigid adherence to Marxist-Leninist principles as practised in the 1960s and 1970s, seemed cast adrift in the Gorbachev era of *perestroika* and peace offensives. The *Sandinista* regime in Nicaragua was in an even more perilous condition. It seemed to be sinking under the weight of its own incompetence and mismanagement, aggravating the consequences of more than a decade of internal conflict, even as the opposing *Contra* forces were fading from the scene.

Earlier years had demonstrated that neither Marxism nor militarism were routes to the promised land of prosperity and modernity. The reins of power have now largely been turned over to democratic leadership, but daunting economic, social and demographic challenges continue to thwart the new leaders. Should they fail, it is not clear whether there is any alternative but to wallow in a period of governmental inefficacy (possibly followed, as one analyst has suggested, by a political 'dark age'). To avert such a fate and help promote democratic prospects for the area, the one clear imperative will be to find a sustainable formula for debt relief.

CENTRAL AMERICAN FERMENT

In 1988, the fortunes of both the *Sandinistas* and the *Contras* declined substantially. The war in Nicaragua wound down, and the conflict in El Salvador heated up. As a result, by early 1989 there was a considerable shift in the pattern of the regional crisis and the challenges for the regional peace process. With the *Contra* rebels seeming to have run their course and the beleaguered *Sandinista* regime offering new concessions, the five Central American Presidents agreed in February 1989 to seek new measures among themselves to ensure an end to the conflict in Nicaragua. In El Salvador, where the trend had seemed inexorably towards polarization and a sharp increase in violence at all levels, a new opportunity for moving towards peace also opened at the beginning of 1989. This consisted of an unprecedented guerrilla offer to participate in, and respect the results of, elections. The prospects for El Salvador remain doubtful, however, as does the capacity of any outside actor to influence the internal situation.

Nicaragua: Can Peace Now be Built on the Ruins?
After more than a decade of conflict that had brought Nicaragua to a state of economic ruin, the peace process was given a new boost. At a regional summit, in El Salvador on 14 February 1989, renewed efforts were made to ensure that the provisional cease-fire reached the year before would be translated into a definitive end to the war.

The armed conflict had been reduced to a low level after the signature on 23 March 1988 in Sapoá, Nicaragua, of a provisional agreement between the *Sandinista* government and the *Contras*. That agreement provided for a 60-day cease-fire from 1 April, during which a final cease-fire was to be negotiated simultaneously with fulfilment of the other commitments under the Esquipulas II agreements. The *Contra* forces would concentrate in agreed zones and then send delegates to a national dialogue. An amnesty would be decreed, with prisoners released in stages. The government guaranteed unrestricted freedom of expression and complete rights for those returning, and it also agreed to discuss the issue of compulsory military service in Nicaragua.

This process quickly ran into trouble. In May, the *Contras* presented new proposals. They offered to incorporate themselves into institutional life and to join an effort for national reconstruction by 31 January 1989, but demanded additional concessions from the Nicaraguan government. The *Sandinistas* responded by accepting many of the proposals for political reforms, while rejecting demands for a new Constituent Assembly, the suspension of military recruitment and a complete amnesty. At the next round of talks, in early June, the negotiations came to an acrimonious halt.

One major disagreement was over timing and guarantees: the *Sandinistas* demanded that discussion and implementation of political changes should be simultaneous with a definitive cease-fire and should involve a guarantee that the *Contras* would disarm; the *Contras* insisted that political changes should be in place before they laid down their arms. The difficulty was exacerbated by the fact that the *Contras* repeatedly increased their demands. Another problem was the emergence of a sharp division within *Contra* ranks. The more intransigent elements clearly opposed the Sapoá accord. Personal rivalries, differences over negotiations, and accusations of corruption led to a rebellion in late April. More moderate commanders and political leaders were purged, and a *Contra* congress in July brought the hard-line military commander, Col. Enrique Bermudez, into prominence in the political leadership. As the US Congress in August again refused to provide military aid, morale deteriorated further. Moderate groups began to split away, arguing that the movement had been taken over by hard-line elements.

At the same time, the economic situation facing the *Sandinistas* was deteriorating to a level that was unacceptable to the population. On preliminary estimates, GDP fell by some 9% in 1988 as agricultural production continued to drop, severe shortages of foreign exchange curtailed imports, and domestic demand sank even further. The country was hit by a devastating hurricane in October, its currency, the *córdoba*, plummeted against the dollar, and inflation began to reach astronomical levels (estimated officially at 5,884% per year, and unofficially at 20,000% and more). New efforts to stabilize the situation only increased popular discontent. Austerity measures adopted in January 1989 cut the state budget by 44%, slashed subsidies, maintained a substantial differential between price and wage increases, and involved the dismissal of some 35,000 state employees. The social consequences also reached unprecedented levels, in terms of malnutrition and the spread of disease.

Internally, the prospects for consensus had not improved. The government clamped down forcefully in July after opposition demonstrations. In August, all except one of the opposition parties refused to participate in the Assembly debate over the new electoral law. There was strong criticism of a new Emergency Law and complaint at the postponement until 1990 of municipal elections scheduled for 1989. The domestic political opposition was little nearer to presenting a credible alternative, both because of official restrictions and because of its own weaknesses and divisions. An effort was made to establish a centrist alliance as a 'third way', with a projected role for Eden Pastora, the one-time *Sandinista* and *Contra* leader. The *Sandinista* Front remained the largest single political force in the country, but its position had become assailable by a coherent, consolidated opposition alliance, and an honest election would present it with a severe challenge.

Without a massive infusion of external resources, there will be no remedy to Nicaragua's crisis. Such an inflow will not occur without stabilization of Nicaragua's internal and external relations – and will certainly not come from the Soviet bloc. The *Sandinistas* have thus been compelled to make a new series of concessionary gestures. The January 1989 austerity measures included, for the first time, a cut in the defence budget. President Ortega also promised that there would be no more nationalizations, and, while not renouncing any 'socialist-oriented project', he did not actually propose a socialist model.

The government also made new offers to facilitate the return of the *Contras*. It asked for US assistance in this process, promising that the *Contras* could return with guarantees of their security and even offering land and credits. It gave new commitments about the mixed economy, political pluralism and freedom of expression. Gestures were also made to the US, including immediate approval of visas for new Embassy personnel, suggestions for direct talks on security issues and proposals for US/Central American co-operation against drug trafficking.

At the summit in El Salvador on 13–14 February, Ortega made unprecedented concessions, not only because he had little option, but also because he saw an opportunity to end the *Contra* presence in Honduras. In view of the improbability of renewed US military aid, an agreement providing for simultaneous concessions and internationally supervised demobilization of the *Contras* appeared possible. Consequently, Ortega announced a 'process of democratization and national reconciliation in the framework of the Esquipulas II agreements' addressing many opposition demands. This included:

– reform of the electoral law and legislation to guarantee freedom of expression, of the media, and of political organization;
– bringing forward presidential elections from November 1990 to 25 February 1990, at which time positions at all levels would be included on the ballot;

– formation of a Supreme Electoral Council with balanced representation for opposition parties;
– supervision of all phases of the election by international observers;
– equal access to state television and radio for all parties during the campaign, and authorization for all media to acquire abroad any materials they might require.

And, he said, imprisoned ex-National Guards would be released.

The *quid pro quo* was that the five Presidents should agree to prepare within 90 days a joint plan for the voluntary demobilization, repatriation or resettlement of *Contra* fighters and their families and to seek UN technical assistance for this process.

Many doubts as well as difficulties remain, and much depends on the willingness of the Bush administration to contribute actively to the process. The concessions did not cover all opposition demands, and reaction from the *Contra* leadership was mixed. Alfredo Cesar, now the most prominent political leader, stated that he was willing to return and take up the battle on the political front if the measures were genuinely implemented. Others may not be so willing, but they may have little choice. The conflicts are not over, but the military situation is unlikely to re-escalate. Neither the *Sandinistas* nor the *Contras* any longer have the means to produce a military solution to the conflict. There is little choice but to attempt to forge some new form of national consensus which would reverse the country's present ruinous course.

El Salvador: The Unextinguished Volcano
In El Salvador the situation has become more explosive. The political centre has been shaken by the sharp rise in armed conflict and political violence, and by the rebels' surprising peace proposals.

The weakening of the Christian Democratic Party (PDC) has accelerated since the party's striking defeat in the March 1988 legislative and municipal elections. This exacerbated a split within the party, which crystallized into rivalry for the 1989 presidential nomination, culminating in the breaking away of a faction led by Julio Adolfo Rey Prendes and the formation of a new party, the Authentic Christian Movement. Although the main body of the party, led by Fidel Chávez Mena, retained some support, it was severely compromised by the failure to bring peace and economic improvements, the corrupt image of many senior party members and the party schism.

At the same time, the political right notably strengthened, and changes in the armed forces indicated a rise of more hard-line elements. The far-right Nationalist Republican Alliance (ARENA), the principal beneficiary in the March 1988 elections and victor in the presidential elections held in March 1989, had strongly opposed the reforms brought in under the Christian Democrat administration and rejected any idea of negotiating with the guerrillas. Although efforts were made to present a more moderate image, the party continued to be associated by many with the most extreme right-wing forces and with the death squads. Party leaders clearly stated their desire for an uncompromising line towards revolutionaries and their supporters, and towards the left in general. Clashes with unions, students and other organizations intensified. Violence from the far right rose, and the government failed to prevent a surge in death-squad activity.

Guerrilla forces of the Farabundo Martí National Liberation Front (FMLN) continued to step up their activities. Although the western departments remained relatively free of conflict, the FMLN succeeded in spreading attacks throughout most of the country, causing significant destruction, tying down the armed forces and carrying out almost constant small-scale attacks on army units and positions. Attacks on larger targets also increased, with assaults on garrisons including, most dramatically, one on the National Guard's national headquarters in San Salvador on 1 November. Urban activity of all types also grew, with an increase in tactics such as car bombing, which for many years the guerrillas had shunned.

By the autumn, as the situation deteriorated, guerrilla leaders were talking openly of the failure of US strategy to build a credible centre, leaving the people with a choice between the army and the revolutionaries. Such views were echoed among the military, within which there had been increasing rumblings of discontent throughout the year. Top commanders openly criticized the inter-party wrangling which followed the March 1988 elections. Col. René Emilio Ponce, who took over as head of the Joint Chiefs of Staff in November, warned in June that weak government and a slide into anarchy threatened to leave people with a choice between the military and the FMLN, either of which, he said, would be bad.

At the same time, however, there was some appreciation on the Left of the problems, and indeed the dangers, that would be caused if they won, whether by the bullet or the ballot. Moreover, the FMLN found itself in a difficult situation because of the decision by the Democratic Convergence (CD) to participate in the elections. The CD is made up of two moderate parties in the Democratic Revolutionary Front (FDR), which is allied with the FMLN, and the Social Democratic Party. There was also some appreciation that intensification of the conflict was not winning the FMLN many friends among the population.

These tensions were reflected in a sudden change in the public position regarding the March 1989 elections. In late January, the FMLN proposed 'to convert the elections into a contribution to peace', by postponing them until 15 September on the following conditions:

– all killings and repression of popular activities should cease, and the Armed Forces should respect the electoral activity of all parties;
– all military, para-military and security forces should remain in barracks during the elections and should take no part in them;

- the CD should be integrated into the Electoral Council, and a broad national Controlling Council should be established;
- a new electoral code should be agreed by consensus among all parties;
- all Salvadoreans living abroad should be permitted to vote;
- the US Government should stay absolutely clear of the process.

If such conditions were met, the FMLN would, among other things,

- respect the activity of all parties and electoral bodies;
- declare a truce from two days before to two days after the elections and withdraw from population centres and voting points;
- call on all its supporters to participate in the elections;
- accept the legitimacy of the electoral results;
- accept that the current government should remain in office throughout the transition period.

The proposals aroused a cautiously positive response in many quarters, including the United States. However, they were rejected by President Duarte, by ARENA and by the armed forces. Indeed, Defence Minister Vides Casanova warned that the armed forces could stage a coup if the government were to take any unconstitutional steps, such as postponing the elections. No progress was made at the February summit, at which the proposal was not even discussed. The only explicit reference to El Salvador was a call for everyone to participate in the forthcoming elections.

A week after the summit a meeting did take place in Mexico between an FMLN delegation and representatives of all the country's political parties; at this meeting the FMLN stressed its willingness to abandon the armed struggle, although adding some conditions. There were, however, strong differences among the parties, with ARENA, like the armed forces, opposing any postponement of the elections. Others, including the PDC (although not Duarte) were more willing to seek a compromise, so long as it did not violate the constitution. No agreement was reached, and the elections took place as scheduled.

Even if the FMLN proposals had been accepted and had proved to be sincere, an end to the war would not have been guaranteed. The rejection of the proposals, however, and the electoral victory by the far-right ARENA party, together with an upsurge in guerrilla activity, make the most likely outcome a substantial increase in violence during 1989. This will sorely test El Salvador's beleaguered political structures.

MEXICO IN TRANSITION

The globe seemed to shift on its political axis in 1988, leaving analysts to ponder whether certain of their long-cherished notions about the international order ought to be revised. Events in Mexico contributed to this iconoclastic trend, although the reasons were far more domestic than external. Long noted for their stability and predictable electoral outcomes, Mexican politics will no longer be characterized by both after the developments of the past year. In fact a veil of uncertainty has descended upon the country as it enters a transition from staid one-party hegemony to a less defined and potentially turbulent future.

As 1988 began, President Miguel de la Madrid faced difficulties on both the political and economic fronts. Because of a schism which had developed in the ruling *Partido Revolucionario Institucional* (PRI) the previous autumn, over selection of its presidential nominee, there was the unusual prospect of a lively challenge in national elections scheduled for July. A reformist faction led by Cuauhtémoc Cárdenas, son of revered former President Lázaro Cárdenas, had defected from the party. Assailing the PRI for abandoning its revolutionary principles, Cárdenas sought to unite the left under the banner of his *Frente Demócrata Nacional* (FDN). This made it all the more imperative for de la Madrid to put the country's economy in order.

His record after five years in power was a dismal one. In 1987 the country's economic output was no greater than it had been when he took office. Per capita income had fallen, and the average wage earner had lost 40–50% of his purchasing power. In 1988 de la Madrid was unable to deliver the standard pre-election fiscal fillip to the economy because the budgetary deficit was already running at 16% of Gross Domestic Product (GDP). Indeed, deficit spending had contributed to an inflationary spiral that had pushed up the price index by 160% in 1987. In the absence of prompt and effective measures to clamp a lid on price increases, the economy appeared to be heading for uncontrolled hyper-inflation. This would have wrecked the President's cherished economic restructuring programme and, more fundamentally, would have jeopardized the PRI's grip on power. Indeed, normally docile government-controlled unions had threatened a general strike in the latter part of 1987 if hefty (and thus inflationary) wage increases were not granted. Squeezing inflation out of the economy thus had become an even higher priority than stimulating economic growth.

President de la Madrid's approach to this problem was to bring labour, business and government together into an anti-inflationary programme called the Economic Solidarity Pact (ESP). The pact went into effect in mid-December 1987. The unions were awarded a phased, 35% increase in the minimum wage, after which wages were to be frozen until March 1988. Business leaders agreed to a price freeze in return for having wages eventually held steady and for having the peso stabilized, which would begin to make their imports less costly. The government pledged to hold the price of public-sector goods and services steady, after an initial 80% increase in certain key areas, and to reduce the budget deficit (in addition to maintaining the value of the peso).

Even though the plan was finely tuned, it had several potential liabilities. Clamping down on government spending risked a recession;

allowing the peso to appreciate made it more difficult for de la Madrid's restructuring scheme, heavily reliant on exports, to bear fruit; and holding the peso steady would put a major strain on government reserves. All parties realized, however, that rampant inflation would have consequences far worse than this.

The programme has proved highly successful in curbing inflation without stimulating serious negative repercussions. Inflation during January 1988 had reached 15.5%; by September it had fallen to 0.6%, and the cumulative total for 1988 was estimated at about 70%, about half the 1987 rate. With such a successful record the pact was extended several times, with minor modifications, until the end of the year.

The End of One-party Politics
While the pieces of the economic puzzle seemed to be falling into place, the political picture was gradually becoming more scrambled. What had appeared in 1987 to be a rather quixotic challenge by Cárdenas slowly gathered momentum during 1988. First he was joined by two parties traditionally considered to be satellites of the PRI. Then he and his entourage became more and more skilled at carrying their campaign to the masses. Although he was at an enormous disadvantage because of the PRI's ready access to governmental resources and the media, Cárdenas nevertheless was able to tap a reservoir of frustration with the regime. He excoriated the government for turning its back on fundamental revolutionary projects. National sovereignty, he alleged, had been subordinated to the dictates of international creditors, and social justice had been sacrificed on the altar of official avarice and economic austerity. Another revolutionary aspiration, effective suffrage, was to be put to the acid test in the July elections.

The PRI official party candidate, Carlos Salinas de Gortari, was widely recognized for his intellectual brilliance. But he was handicapped by having been a chief architect of the government's economic restructuring and austerity programme, as de la Madrid's Minister of Planning and Budget. Rather than running on the record of past hardships, Salinas opted to appeal to the electorate's hopes for the future. He promised to modernize both the country's economic and political processes (appearing to define the latter as seeking legitimacy through 'effective suffrage'), acknowledging deficiencies in recent elections in the north and proclaiming that 'modern politics demands clean elections, and I reject the old thesis of the clean sweep'. The legitimacy of any future Salinas administration was thus made virtually synonymous with public perceptions of the conduct of the July elections.

Cárdenas and his closest advisers, intimately familiar with PRI electoral methods from their years as party militants, were too wary to put their trust in sweeping campaign promises. In conjunction with other opposition elements, they formed a watchdog group (Democratic Assembly for Effective Suffrage) with the aim of placing an independent observer in each of the country's 56,000 polling stations. Indications of planned electoral manipulation began to surface well in advance of election day, as reams of forged voting forms were discovered in circumstances indicating that they were to be used for stuffing ballot boxes. Far more shocking was the assassination of Francisco Ovando, a close Cárdenas aide and key organizer of an electoral observer group. The opposition saw this as a brazen attempt to deter it from exercising vigilance at the polls.

The greatest damage to the credibility of the election, however, came when the vote was counted. Although the government had promised to release official results within a day, its central election computer mysteriously broke down after initial returns had begun to come in. The FDN claimed that its information indicated a Cárdenas victory. The Federal Electoral Commission's announcement of the outcome was delayed for an entire week, causing widespread speculation that the government was 'cooking' the returns. This was reinforced by the many allegations of irregularities in the actual conduct of the voting and the discrepancies between the totals given for the country's 300 voting districts and the 56,000 polling stations.

The final figures gave Salinas 50% of the vote against 31% for Cárdenas and 17% for Manuel Clouthier of the right-wing PAN party. In addition to suffering the weakest announced showing ever by a PRI presidential candidate, the party lost four seats in the 64-member Senate (only one non-PRI member had ever sat there before) and retained only a slim majority in the Chamber of Deputies. If these historic results had been announced promptly, as promised, Salinas might have garnered a measure of credibility for winning a surprisingly tough, but seemingly honest, election. But the delay and the suspicions surrounding the conduct of the vote left him without a cloak of legitimacy to shield himself from future adversities.

Before Salinas' tainted election was legally recognized, left- and right-wing opposition elements exerted strenuous efforts to overturn it. The ruling party's total control over the certification process, extending from the local level all the way to the Chamber of Deputies sitting as an electoral college, ensured that these efforts were in vain. Nevertheless, the vociferous crusade, which also included mass rallies to denounce Salinas' election, did serve the secondary purpose of heaping further discredit on the entire process.

The government's problem of having to contend for the first time with a considerable opposition block in the legislature was compounded by restiveness within its own ranks. The most unruly element was the oil workers' union under the iron rule of Joaquín ('La Quina') Hernández Galicia. Through its control over oil production, this notoriously corrupt union functioned as a state-within-a-state, and 'La Quina' (as he is universally called) behaved as though he were a sovereign. The seeds of discontent had been sown earlier in the de la Madrid administration, when Salinas spearheaded a successful effort to slash the union's privilege of receiving half of all oil industry contracts (the figure was cut to

2%). Subsequently, 'La Quina' opposed Salinas' bid for the party's presidential nomination and, when this failed, reportedly told his union members they were free to vote their consciences in the election. For most this surely meant a Cárdenas vote, since Cuauhtémoc's father had taken the enormously popular step of nationalizing the oil industry when he was President.

After the election 'La Quina' mounted a further challenge by instigating oil union members of the Chamber of Deputies to join the opposition in calling for an investigation into alleged misdeeds by the former head of the state-owned oil company, PEMEX. This was a clear signal that the oil union, and other hard-line labour elements, could be used to obstruct Salinas' future legislative initiatives. Thus, when Salinas finally donned the presidential sash on 1 December 1988, he entered office with greater political liabilities and fewer apparent assets than any Mexican President in the post-war era.

The Economic Conundrum

Salinas is firmly committed to carrying forward even more vigorously the economic restructuring programmes he helped to initiate under de la Madrid. This will entail reducing state-owned businesses to a minimum strategic core and continuing to rely on growth in the export sector to energize the economy. Persistent weakness in oil prices and any further appreciation of the peso would make this task especially difficult. The immediate problem, however, will be to remove the Economic Solidarity Pact's wage/price/exchange-rate controls without rekindling inflation. But even a success on this count will be insufficient, for he must also stimulate growth in an economy that has been essentially flat for the past six years. If Salinas fails in this task, his presidency could be gravely imperilled.

Many of the measures taken to restructure the economy have been immensely unpopular, even within the PRI itself. Labour leaders have been especially opposed to reductions in the size of the public sector. Nor are Salinas' pronouncements about the need for political modernization liable to receive support from this group. Indeed, Fidel Velázquez, who for fifty years has headed the labour wing of the party, has bitterly denounced even the limited political reforms that have taken place to date as having caused the party's debacle in the 1988 election. Opposition parties, on the other hand, have been energized by their showing, and the populace has been mobilized by the prospect of a genuine choice in future elections. Paradoxically, the only way the PRI will be able to win in the future will be by losing: it will be unable to gain popular legitimacy until it is prepared to take its chance in open and honest elections – even if (as is probable) that means it will forfeit the tight grip on power that it has always had. But even limited concessions will be resisted by those entrenched elements in the PRI which would lose positions and patronage as a result.

The essence of the challenge facing Salinas is that he must proceed simultaneously with basic reforms to both economic and political systems, something his predecessor backed away from. The economic restructuring programme to which he is wedded has so far brought the Mexican people nothing but hardship. Yet, even before these measures have had a chance to bear fruit, he has come under intense pressure to open the political system to genuine competition and honest elections. If he cannot restore vigorous, non-inflationary growth to the economy by the crucial 1991 mid-term elections, Salinas will face two highly undesirable alternatives. If he opted to heed the will of the majority, he would risk repudiation of his economic programme, and would probably also lose control of the Chamber of Deputies and of numerous senatorial and gubernatorial seats. This might well leave him incapable of governing effectively during his final three years in office. If, on the other hand, he felt compelled to retain control by manipulating the vote, this would create a serious risk of unrest. A portion of the opposition would no doubt conclude that peaceful change was no longer possible; and the potential for spontaneous mass demonstrations could not be discarded either. The stability of the regime would be severely tested in any event. Either outcome would cause grave concern in the United States.

In his first few months in office, President Salinas has moved boldly to demonstrate that his presidency will not be crippled by the controversy surrounding his election. He jailed his arch rival 'La Quina', using the army to storm the union leader's home, which was in fact a heavily armed bastion. He has also replaced the Economic Solidarity Pact with his own programme, which will gradually ease controls on wages, prices and exchange rates.

The most crucial task, however, will be to bring about a resumption of non-inflationary economic growth, a task he will find difficult to achieve because he is not in total command of the necessary resources. Leaving aside his obvious inability to influence oil prices or international interest rates, the core of Salinas' problem is that Mexico has become a net exporter of capital. The external debt is so high that the country pays its creditors 5–6% of GDP each year. Unless mechanisms for substantially reducing this outflow are soon implemented, the prospects are poor that the Mexican economy will be healthy again before the crucial 1991 elections.

Debt Relief: A Strategic Imperative

The political ramifications of such a situation have already been suggested. It is also worth noting, however, that the essential elements of the de la Madrid/Salinas restructuring programme were urged upon Mexico by its commercial creditors, the IMF and the US. Should the economy remain sluggish for much longer, the search for scapegoats will not be confined to Mexico. Indeed, the one issue on which all shades of the political spectrum can agree is the urgent need for debt relief. Failure to devise a workable formula would strengthen highly nationalistic elements eager to exploit resulting anti-American feelings.

Recognizing the need to ease the economic restraints that Salinas would have to face, the Reagan administration provided Mexico with a $US 3.5-bn 'bridging loan' in November 1988. Politically, this was a potent symbol of Washington's confidence in the incoming Salinas administration. Economically, it helped to compensate for the billions Mexico had lost during 1988 to the sharp decline in oil prices and the defence of the peso from a wave of capital flight. However, it also meant that the new government became the second Mexican administration in a row to have received a multi-billion-dollar bail-out from the US, an unenviable trend to have perpetuated. And, despite the advantages it brought, the loan was at best only a palliative and hardly a solution for the country's towering burden of debt.

If Mexico and its creditors could develop a scheme to make available sufficient capital resources to allow the country's restructuring pro-gramme to work, the dividends would be both economic and political. In addition to placing Mexico on the path towards future prosperity, it would also give President Salinas sufficient latitude to liberalize the pol-itical process as well. Assuming he is, in fact, committed to the latter, Mexico could emerge at the end of his six-year term both more vibrant economically and more pluralistic politically. Neither of these optimis-tic outcomes is assured, however. Indeed, the only certainty is that Mexico is in the midst of a pervasive process of change. If domestic events go seriously awry, this could affect the country's relationship with the US, which would see two prized strategic assets that it has enjoyed throughout the post-war era – stability on its southern border and friendly bilateral relations – as coming into jeopardy. Salinas is clearly a transitional president, but what lies beyond the transition is very far from clear.

SOUTH AMERICA UNDER STRAIN

Overall economic performance in Latin America was profoundly dis-couraging in 1988. The region's GNP rose by only 0.7%. On a per capita basis, this translated into a decline of 1.5%, which perpetuated a trend that had seen per capita income fall by 6.5% during the 1980s. In Brazil, the largest and most diversified economy in the region, per capita income fell by over 2%, industrial output declined by 3%, and invest-ment fell to the lowest levels registered since the onset of the debt crisis. Of even greater concern was the fact that economic stagnation was accompanied by a dramatic acceleration of inflation. This increased from a regional average of 200% in 1987 to 470% in 1988. In

Argentina inflation doubled from 175% to 370%, and in Brazil it reached the unprecedented level of over 800% by the end of the year.

On the external side, there was a sharp deterioration in the level of new loans and investment, down to two-thirds of an already very low 1987 figure. Apart from Brazil, which registered a record trade surplus of $US 19 bn, there was little sign of the increase in export revenues so essential for recovery from economic stagnation. Total dollar earnings were little higher than in 1984 and in real terms remained well below pre-1982 levels. Moreover, Latin America's share of world exports fell below 4% for the first time this century. As a result, the region continued to be a net exporter of capital on an enormous and debilitating scale. The net outflow of capital rose from $US 21.4 bn in 1987 to $US 28.9 bn in 1988.

Political Developments
In Brazil, dissatisfaction with President Sarney and the party most closely associated with his government (the PMDB – Brazilian Democratic Movement Party) was graphically illustrated in the results of the November 1988 municipal elections. The Workers' Party (PT) made major gains, collecting 4.3 million votes in Brazil's largest 100 cities and winning control of three state capitals – Porto Alegre, Vitoria and Brazil's largest city, Sao Paulo. The other major left-wing party, the Democratic Workers' Party (PDT) led by Leonel Brizola, also did well, capturing 3.2 million votes and three state capitals. These results gave further impetus to the realignment of political forces on both Right and Left as the country moves towards the first direct presidential election in nearly thirty years in November 1989.

The autumn also saw a wave of industrial unrest in the state sector which effectively ended the chances of negotiating a social pact similar to the one developed in Mexico. After months of drift and uncertainty, President Sarney finally outlined a new counter-inflation plan in January 1989. The 'Summer Plan' involved a freeze on wages and prices together with the abandonment of wage indexation and an extremely tough monetary and fiscal shock. However, the political difficulties of implementing such a policy became apparent almost immediately, for the government was unable to dismiss 90,000 state sector workers or close five ministries, as the plan envisaged.

In Argentina economic difficulties led to a similar weakening in the position of President Alfonsín and his Radical Party. In July 1988 the opposition Peronist party chose a populist from its traditional wing, Carlos Saúl Menem, as its candidate for the May 1989 presidential election. Throughout the rest of the year Menem was able to exploit the government's economic difficulties to the detriment of Radical Party candidate Eduardo Angeloz. The country's economic problems were aggravated by the worst drought since 1871, which led to electricity shortages and a decline in agricultural production.

Of greater concern was the continuing unrest in the military, which in December 1988 led to the third and most serious rebellion of Alfonsín's presidency. This was led by Col. Seineldin, an officer who, unlike the earlier rebel leader Aldo Rico, was greatly respected in the army. The rebels did not aim to seize power, but rather demanded the dismissal of the Army Chief of Staff, greater spending on the army and an amnesty for those implicated in the 'dirty war' of the 1970s; after initial hesitation, Alfonsín was forced to concede the first two of these demands. In January 1989 an attack by left-wing guerrillas on the barracks at La Tablada, outside Buenos Aires, revived disturbing memories of the civil war of the 1970s, though there was little to suggest that this was more than an isolated incident.

In Peru, by contrast, there was a worrying increase in the intensity of political violence. President García announced tough new counter-insurgency laws in August 1988. Yet the chances of militarily defeating either *Sendero Luminoso* or the Tupac Amaru guerrilla group appeared as remote as ever. *Sendero*'s influence has continued to grow, and the movement is well established in most of the country's highland departments, in the coca-producing Alto Huallaga valley and in Lima itself (its improved position in the capital representing an important modification of its earlier rural-based strategy). The continued deterioration of Peru's economy in 1988, the decline in García's personal position and the army's increasingly evident inability to fight a counter-insurgency war on five or six fronts at once make the threat posed by political violence the most serious in the region.

Serious social disorder continued to plague Colombia as well. President Barco's peace plan, announced in August 1988, met with little success. The renewed peace initiative followed the kidnapping in June of the prominent Social Conservative politician Dr Alvaro Gómez, who was held for 53 days by the M-19 guerrilla group, and was also motivated by mounting criticism of both the inefficiency and brutality of the armed forces. The three largest guerrilla groups, loosely united under the *Coordinadora Guerillera Simón Bolívar* (CGSB), responded by launching a new offensive in September both in rural areas and in the cities; the death toll reportedly reached 1,200, including 250 soldiers. To this must be added both the violence related to the drug mafia and increased activity of the para-military death squads (aimed largely at the left-wing coalition, the *Unión Patriótica*), which claimed around 500 lives in 1988.

While Peru and Colombia provide the clearest examples of the growing influence of the drug trade, concern about drugs has spread far wider. There was greater awareness that, as new trafficking routes have been opened, more countries have become directly involved. There was also an alarming increase in local consumption, particularly in large cities, a problem that is related to the rapid spread of AIDS in Latin America. Although the links between *narcotraficantes* and guerrilla groups are complex (and often conflictual), the stimulus that the drug trade

221

provides to both urban and rural violence and the threat it poses to already weak state structures is clearly established.

There were also important developments in two countries clearly out- side the democratic fold. In Chile, President Pinochet was defeated in the 5 October plebiscite, thereby ending his hopes of remaining in office for a further eight years on a constitutional basis. Although Pinochet did win 46% of the vote, largely on the basis of the country's economic advances, he was unable to garner the necessary majority. He lost because of his own unconvincing standing as a prospective democratic President, and because of a crucial loss of support amongst the right- wing parties and business groups. Another crucial factor was the mod- erate and unified performance of the 16-party opposition alliance. Under the Constitution, elections will have to take place before the end of 1989, with a democratically elected President assuming office in March 1990.

In Paraguay, President Alfredo Stroessner, the world's longest-ruling dictator, was toppled on 2 February 1989 in a coup led by Gen. Andrés Rodríguez. The revolt followed a build-up of popular opposition to the regime throughout 1988, with large numbers of people taking to the streets despite heavy repression. The coup was organized by the tra- ditionalist wing of the ruling *Colorado* party, a faction which had lost formal control of the party in August 1987 to the so-called *militantes*, the most extreme element within the Stroessner regime. Although Gen. Rodríguez has promised to hold elections, his own very close associ- ation with the previous regime places a question-mark over the extent of future democratization. More ominous still, especially for the US, are Rodríguez's reputed connections with the country's extensive drug business. In the early 1970s he was implicated in the case of a leading heroin smuggler and declared *persona non grata* in the US.

In spite of the many domestic problems facing the region, political and electoral systems continued to function. However, the incorpor- ation of new social forces into the political process (represented, for example, by the PT in Brazil) remains a necessary condition for consoli- dating democracy. Although many centrist governments were weak- ened by developments in 1988, the alternatives appeared even less viable. Memories of past repression and the disastrous record of mili- tary governments in managing the economy continued to make a return to military rule very much an option of last resort. On the other hand, although 1988 saw elected gains for the left and centre-left in Ecuador, Venezuela, Chile and Brazil, the overall attractiveness of extreme left-wing policies is probably lower than at any time since before the Cuban Revolution. Indeed, there was substantial consensus (even amongst many so-called populists) on the need to increase the efficiency of the public sector, control budget deficits, modernize the tax system, and to give a high priority to exports. Events in March 1989 in Venezuela – long regarded as the most stable country in the region – provided an ominous indication of what might happen if there is no improvement in the overall economic climate. Austerity measures introduced in February 1989 by the newly-elected government of Carlos Andrés Peréz resulted in two days of rioting in and around Caracas which cost the lives of over 300 people.

International Developments
Latin America's foreign debt remained the most important aspect of the region's relationship with the rest of the world. Although the threat to the international banking system has been reduced by the strengthening of the financial positions of most of the major banks, Western economic interests continued to be damaged by protracted economic stagnation in the region. There were, however, only a few new developments in 1988. In June and July Brazil returned to the path of orthodoxy by signing agreements with its private creditors, the IMF and the Club of Rome. There also was some progress in reducing foreign debt by means of debt-for-equity swaps and the exchange of old debt for new bonds – this reduced the Brazilian debt by around $US 4 bn and the Mexican debt by around $US 5 bn. Finally, the US made emergency short-term loans available to Argentina in December 1987, to Mexico in October 1988 and to Venezuela in March 1989.

While tangible progress towards a programme of debt relief was lacking, there were some signs of movement, particularly from Japan. This reflected both Tokyo's increased economic power (in 1988 it overtook the US as the world's largest aid donor) and the size of its own economic interests in Latin America, particularly in Brazil and Mexico. At the Toronto summit in May 1988 Japan repeated its proposals for a multilaterally supervised reduction of middle-income country debt; although this was opposed by the US, the UK and West Germany, the underlying principle was supported by France, major US banks and a growing lobby in the US Congress. By early 1989 pressure for debt relief was multiplying throughout the region. The seriously deteriorating economic situation in Brazil and Argentina, Brazil's suspension of debt-for-equity swaps, the prospect of a sizeable fall in the region's trade surplus in 1989, and the appearance of a possible regional leader on the debt question in Venezuela's newly-elected President combined to produce a sense that siginificant debt relief could no longer be avoided.

If Latin America remains of major concern in economic terms, its salience in East–West relations declined appreciably in 1988. This was partly the result of the Reagan administration's failure to secure domestic support for its Central American policy and of US preoccupation with the presidential election. It also reflected the impact of Gorbachev's 'new thinking' and Moscow's evident determination to encourage negotiated settlements to regional disputes.

These changes in Soviet policy had important repercussions for Cuba. Not only has its importance in Soviet foreign policy been downgraded somewhat, there was increased pressure on Castro to reform the Cuban economy (thus allowing Moscow to reduce its esti-

223

mated $US 4.5-bn annual subsidy) and to emulate Gorbachev's policy of *perestroika*. Gorbachev could have been expected to discuss these issues during his visit to Havana in early April 1989. In addition, although Cuba agreed to withdraw from Angola on the back of significant military success against South Africa, this necessarily represented a substantial reduction of its international role. These developments served to increase Cuba's interest in seeking to bolster its ties with Latin America.

The greater priority given to economic issues in the Soviet Union's third-world policy attracted considerable Latin American interest in 1988. In October 1988 President Sarney made the first visit by a Brazilian president to Moscow and signed eight accords on technical, economic and scientific co-operation. In late 1988 Chile re-established diplomatic relations with Moscow and signed trade agreements with Poland and Romania. Despite such diplomatic activity, though, the scope for expanding economic ties remained limited by the USSR's inability to supply the goods, services and technology that Latin America needs. In 1987, for example, Brazilian exports to the Soviet Union totalled $US 390 m, compared with imports of $US 19 m. This structural imbalance will remain a major constraint on the expansion of trade ties.

Concern about the impact of Amazonian deforestation on the global environment emerged as a new, and potentially contentious, issue on Latin America's international agenda. By the end of 1988 such environmental pressure had forced changes in the lending practices of both the World Bank and the EC (a prime financial backer of a major Amazonian mineral development project) and had led to the growth of a sizeable lobby in the US Congress. There was much discussion of how common interests between Latin America and its international partners might be realized, particularly via some form of extended 'debt-for-nature' swap. There is also a growing domestic environmentalist lobby, made more vocal and given more prominence by the murder of the environmentalist leader Francisco Mendes Filho. Yet Brazilian reactions to environmentalist demands – particularly President Sarney's speech of early March 1989, accusing foreign powers of trying to turn the region into 'a green Persian Gulf' – also underlined how easily increased external pressure runs the risk of producing a nationalist backlash.

Chronologies: 1988

THE UNITED STATES AND CANADA

January

2– US and Canada sign agreement eliminating trade and tariff barriers; sign Arctic co-operation agreement (11).

12 Prime Minister Takeshita of Japan arrives in Washington on his first visit.

25 President Reagan's State of the Union address pledges continued efforts for prosperity and freedom at home and abroad.

27 Egyptian President Mubarak arrives in US seeking support for Middle East peace plans.

February

3 House of Representatives defeats (219–211) President Reagan's aid package to *Contras*.

7 US warns of possible withdrawal of American troops in Europe if West Germany insists on eliminating nuclear weapons from its territory.

8– US successfully conducts major SDI test in space; announces new space policy encouraging commercial space developments (11).

18– President Reagan presents to Congress FY 1989 budget of $1.1 trillion, proposing heavy defence cuts; Navy Secretary James Webb resigns (22); William Ball nominated as successor (23).

March

9 As Chinese Foreign Minister Wu Xueqian ends official visit to US, lifting of restrictions on high-technology sales to China is announced.

14–16 Israeli premier Shamir visits Washington, fails to reach agreement on Middle East peace plan.

20 Soviet Foreign Minister Shevardnadze arrives in US for talks on Soviet withdrawal from Afghanistan.

31 US Congress approves $48 m in food and medical aid for *Contras*.

April

17 French ambassador to Ottawa recalled as long-running fishing dispute between Canada and France worsens.

19 House of Representatives approves INF Treaty (393–7).

May

17 US Senate begins considering INF Treaty for ratification.

June

19–21 Fourteenth Group of Seven economic summit held in Toronto.

21– Canada expels 17 Soviet diplomats for industrial espionage; series of tit-for-tat expulsions follow (22–).

24 2 Egyptian officers and 3 Americans, arrested in Washington, Baltimore and Sacramento, charged with trying to smuggle missile material to Egypt.

29 During US visit, Israeli defence minister Rabin signs memorandum of understanding on joint development of anti-tactical missile.

July

19 Karoly Grosz begins first visit by a Hungarian leader to US for 41 years.

August

10 Senate approves $27 m in humanitarian aid for *Contras*.

September

13 US begins paying its UN arrears.

27 Congress drops ban on sale of *Maverick* air-to-surface missile to Kuwait.

28 Congress passes $300-bn military authorization bill for FY 1988–9, removing spending restrictions on SDI.

29   Revamped space shuttle *Discovery* successfully launched.
29   US and 11 allies sign agreement to build permanently-manned space station.
October
4   Pentagon announces decision to halve number of space-based weapons in SDI programme in favour of ground-based weapons.
November
7–   George Bush elected US President.
10–   USAF announces existence of 'stealth' fighter; 'stealth' bomber displayed for first time (22).
21   Conservative party wins second successive term in Canadian general election.
26   US refuses Yasser Arafat visa for visit to address UN in New York.
27   US and Japan sign agreement for joint building of new fighter aircraft; Japanese foreign minister visits US for wide-ranging talks (30–2 Dec).
December
2   Space shuttle launched with spy satellite on board.
6–8   During trip to US, Gorbachev addresses UN; curtails visit after earthquake in Armenia.
9   GATT talks in Montreal adjourned until April 1989.
28   US extends sanctions against Libya for another 6 months.

THE SOVIET UNION

January
7   USSR announces it will test a reusable space shuttle in 1989.
11   New Czech leader, Milos Jakes, arrives in Moscow on official visit.
21   USSR proposes special UN Security Council meeting to discuss an international Middle East peace conference.
February
6   Head of Gosplan, Nikolai Talyzin, dismissed for failing to implement economic reforms.
18   Central Committee plenum removes Boris Yeltsin as non-voting Politburo member, Gorbachev attacks NATO's nuclear moderization proposals.
24–   Party leader of Nagorno-Karabakh region of Azerbaijan, Boris Kevorkov, dismissed after 5-day riots by ethnic Armenians; disturbances spread to Sumgait (28); curfew imposed by Soviet troops, government commission formed to maintain order (1 March).
March
13–   Armenians demonstrate in Moscow against lack of information on events in Armenia and Azerbaijan; Gorbachev refuses to annex Nagorno-Karabakh into Armenia (23); widespread strike in Armenia results.
April
21   During US Secretary of State Shultz's visit to Moscow, USSR presents draft treaty on space arms.
May
8   KGB detains 47 members of newly-formed opposition party, Democratic Union.
21   Party leaders of Armenia and Azerbaijan dismissed.
29   President Reagan and Soviet leader Gorbachev hold their fourth superpower summit in Moscow; ends 2 June.
June
16   Estonian Communist Party leader Karl Vaino dismissed as Moscow tries to restrain Estonian separatist tendencies.

17– Azerbaijani parliament refuses to cede Nagorno-Karabakh to Armenia; fighting breaks out in the region (18–20).

28 Special party conference in Moscow passes 7 resolutions endorsing reforms and establishing an executive Presidency; ends 1 July.

July

7 Unmanned space probe launched to Mars' moon.

12– Nagorno-Karabakh votes to secede from Azerbaijan and join Armenia; Azerbaijan rejects this (13).

28 First official Israeli delegation for 21 years arrives in Moscow.

August

1 USSR and Qatar establish diplomatic relations.

2 US Defense Secretary Carlucci examines *Blackjack* bomber in Moscow.

3 Mathias Rust freed after one year of three-year sentence for landing light aircraft in Red Square in May 1987.

September

16 In Krasnoyarsk, Gorbachev unveils 7-point plan to reduce super-power rivalry in Asia and Pacific.

18– More clashes in Nagorno-Karabakh; curfew and state of emergency declared (21); troops deployed in Armenia (22).

27 In foreign-policy speech to UN, Foreign Minister Shevardnadze suggests new role for Security Council.

30– In Central Committee meeting changes, Andrei Gromyko is dropped from Politburo and Yegor Ligachev loses some of his functions; at Supreme Soviet meeting Gorbachev replaces Gromyko as President (1 Oct).

October

4 President Ceausescu of Romania makes brief official visit to Moscow.

17–21 President Sarney makes the first visit to Moscow by a Brazilian President.

24–26 West German Chancellor Kohl visits Moscow, grants economic aid to support Soviet economic reform; announces Soviet promise to release all political prisoners in USSR before year end.

November

11– Politburo members arrive in Latvia, Lithuania and Estonia, alarmed at Baltic opposition to proposed constitutional changes; Estonian parliament votes to reserve right to veto national legislation (16); Lithuanian parliament postpones such a decision (18); Latvia decides not to operate veto (22).

22– Armenians and Azerbaijanis clash in Baku and other Azerbaijani cities; 3 soldiers die (23); Party leaders of 2 Azerbaijani cities sacked (26–7).

25–26 During visit to Moscow, President Mitterrand extends French credit worth $2.1 bn, sees launch of Franco-Soviet space mission.

December

1–3 Chinese and Soviet foreign ministers Qian Qichen and Shevardnadze hold talks in Moscow, agree to Sino-Soviet summit meeting in 1989.

7– Chief-of-Staff Akhromeyev resigns; replaced by Col.-Gen. Moiseyev (15).

7– Severe earthquake hits Armenia; Gorbachev abandons trip to US, Cuba and UK and returns home (8).

21 2 Soviet cosmonauts return to earth after record 366 days in space.

EUROPE

January

7 East German leader Erich Honecker begins 3-day visit to Paris.

10– West German foreign minister Genscher begins 3-day visit to Poland; meets Solidarity leader Lech Walesa (12).

12–	Spain's ETA terrorists isolated as 6 other Basque parties sign anti-terrorist pact; ETA offers government a truce if talks between the 2 sides resume (29).
13	Sweden and USSR sign agreement settling disputed fishing zones in Baltic.
15	Spain announces US will withdraw from Torrejón air base within 3 years.
27	Chancellor Kohl ends 2-day visit to Czechoslovakia aimed at improving bilateral relations.
31	2-day Greek–Turkish summit ends with announcement of confidence-building measures to improve bilateral relations.

February

10	UK withdraws from European manned space station programme.
13	At emergency meeting in Brussels, EC leaders agree 5-year budget plan.
17	UK premier Thatcher urges NATO permanent representatives to modernize the Alliance's nuclear arsenal.
21	George Vassiliou elected new President of Cyprus.
24	Foreign ministers of 6 Balkan states begin inaugural meeting in Belgrade.

March

2–3	NATO leaders meet in Brussels to discuss Alliance approach to conventional arms reductions but postpone detailed planning for nuclear force modernization.
4–	Greece and Turkey hold further round of reconciliation talks; first of a regular series of bilateral talks starts in Athens (30).
13	New President of Cyprus visits Athens to formulate joint Greco-Cypriot approach to reuniting Cyprus.
18	Four-day Gorbachev visit to Yugoslavia ends with joint communiqué pledging respect for each other's political views.
29	Head of African National Congress in France assassinated in Paris.
30	Warsaw Pact foreign ministers' meeting ends with call for strategic nuclear missile treaty and separate talks on tactical nuclear weapons.

April

6	Mrs Thatcher begins first official visit by a British Prime Minister to Turkey.
6	Supreme Allied Commander, Europe, begins historic 3-day visit to Spain.
13–	New Italian government headed by Ciriaco de Mita sworn in; aide of new Premier assassinated by Red Brigade terrorists (16).
18	UK announces it will join 3 projects in European Space Agency programme.
19	Yugoslavia announces economic austerity plan.
26	Rupert Scholz officially confirmed as new West German defence minister with effect from 19 May.
28	At the end of a NPG meeting, NATO ministers support modernization of their nuclear arsenal, but make no decisions on deployment.
29–	Japanese Prime Minister begins trip to Europe; stops in Italy (2 May), UK (3–4 May), Netherlands, France (6 May) and West Germany (5 May).

May

2	Solidarity leaders arrested in Poland after a week of labour unrest.
8–	François Mitterrand re-elected President of France; appoints Socialist, Michel Rocard, Prime Minister (10); snap general election called when he fails to form a government (14).
9	Dr Wilfred Martens sworn in as Belgian Prime Minister, ending 145 days with no official government.
11–	Yugoslav austerity plan postponed; attempted Slovenian no-confidence vote fails (15); austerity measures introduced (28).
22	At end of 3-day Party conference in Hungary, Janos Kadar is ousted as leader and replaced by Karoly Grosz.
27	2-day meeting of NATO's Defence Planning Committee ends with no practical decisions reached.

June

3–   In Denmark, Poul Shluter forms 3-party coalition government; declares US and British warships can resume routine visits to Danish ports (7).

9   EC and COMECON sign mutual recognition accord.

9–10 NATO foreign ministers meet in Madrid, welcome results of Moscow super-power summit but reach no decisions on contentious issues.

12   Parliamentary elections in France result in hung parliament for first time in 30 years.

13–15 First visit by Turkish Prime Minister to Greece for 36 years passes with few concrete results.

16   France resumes diplomatic relations with Iran, severed in July 1987.

18   Attempt to assassinate Turkish premier Ozal fails in Ankara.

24–   NATO creates multinational army brigade to defend Norway, replacing disbanded Canadian unit; Italy agrees to accept transfer by 1991 of NATO F-16 planes from Spain (30).

27–   Rally in Budapest protests at Romanian plans to destroy 8,000 mainly Hungarian-populated villages; Romania closes Hungarian consulate in affected region (28).

July

8   UK signs arms contract with Saudi Arabia worth $6 bn.

9   Demonstrations in Yugoslav provinces of Kosovo and Vojvodina against curbs on their autonomy; sacking of provinces' leaders demanded (16–17); Serbian Assembly passes amendments to limit provinces' autonomy (26).

11   Gorbachev begins 4-day official visit to Poland, during which he makes new arms-control proposal (see *East–West Arms Control*).

12   President Evren of Turkey begins 3-day visit to London, first by a Turkish head of state for 21 years.

August

15   East Germany and EC establish diplomatic relations.

16–   Polish workers strike over pay and recognition of Solidarity trade union; Lech Walesa meets government officials for first time in 6 years, calls for return to work (31).

24   Greek and Cypriot community leaders meet in Geneva under UN auspices to discuss ending Cyprus conflict.

September

18   In Swedish general election, Green party win seats but ruling Social Democrats retain power.

19–   Polish premier Messner resigns and is replaced by M. Rakowski.

20–   UK premier Thatcher makes speech on European co-operation in Bruges; continues European tour in Luxembourg (21) and Spain (22–23).

27   UK and Malaysia sign $1-bn arms deal.

28   New 8-year pact agreed providing US with 3 military bases in Spain, with no economic or military aid involved.

October

10–11 Czech premier Strougal resigns, replaced by Ladislav Adamec; cabinet reshuffled.

17   Yugoslav Communist Party Central Committee meets; 4 Politburo members resign and other Committee members are removed (19); further economic, social and political reforms announced (23).

31   Polish government announces closure of Gdansk shipyard, Solidarity's HQ.

November

2–4   During 3-day visit to Poland, the first by a British premier, Mrs Thatcher meets Solidarity leader Lech Walesa.

4   Spain becomes fourth partner in European Fighter Aircraft programme.

10   UK and Iran agree to restore full diplomatic relations.
14   Spain and Portugal become members of WEU.
17   2 Albanian leaders in Yugoslavia's Kosovo province sacked.
23–   Miklos Nemeth appointed as Hungarian Premier; extensive reform pro-
      gramme unveiled, including new constitution for 1990 (24).
25   Yugoslavia amends one-third of its constitution to hasten economic and
      social reform.

December
1   West Germany announces 50% cut in training manoeuvres starting in 1990.
2–3   EC heads of government hold summit in Rhodes.
8–9   French President Mitterrand continues his *Ostpolitik* with visit to
      Czechoslovakia.
12   NATO suspends fighter aircraft training in West Germany.
21   Terrorist bomb blows up US airliner over Scottish town, killing 270.
21–   6 Polish Politburo members removed in reshuffle; radical economic laws
      adopted (23).
30   Yugoslavia's government resigns after Parliament blocks economic reform.

THE MIDDLE EAST

January
2–   Israeli jets bomb 3 Palestinian guerrilla command centres in south Lebanon,
      killing at least 19; 3 Palestinian guerrillas killed by Israeli army after pen-
      etrating Israel–Lebanon border fence (20).
5–   At UN, US endorses resolution condemning Israel's plans to deport
      Palestinians from occupied territories; UN Under-Secretary, touring area, is
      barred by Israel from visiting refugee camps (12); unrest spreads to
      Jerusalem, where curfew is imposed in one suburb (22–3).
9   President Mubarak marks Egypt's re-integration into Arab world with visit
      to 6 Gulf Co-operation Council states.
14/15– Iran attacks 3 tankers in 2 days; French navy hardens its rules of engagement
      in Gulf waters (20).
16–   Shi'ite Muslim *Amal* fighters lift their 3-year siege of refugee camps in Beirut
      and south Lebanon.
23   Tunisia and Egypt resume diplomatic relations.
February
4   PLO guerrillas infiltrate the Israel–Lebanon border, killing 2 Israeli soldiers.
5–   2 UN relief workers kidnapped in south Lebanon (released in Beirut, 1
      March); US head of UN Truce Supervision Organization kidnapped (17).
16   US withdraws 1 battleship and 2 other warships from Gulf, reducing its flo-
      tilla to 25 vessels.
25–   US Secretary of State Shultz arrives Israel on peace mission: Jordan and
      Syria (27); Egypt (28); Jordan (29).
29–   Missile attacks on Iraqi and Iranian cities resume; Iraq fires 17 missiles in
      one day, striking Tehran for first time (1 March).
March
1–   Shultz meets King Hussein in London; presents peace plan to Israel, Egypt
      (which endorses it) and Syria (9); Syria rejects it (8) as does Israel (11).
3–   In Lebanon, West German hostage kidnapped in January is released; 2
      Oxfam workers kidnapped (4); released (8).
9–   General strike disrupts Israeli occupied territories; 400 of 1,000 Arab police-
      men resign (13); Israel imposes curfew and economic sanctions (14); 4
      Palestinians die in Land Day clashes with Israeli soldiers (30).

230

10–   Iraq and Iran call separate cease-fires in the 'War of the Cities'; cease-fires broken (13); Iraqi planes attack 2 Iranian supertankers in Gulf, killing 51 sailors (19); 2 Kuwaiti servicemen killed as Iran attacks Bubiyan island in first Iranian–Kuwaiti clash of Gulf War (19).

15   Iran captures Halabja, north-eastern Iraqi border town; Iraq uses chemical weapons on town (16), killing thousands of Kurdish civilians.

17   Israeli air force begins repeated attacks on Palestinian guerrilla positions in south Lebanon.

April

5   Heavy fighting breaks out between Syrian and Iranian allies for control of south Lebanon.

5–   Kuwaiti airliner en route Bangkok to Kuwait hijacked to Mashad, Iran, release of 17 terrorists imprisoned in Kuwait demanded; two killed (9,11); plane flies to Cyprus (8) and Algiers (12); remaining hostages released in return for safe passage of hijackers (20).

6–   In disputed circumstances, the first Israeli civilian death since unrest in occupied territories began leads Israel to seal off West Bank and Gaza strip and impose curfew; restrictions lifted (24).

18   Iraq recaptures Fao Peninsula after 2 days' heavy fighting.

22–   Israeli air force attacks PLO bases in south Lebanon; Palestinians carry out cross-border raids into Israel (26–7).

24   Yasser Arafat visits Damascus, ending 5-year rift between PLO and Syria.

26   Saudi Arabia breaks diplomatic relations with Iran.

May

2–4–   Israeli troops cross into south Lebanon and clash with Shi'ite militiamen; Israeli helicopters raid villages and refugee camps (25).

4–   Last 3 French hostages in Lebanon released; fighting erupts between Shi'ite militias for control of Beirut's southern suburbs (6); Syria and Iran supervise truce (12); Syria sends in troops to end fighting (27).

6   6 Kurdish groups form coalition to fight for self-rule in northern Iraq.

25   Iraq recaptures territory around Shalamcheh, held by Iran since January 1987.

June

3–   US Secretary of State Shultz starts fourth Middle East peace shuttle, including talks in Egypt, Jordan (4), Israel (5), Syria (6).

7–9   Arab summit meeting in Algiers pledges money to support Palestinian uprising in Israel.

25   Iraq drives Iranian troops from Majnoon island.

July

3   USS *Vincennes* shoots down Iranian airliner in Gulf, mistaking it for fighter.

7   Supporters of Yasser Arafat driven from their last Beirut stronghold by dissident Palestinian fighters.

13–   In Gulf War, Iraq pushes into Iranian territory for first time since 1982; withdraws its troops and offers peace (17); Iran implicitly agrees cease-fire by unconditionally accepting UN Resolution 598 (18); official truce takes effect (20); Iraq continues offensive on northern, central and southern fronts (22–24).

28–   Jordan terminates 5-year economic plan for West Bank; Hussein dissolves parliament, ending representation for Palestinians in West Bank (31).

August

18   Lebanese parliament fails to elect a new President, due to lack of quorum.

20–   Gulf War cease-fire begins; Iranian and Iraqi foreign ministers open talks in Geneva (25).

25   Israeli navy and air force attack Palestinian targets in south Lebanon.

231

September

4– France and Italy reduce naval forces in Gulf; US stops escorting US-flagged ships in Gulf waters (26); Italy stops escorting Italian ships (29).

19 Israel launches communications satellite.

22– President Gemayel appoints Gen. Aoun as head of military government; Sunnis refuse recognition, claiming premier al-Hoss leader of Lebanon (23).

29 International arbitration panel awards Taba strip to Egypt.

October

19 UK announces Royal Navy will stop escorting British merchant ships through Strait of Hormuz from end of October.

21 Israel launches air and ground raids on PLO and *Hizbollah* strongholds in Lebanon.

22– King Hussein and Yasser Arafat meet in Jordan to heal Jordan–PLO rift; Arafat meets President Saddam Hussein in Iraq (23).

November

1– UN-mediated Iran–Iraq peace talks resume in Geneva; agreement reached on exchange of wounded prisoners (8); talks adjourned (11); prisoner exchange suspended (27).

1 No party wins majority in Israeli general election.

12–15 Palestine National Council meets in Algiers, endorses UN Resolution 242 as basis for Middle East peace settlement; declares an independent Palestinian state in West Bank and Gaza Strip.

13 In Lebanon, Finnish peace-keeping forces end siege of their post by Palestinian guerrillas; Red Cross worker kidnapped (17); fighting between *Amal* and *Hizbollah* in West Beirut (24); Syria arranges cease-fire (28).

27–28 West German foreign minister makes 2-day visit to Iran.

30 Iraq announces it has developed new missiles able to destroy medium-and short-range surface-to-surface missiles.

December

4 British embassy reopens in Tehran after 8 years.

7 Yasser Arafat explicitly recognizes state of Israel and denounces terrorism, clarifies these points in speech to UN in Geneva when launching peace plan (13) and at press conference (14); US envoy meets PLO officials in Tunis (16).

8– General strike called to mark first anniversary of *intifada*; Israel seals off occupied territories (9).

9– Israel launches combined-arms attack on Palestinian camp near Beirut, first land attack outside south Lebanon security zone; attacks *Amal* base in south Lebanon (29).

16 Gulf War peace talks postponed indefinitely.

16 Red Cross worker, kidnapped in November, released in Lebanon.

22 *Likud*-Labour coalition government sworn in Israel: Shamir made premier; Peres finance minster, Rabin defence minister, Arens foreign minister.

AFRICA

January

4 British premier Thatcher starts 5-day visit to Kenya and Nigeria, her first trip to Africa since 1979.

6 Gen. Holomisa assumes control of Transkei after coup.

8 In South Africa, United Democratic Front and Zulu *Inkatha* movement, sign document to curb violence amongst their supporters in Natal province.

23 President Idris Abdul Wakil of Zanzibar dismisses cabinet, accusing members of plotting against him.

29   Annual meeting of Southern African Development Co-ordination Confer-
        ence ends with $1 bn economic aid pledged by western donors.

February

4   Col. Gaddafi arrives in Tunisia for his first visit in 4 years.
10   Attempted coup in Bophuthatswana crushed by South African troops.
19–   Bomb explosion in bank in Namibia kills 15; South Africa blames SWAPO,
        retaliates with attacks on 3 SWAPO bases in southern Angola (20).
24   South Africa introduces legislation effectively closing 17 anti-government
        organizations and curtailing activities of black trade union movement.
29   State of emergency declared in Senegal after rioting as President Diouf
        elected for another 5-year term.

March

4   Tigrean guerrillas capture Eritrean strategic town of Wukro.
14–   South Africa and US meet on diplomatic solution to Angolan civil war;
        Front-line states summit approves Angolan peace initiative (24).
21   Ugandan People's Democratic Army joins government's National Resist-
        ance Army to form a new national army.
24   After general elections, Kenya's President Moi shuffles cabinet, removing
        Vice-President Kibaki from office.

April

3   Ethiopia and Somalia restore diplomatic relations after 11-year break,
        pledge ministerial-level talks on border dispute.
7   Senegal President Diouf reshuffles government to curb continuing unrest.
9   Chairman of OAU and UN Secretary-General open talks on peace plan for
        Western Sahara.
16   Second-in-command of PLO, Abu Jihad, killed in Tunis.
21   South African President Botha proposes limited improvements to black par-
        ticipation in regional and national government.

May

3–   Angola, Cuba, South Africa and US hold 2-day talks in London on ending
        war in Angola; Angola and Cuba continue these talks (12–13).
16   Algeria and Morocco resume relations after 12 years.
22   Libya and Tunisia sign economic and social co-operation pact.
26   Mozambique and South Africa agree to revive Nkomati Accord.
27–   Rebels launch offensive in northern Somalia; claim capture of Burao (28)
        and Hargeisa (31).

June

9   South Africa declares new year-long state of emergency.
10   Algerian, Libyan, Mauritanian, Moroccan and Tunisian heads of state meet
        in Zeralda, Algeria, set up committee to explore Maghreb unification.
24/5–   Second round of Angolan peace talks held in Cairo between Angola, South
        Africa, Cuba and US; South African raid in Angola kills 200 Angolan and
        Cuban troops (27).

July

13   Maghreb unification committee holds first meeting.
13–   US announces plan to end Angolan conflict: Cuba to pull out of Angola in
        return for Namibian independence; Angola, Cuba and South Africa endorse
        it, but differences remain on withdrawal time-scale (20).

August

8–   Angola, Cuba and South Africa declare cease-fire in Angola, recommend 1
        November for implementation of UN Resolution 435 on Namibian inde-
        pendence; South African troops leave Angola (10–30); formal cease-fire
        accord, to be supervised by joint monitoring committee, signed (22); talks to
        discuss withdrawal of Cuban troops begin in the Congo (24).

13   South Africa admits it has capacity to produce nuclear weapons.
14   Tribal warfare in Burundi between Hutu and Tutsi.
30   UN Western Sahara peace plan conditionally approved by Morocco and Polisario.

September

10–   British Foreign Secretary Howe, starts 10-day African tour in Sudan; visits Ethiopia, Kenya (11–12), Uganda (14), Tanzania and Mozambique (17–19).

12–13 South African President Botha makes first trip to Front-line states, visiting Mozambique and Malawi.

22–   Talks between UN Secretary-General and South Africa agree all Namibian political parties can participate in peace process; South Africa, Angola and Cuba begin Namibian independence talks in Brazzaville (26).

October

1–   President Botha continues African diplomatic offensive, visiting Zaire and Ivory Coast (15).

3   Libya and Chad announce end to hostilities and renewal of diplomatic ties.

6–   President Chadli Bendjedid announces state of siege and curfew in Algeria after rioting; restrictions lifted (12).

24   4-day meeting opens in West Germany between ANC representatives and Afrikaner academics.

26   Conservative Party makes gains in South African local government elections.

November

5–   New Algerian premier Kasdi Merbah appointed to reform economy; ruling party congress endorses President Chadli's political reforms (28–29).

6–   Riots in Sokoto, northern Nigeria, after Ibrahim Dasuki appointed leader of Nigerian Muslims; 24-hour curfew imposed (9).

10–   Namibia independence talks resume in Geneva; Cuba and Angola accept terms for withdrawal of Cuban troops (18); South Africa also accepts (22).

16–   Sudanese rebels and Democratic Unionist Party (DUP), part of ruling coalition government, sign peace plan; approved by cabinet (1 Dec).

23   President Botha of South Africa commutes death sentences on 'Sharpeville Six'.

24   Algeria and Egypt agree to renew diplomatic ties.

December

8   Polisario rebels in Western Sahara accidentally shoot down US aid plane on locust-spraying flight to Morocco, killing 5.

20–   Khartoum placed under state of emergency after coup attempt; Parliament rejects peace pact signed in November, preferring premier's el-Mahdi's vaguer proposals (21); DUP quits ruling coalition in protest at price rises (28); these reversed, but anti-government demonstrations continue (29).

22   President Chadli of Algeria elected for third term of office.

22   South Africa, Cuba and Angola sign treaties giving Namibia independence and withdrawing Cuban troops from Angola by 1991, South Africa agrees to halt military aid to UNITA.

27   Front-line states summit in Angola urges US to end military support for UNITA.

ASIA AND AUSTRALASIA

January

13   Taiwan President Chiang Ching-kuo dies, Vice-president Lee Teng-hui sworn in as successor.

21   Filipino President Aquino reshuffles cabinet, appoints armed forces chief, Fidel Ramos, as new defence minister.

26   Japan imposes diplomatic sanctions against North Korea.

February

1   Prince Sihanouk meets Chinese premier Zhao Ziyang to brief him on recent Kampuchean peace talks in Paris.

4   Filipino army seizes 20 top rebel leaders in series of raids.

6–   UN mediator on Afghanistan meets Afghan guerrilla leaders for first time in Pakistan; Gorbachev nominates 15 May as a possible date for beginning of Soviet troop withdrawal from Afghanistan (8).

8–   In South Korea, Kim Young Sam resigns as head of his party; Roh Tae Woo sworn in as new President (25); announces political amnesty (26).

10   UK White Paper on political reform in Hong Kong published, envisages direct elections for some legislature seats in 1991.

12–   Indian army begins 3-day offensive against Tamil Tiger rebels in eastern Sri Lanka, capturing 60; opposition party leader assassinated (16).

17   Thailand and Laos agree cease-fire in their 6-month border conflict.

25   India announces successful test of nuclear missile with 150-mile range.

March

3   In Geneva, Soviet Deputy Foreign Minister announces agreement for Soviet troops to leave Afghanistan over 9 months (half leaving in first 3 months).

5   Anti-Chinese disturbances in Tibet, up to 9 feared killed.

10   Vietnamese Prime Minister, Pham Hung, dies, position filled by First Vice Premier until National Assembly elects successor.

14   China protests to Vietnam over firing on Chinese ships in Spratly Islands in South China Sea.

16   For first time since signing of Indo-Sri Lankan peace accord, Sri Lankan troops attack Tamil Tiger rebels in eastern Sri Lanka, killing 8.

17   In South Korea Kim Dae Jung resigns as head of his party.

April

9–   Chinese National People's Congress opens; Li Peng confirmed as Premier and cabinet reshuffled to strengthen pace of reform (12).

13–   Former South Korean President, Chun Doo Hwan, resigns all public offices; in elections Democratic Justice Party loses majority in legislature (26).

14   US and USSR act as guarantors as Pakistan and Afghanistan sign agreements for Soviet troops to begin to withdraw from Afghanistan on 15 May (half to go by 15 August, all by 15 February 1989).

22–   Kanak militants on Pacific island of Ouvea kill 4 and capture 26 French *gendarmes*; 11 released (24); 8 more hostages taken (27); 1 released to act as mediator (28); all freed as special forces storm militants' position (15 May).

May

4   President Najibullah of Afghanistan begins his first official visit to India.

9–   Sikh separatists besiege Golden Temple in Amritsar; surrender to government troops (15, 18).

10   Sri Lankan government and Sinhalese extremist group, JVP, sign a peace accord giving JVP formal recognition in return for surrendering its arms.

15   USSR begins withdrawing troops from Afghanistan.

29   Pakistan President Zia dissolves Parliament and announces elections will be held in 3 months.

June

7   India begins withdrawing its peace-keeping troops from Sri Lanka.

15   President Zia proclaims Islamic law in Pakistan.

21   Curfew imposed in Burmese capital, Rangoon, after protesters and riot police clash.

22   Do Moui appointed Prime Minister of Vietnam.
25   Peace formula for Pacific island of New Caledonia announced by French government.
30   Vietnamese high command leaves Kampuchea in phased troop withdrawal.

July
4–   UN Secretary-General presents draft Kampuchean peace plan to ASEAN Foreign Ministers' meeting; ASEAN countries agree to attend talks between Kampuchean resistance factions and government (5); Prince Sihanouk quits as head of resistance coalition (11); talks make no progress (25–28).
6   US Secretary of State Shultz starts 18-day tour of Asia including stops in South Korea, Philippines, Hong Kong, Japan and China.
23–   Burma's leader Gen. Ne Win resigns; replaced by Sein Lwin (26).
24–   Ruling coalition wins Thai election; Prem Tinsulanonda refuses another term as premier (27); Gen. Chatichai replaces him (4 August).

August
3–   Martial law imposed in Burma; Sein Lwin resigns (12); replaced by Maung Maung (19); martial law lifted, special party congress called for September (24); opposition coalition, Alliance for Democracy and Peace, formed (29).
17   Pakistan's President Zia, US Ambassador and several Pakistani generals killed in aircraft explosion; Ghulam Ishaq Khan becomes Acting President.
17   Bill Hayden confirmed as next Australian Governor-General.
19–   North and South Korean government officials meet to discuss Olympic games; meeting concludes with no agreement (26).
20   New Caledonian peace accord signed, referendum on self-determination to be held in 1998.

September
3   Singapore's Premier Lee Kuan Yew wins general election.
9–   Burmese opposition forces form provisional government; announce free elections to be held (10); armed forces chief, Gen. Saw Maung mounts military coup, assumes power (18); names military-dominated cabinet (20); another opposition party, League for Democracy, formed (24); ruling party renamed National Unity Party (26).
30   At end of 5-day Party meeting, premier Li Peng announces slow-down in decentralization of Chinese economy.

October
16   In Pakistan, official inquiry rules that sabotage caused plane crash which killed President Zia.
17   US and Philippines sign 2-year bases deal – US to pay $481 m a year in economic, military and development aid for Clark and Subic Bay bases.
17   3-day meeting in Indonesia to follow up July Kampuchean peace initiative, boycotted by *Khmer Rouge*, agrees on further meeting.
18–   In first address by South Korean President to UN General Assembly, Roh Tae Woo calls for international conference on Korean reunification; North Korean President in his address ignores proposal (19).

November
3–   Coup attempt in Maldives fails after India sends in troops.
16   Pakistan People's Party wins general election in Pakistan, but without absolute majority.
18–   Gorbachev begins 3-day visit to India; signs $5.3-bn credit agreement.
22   Australia and US extend space satellite bases agreement for 10 years.
27   Soviet officials and *Mujaheddin* rebels hold first meeting for 9 years in Islamabad.
29   US–Japanese agreement signed on joint development of FSX.

December

1–   China appoints new Communist Party leader in Tibet; 1 killed, 13 injured in Tibetan unrest (10).

1–   State of emergency lifted in Pakistan; Benazir Bhutto sworn in as premier (2); names cabinet retaining General Zia's foreign minister (4); Ghulam Ishaq Khan elected President for 5 years (12).

2–   Australia expels all staff of Yugoslav consulate in Sydney; Yugoslavia expels 3 Australian diplomats from Belgrade (5).

4–   High-level talks between USSR and Afghan rebels take place in Saudi Arabia; rebels agree not to harass Soviet troops as they withdraw (5); reject Gorbachev's call for cease-fire (8); searching for political solution, USSR talks to ex-king Zaher, who refuses peace talks with Kabul regime (24).

5   South Korean President Roh Tae Woo shuffles his cabinet, appoints 23 new ministers.

9–   Japan's finance minister resigns over Recruit scandal; premier Takeshita shuffles cabinet (27); after 2 days, justice minister resigns over scandal (29).

12   Yon Hyong Muk appointed premier of North Korea after Li Gun Mo's resignation on health grounds.

13–   Vietnam announces demobilization of 300,000 soldiers; continues withdrawal of troops from Kampuchea (15).

18–   Soviet Foreign Minister Shevardnadze fails to resolve Kurile Islands dispute during 4-day visit to Japan; goes on to Philippines (21–22).

19   Ranasingh Premadasa narrowly wins Sri Lanka's presidential election.

19–   Rajiv Gandhi makes first visit by an Indian premier to China for 34 years; joint working group to resolve border disputes agreed upon (22).

29–31   Indian and Pakistani premiers Gandhi and Bhutto meet at South Asian Association for Regional Co-operation summit in Islamabad, agree not to attack each other's nuclear facilities.

LATIN AMERICA AND THE CARIBBEAN

January

15   Costa Rica, El Salvador, Guatemala, Honduras and Nicaragua hold 2-day Central America summit in Costa Rica to discuss implementation of August 1987 regional peace plan.

16–   Nicaraguan government lifts state of emergency; talks face-to-face with *Contra* rebels for first time, reaching agreement to reconvene in Guatemala in February (28).

16–   Argentina suffers second military rebellion in 9 months; rebellion collapses, and its leader, Col. Rico, surrenders (18).

24   Leslie Manigat wins Haitian presidential election with 50.3% of vote.

25   Eight years of military rule in Suriname formally end as Ramsewak Shankar is inaugurated as President.

25   Colombian Attorney-General Carlos Mauro Hoyos kidnapped and murdered by drug traffickers.

February

4–   Panamanian leader Gen. Noriega indicted by US jury on drug-related charges; recalls Panamanian diplomats from US (8); President Delvalle dismisses Noriega as leader (25); is himself ousted by Noriega, and a temporary President sworn in (26).

14   Gen. Stroessner wins 8th consecutive term as Paraguayan President.

19   Second round of direct negotiations between *Contra* rebels and Nicaraguan government suspended after failure to agree on 30-day truce.

March

11–   President Reagan imposes new economic sanctions on Panama; rioting and general strike in Panama City (14); police chief leads abortive coup (16); national state of emergency imposed (18).

16–   Honduras claims Nicaraguan troops have crossed its border; heavy fighting breaks out (17); US sends 3,200 troops to Honduras for joint exercises (17); having overrun several *Contra* bases on both sides of the border, *Sandinista* forces return to Nicaragua (20).

20   Municipal elections in El Salvador give ARENA majority over Christian Democrats in Legislative Assembly.

21–   *Sandinista* government and *Contras* hold talks, announce temporary cease-fire; sign agreement on 60-day cease-fire from 1 April, amnesty for rebels and release of political prisoners (23); first 100 prisoners released (27).

22   Brazilian Assembly votes 344–212 to retain strong executive Presidency in the new constitution.

April

8   Honduras declares state of emergency in 2 main cities after anti-US riots.

15–19   Second round of *Sandinista–Contra* peace talks only agrees to meet again.

20   Panama lifts state of emergency imposed in March.

May

4–   In co-ordinated attacks throughout Colombia, journalists and foreign diplomats kidnapped by left-wing guerrillas; all released unharmed (10–14).

11   Attempted army coup in Guatemala foiled bloodlessly.

23   Nicaraguan President Ortega unilaterally extends cease-fire to allow further peace negotiations with *Contras*.

29   Colombian Social Conservative leader Alvaro Gómez kidnapped by M-19 guerrillas; freed after 53 days (20 July).

June

20   Gen. Namphy stages coup in Haiti, overthrowing civilian President Manigat.

24   Talks to review Esquipulas II peace proposals between foreign ministers of Costa Rica, El Salvador, Guatemala, Honduras and Nicaragua end abruptly, achieving nothing..

July

6   Carlos Salinas de Gortari, ruling PRI candidate, narrowly wins Mexican presidential election with 50.4% of vote; in legislative election National Democratic Front wins 240 of 500 seats and gains its first 4 Senate seats.

11–12   US and Nicaragua expel 8 of each other's diplomats.

19–   Nicaraguan President Ortega unilaterally extends cease-fire with rebels for a month; 7 southern-front *Contra* military commanders resign and seek separate peace talks with government (20); political and military sections of the resistance reorganized (26).

August

1–   US Secretary of State Shultz begins 10-day, 9-country Latin American tour to promote US policy towards Central and South America in Guatemala; survives assassination attempt in Bolivia (8); ends tour at inauguration of new Ecuadorean President Rodrigo Borja (10).

31   Gen. Pinochet nominated as sole Chilean Presidential candidate; 3 die in subsequent anti-government protests.

September

1   Colombian President Barco announces 3-phase domestic peace initiative, proposing dialogue with guerrillas, constitutional reform and pardon for guerrillas laying down their arms.·

17–18   Gen. Prosper Avril named as Haitian head of state after coup.

19   3-hour *Sandinista–Contra* meeting fails to agree on where to hold next round of talks.

October

5–   Chile's President Pinochet, seeking another 8-year term, is defeated in plebiscite; his cabinet resigns (20).

5   New Brazilian constitution comes into effect.

28–29   Seven Latin American heads of state meet in Uruguay to discuss regional problems.

November

14   Annual OAS meeting begins in El Salvador.

15   In Brazilian municipal elections, Workers' Party and Democratic Workers' Party win several cities at expense of ruling Democratic Movement.

28   New Peruvian finance minister, the fourth in seven months, appointed after resignation of Abel Salinas.

29   Presidents of Costa Rica, El Salvador, Guatemala, Honduras and Nicaragua, at 3-day meeting in Mexico, agree to reconvene in January to revive Arias peace plan.

December

1   Carlos Salinas de Gortari inaugurated as Mexican President, amid opposition claims of electoral malpractices.

3–   In Argentina's third army mutiny in 18 months, rebels demand resignation of army chief, Gen. Caridi; rebels surrender (6); Caridi resigns (20); replaced by Gen. Gassino (21).

4   Ruling party candidate, Carlos Pérez, elected President of Venezuela.

12/13– 7 Latin American finance ministers meet in Brazil to co-ordinate debt strategy; Venezuela suspends repayments of principal on foreign debt (31).

EAST–WEST ARMS CONTROL

January

6   Warsaw Pact offers to stop modernizing short-range nuclear weapons in Europe if NATO does likewise.

14   START arms-control talks resume in Geneva.

18   Soviet Foreign Minister Shevardnadze proposes removal of all tactical nuclear weapons in Europe and significant cuts in conventional arms.

22   US tables draft treaty on space weapons at super-power talks in Geneva.

February

15   US and USSR resume nuclear test ban talks in Geneva.

25   USSR begins withdrawing SS-12 missiles from East Germany and Czechoslovakia before INF Treaty ratification.

March

15   At UN Disarmament Conference in Geneva, USSR offers compromise solutions for negotiating chemical weapons ban.

16   Speaking to Yugoslav parliament, Gorbachev proposes freezing super-power warship numbers in Mediterranean in 3-point plan to reduce tension.

25   CSCE review conference in Vienna recesses with little progress made on humanitarian issues.

April

5   West German Social Democrats and Communist parties of East Germany and Czechoslovakia issue joint call for chemical-weapon-free zone in Central Europe.

May

27–28   US Senate (27) and the Supreme Soviet (28) ratify INF Treaty.

June

1   In Moscow, Reagan and Gorbachev sign INF Treaty.

26   Special UN session on disarmament ends without agreeing a final document.

July

11   Speaking to Polish Parliament, Gorbachev proposes East–West summit on conventional arms control.

12   US–Soviet talks on strategic arms reductions resume in Geneva.

16   After 2-day summit, Warsaw Pact proposes new East–West nuclear disarmament talks and alters position on conventional force reductions.

August

17–   USSR monitors US underground nuclear test, first of joint series conducted to agree methods of verifying a test ban treaty; US–Soviet nuclear test talks open in Geneva (29).

25   ABM Treaty review conference opens.

29   CSCE talks in Vienna resume after 3-week break.

September

8–   2 cruise missiles leave RAF Molesworth, UK, (first to be eliminated from Europe under INF Treaty); first *Pershing* II missiles also removed from Ramstein, West Germany (12).

14   US monitors Soviet underground nuclear test in follow-up to August monitoring of US test.

26   At UN, President Reagan suggests global conference to reinforce 1925 Geneva Protocol's ban on chemical warfare.

15   START talks in Geneva adjourned.

25–   NATO publishes figures on conventional military force balance in Europe; USSR rejects them (29).

December

5   USSR agrees to drop demand for human-rights conference in Moscow as precondition for ending CSCE conference in Vienna.

7–   In UN speech Gorbachev proposes unilateral cuts in Soviet conventional forces in Europe; NATO foreign ministers welcome this and propose own conventional arms reductions of 50% (8).

Subscriptions to IISS Publications

Three alternative forms of annual subscription are available, covering publications which are issued during the year from the subscription commencement date

COMBINED
1 *The Military Balance*
1 *Strategic Survey*
About 12 Adelphi Papers
6 issues of *Survival*.
Subscription price:
£70.00 ($US 126.00)

Published during year from subscription commencement date to be entered below.

SPECIAL
1 *The Military Balance*
1 *Strategic Survey*
About 12 Adelphi Papers
Subscription price:
£65.00 ($US 117.00)

If you would like to take out one of these subscriptions, please fill in and mail the card below.

SURVIVAL
6 issues of *Survival*.
Subscription price:
£21.00 ($US 38.00)

SUBSCRIPTION CARD

Please enter me for a 1989 subscription

Combined	☐	£70.00 ($US 126.00)
Special	☐	£65.00 ($US 117.00)
Survival	☐	£21.00 ($US 38.00)

Payment: ☐ Payment enclosed
☐ Bill me

I am a **new subscriber** ☐

I already have: Combined subscription ☐ } (please enclose IISS
Special subscription ☐ } mailing label)
Survival subscription ☐ }

PLEASE PRINT NAME AND ADDRESS CLEARLY

Name _____

Address _____

City _____ Country _____

BRASSEY'S DEFENCE PUBLISHERS
(JOURNAL SUBSCRIPTIONS DEPARTMENT)
HEADINGTON HILL HALL
OXFORD
OX3 0BW
UK